Why
Atheism?

Also by George H. Smith

Atheism: The Case Against God

Atheism, Ayn Rand, and Other Heresies

Why Atheism?

George H. Smith

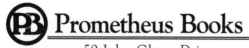

Prometheus Books

59 John Glenn Drive
Amherst, New York 14228-2197

Published 2000 by Prometheus Books

Inquiries should be addressed to
Prometheus Books
59 John Glenn Drive
Amherst, New York 14228–2197
VOICE: 716–691–0133, ext. 207
FAX: 716–564–2711
WWW.PROMETHEUSBOOKS.COM

07 06 05 04 03   7 6 5 4 3

Library of Congress Cataloging-in-Publication Data

Smith, George H., 1949–
    Why atheism? / George H. Smith.
        p. cm.
    Includes bibliographical references and index.
    ISBN 1–57392–268–4 (pbk. : alk. paper)
    1. Atheism. 2. Christianity and atheism. I. Title.

BL2775.2 .S55 2000
211'.8—dc21   00–055373

Printed in the United States of America on acid-free paper

"[I]nto the subtleties of the mythologists it is not worth our while to inquire seriously; those, however, who use the language of proof we must cross examine. . . ."

Aristotle, *Metaphysics*

To

Jeff Riggenbach

Philosophe and Friend

Contents

Acknowledgments

I owe more than the customary nod of appreciation to many friends who, acting above and beyond the call of philosophy, enabled me to write this book: Ross Levatter, Greg Morris, Vince Miller, Mark Valverde, Anton Sherwood, Tim Starr, Vincent Cook, Ellen Young, Mike Mayakis, Betty Huneycutt, Jean Kennedy, and Dick and Rennie Riemann.

My thanks also to:

Mark Read Pickens, for his advice and endurance;

Richard Martin, who shared my curiosity about heaven and hell;

Sharon Presley, a paradigm of independent thinking, for her indomitable spirit;

Robert Kephart and Andrea Rich, for being there;

Suzanne and Jeff Riggenbach, the irresistible force and the immovable object;

Steven Mitchell, editor in chief of Prometheus Books, for his ungodly patience and occasional diplomacy;

Brekke Kroutil-Mueller, my stepdaughter and philosophical companion, for proving that public education cannot kill intelligence; and Laura Kroutil, my wife, for her love and much, much more.

George H. Smith
January 26, 2000

Coming to Terms

THE CREDIBILITY OF ATHEISM

The title of this book, *Why Atheism?*, may be construed in several different ways. It may be understood as a philosophical roll call wherein arguments for atheism are lined up and presented. Or it may be interpreted pragmatically as an inquiry into the benefits of atheism for the individual and society. Or we may view it as a historical investigation into the conditions and causes of modern atheism.

I shall touch on some of these issues later in this book, but I now wish to discuss another interpretation of *Why Atheism?*—namely, why should anyone, especially the religious believer, take the time and trouble to consider the atheistic point of view? We cannot, after all, explore every new idea that happens our way; we must be selective, focusing on some while ignoring others.

Assertions, arguments, doctrines, and the like (which, for the sake of convenience, I shall call *propositions*) must strike us as both *relevant* and *credible* before we will take time to investigate them further. A proposition is relevant if it is related to our intellectual interests, whether theoretical or practical. A relevant proposition is one whose truth or falsehood would have a significant impact on what we believe or how we act.

A proposition must also appear credible before we will take it seriously. If I am told, for example, that American astronauts did not really land on the moon but that this event was an elaborate hoax concocted by NASA to secure funding for the space program, I would likely reject this assertion outright—because, though interesting, it does not strike me as credible. True, I do not have the evidence in hand to prove that the moon landing was authentic, and we have abundant evidence of other governmental frauds; nevertheless, I would not take the time and effort to investigate this claim unless I were presented with enough presumptive evidence to establish its credibility. Only if I took it seriously enough to merit further investigation would I seek more detailed information that would resolve the issue one way or another to my own satisfaction.

To assess a proposition as credible is to say not that it is justified but that it is worthy of being justified. A credible proposition is one that we regard as worthy of further consideration. Without credibility a proposition will simply pass through our consciousness without stopping long enough to be examined. Credibility is like an Ellis Island of cognition, a checkpoint for immigrating ideas that are seeking permanent residence in our minds. Whether a proposition is turned away or admitted for further investigation will depend on how we assess its credibility.

The same point can be made by differentiating between a reasonable belief and a justified belief. A reasonable proposition is one that does not strike us as impossible or highly improbable, even though it may lack sufficient justification to warrant our assent. Of course, given the vast number of reasonable beliefs, we cannot examine every proposition that falls into this category. Severe limitations of time require that we narrow our focus, selecting only those propositions that we regard as reasonable *and* relevant.

But even these conditions are sometimes insufficient, as when a proposition, though both reasonable and relevant, conflicts with our most strongly held beliefs. Consider, for instance, an intelligent Christian who confronts the agnostic's claim that God's existence cannot be proven one way or the other, so we should suspend judgment. This proposition is of great interest to the Christian, and it may even strike him as reasonable inasmuch as he can understand why other intelligent people might adopt this view. Nevertheless, the Christian might decline to investigate the arguments for agnosticism in any detail, because his own belief in God is so strong, his degree of certainty so high, as to render any further investigation unnecessary.

Much of this book is more concerned with the credibility of atheism than its justification. I shall argue that atheism is credible and should therefore be seriously considered by theists and agnostics alike. This is an essential link in the process of persuasion. If most Christians (and other religious believers[1]) dismiss atheism outright, this is not because they have examined the arguments for atheism and found them wanting, but because they do not take atheism seriously enough to examine its arguments in detail. Atheism, in their view, lacks credibility, so they have no motive to explore it further.

To portray atheism as utterly lacking in credibility has long played a crucial role in religious propaganda. Atheism must be rendered *unthinkable*, because doubt, if left unchecked, can easily propel the believer down the path of deconversion. (By *deconversion*, I mean the process by which a religious believer becomes an atheist.) Dire accounts of atheism, which portray deconversion as a descent into spiritual and moral oblivion, are propaganda born of religious necessity. Atheism lies at the end of a slippery slope, so the process of deconversion, if not immediately blocked, can easily advance to its final destination.

To say that atheism is credible is to suggest that the atheist may be right; to say that the atheist may be right is to suggest that the Christian may be wrong; to say that the Christian may be wrong is to suggest that faith may be an unreliable guide to knowledge; to say that faith may be an unreliable guide to knowledge is to suggest that each and every tenet of Christianity should be reexamined in the light of reason—and from here all hell breaks loose as the process of deconversion rushes headlong to its logical destination.

When reason is liberated from the shackles of faith it will inevitably claim sovereignty, the right of critical jurisdiction, over every sphere of knowledge. This inner logic of ideas (for which we have many historical examples) is one reason why so many theologians have found it necessary to dismiss the case for atheism as unworthy of serious consideration. To move from the position that atheism is unreasonable to the position that it is credible is a bigger step than the step from credibility to justification—for it may require the Christian to question God himself by subjecting his divine revelation to critical analysis. Thus has the slander of atheism and atheists played a major role throughout the history of Christian propaganda.

A BUGABOO EPITHET

In 1623, the Friar Mersenne declared that there were fifty thousand atheists in Paris alone. Yet just two years later another Catholic theologian, Father Garasse, could count only five atheists in all of Europe (two Italians and three Frenchmen). How can we explain this discrepancy? Either thousands of atheists had suddenly converted within a two-year period, which is highly unlikely, or these Catholic observers had radically different things in mind when they used the term *atheist*.

The word "atheist" has traditionally been used as a smear word—or "bugaboo epithet," as the historian Preserved Smith once described it. To call someone an atheist was more often an accusation than a description, an invective hurled by orthodox Christians against any and all dissenters, including other Christians.

Derived from the Greek *atheos* (meaning "godless, not believing in the existence of gods"), an *atheist* is "one who does not believe in the existence of a deity."[2] Atheism, or the absence of theistic belief, is therefore a perspective, not a philosophy. Although there can be atheistic philosophies that are based solely on naturalistic principles, there cannot be a "philosophy of atheism" per se, because a negative position can never serve as a satisfactory foundation for a philosophical system.

Since an atheist is a person who does not believe in any god or number of gods, how we define atheist will depend on how we define the word *god*. Some theists have been called atheists for disbelieving in the god (or gods) of the orthodox majority. Early Christians, for example, were frequently accused of atheism by their pagan critics. "We are called atheists," wrote Justin Martyr in the second century, "[a]nd we confess that we are atheists, so far as [the pagan gods] are concerned, but not with respect to the most true God. . . ."[3] Another apologist, Athenagoras, dismissed as "exceedingly silly" the charge that Christians are atheists, because pagans disagree among themselves, some believing in gods that others do not. Hence if Christians qualify as atheists owing to their disbelief in the pagan gods, then everyone is an atheist of some sort, since those who believe in the god (or gods) of one religion will necessarily disbelieve in the god (or gods) of other religions.[4]

Atheism was sometimes used to describe a doctrine that, if carried to its logical conclusion, would allegedly result in disbelief. Michel de Montaigne, one of the most intelligent and sophisticated Catholics of the sixteenth century, had this in mind when he condemned the teachings of Martin Luther as implicitly atheistic. Protestants had rejected the church as an intermediate authority between God and man, arguing instead that individuals should search their own conscience for divine inspiration. But this was a dangerous innovation, according to Montaigne, because the feeble and unreliable judgments of individuals will generate diverse and conflicting religious beliefs, and eventually terminate in atheism. The "novelties of Luther" were "shaking our old religion," and this "new disease would soon degenerate into loathsome atheism."[5]

It was rare to find atheism mentioned in the sixteenth and seventeenth centuries without being preceded with adjectives like "loathsome" and "wicked." Montaigne was also following the custom of his day in referring to atheism as a "disease." Equally common was to label atheists as "monsters" of one kind or another. Post-Reformation Christians, Catholic and Protestant alike, regaled their readers with dire accounts of how the disease of atheism was rapidly infecting many thousands of people, and how atheistic monsters were stalking the land, devouring all morality and decency that lay in their path. The Elizabethan writer Roger Ascham blamed the freethinking Italians for infecting many of his countrymen with atheism. These "Italianate Englishmen are incarnate devils . . . for they first lustfully condemn God, then scornfully mock his word, and also spitefully hate and hurt all the well wishers thereof. . . . They count as fables the holy mysteries of religion." Another Englishman of that era claimed to have found more atheists in Oxford and Cambridge alone than in all of the rest of Europe.[6]

In 1645, the Presbyterian Thomas Edwards expressed alarm at a new breed of atheistic monsters who were "now common among us—as denying the Scriptures, pleading for a toleration of all religions and worships, yea, for blasphemy, and denying there is a God." (The advocate of religious toleration was sure to find himself condemned as an atheist, for who else would dare call for the legalization of blasphemy, heresy, and other heinous sins?) In 1652, Walter Carleton, formerly a physician to the king, complained that England had produced and fostered "more swarms of atheistical monsters" than any other age or country. A decade later Bishop Stillingfleet noted an alarming but fashionable trend of atheism among educated Englishmen, who considered disbelief in Christianity to be a mark of wit and good judgment. Sir George Mackenzie—nicknamed Bloody Mackenzie for his zeal in persecuting heretics—was perplexed because "the greatest wits are most frequently the greatest atheists," while in 1665 Joseph Glanville similarly noted that it is "now accounted a piece of wit and gallantry to be an atheist." Matters had apparently become even worse by 1681, when Archdeacon Parker testified that "atheism and irreligion are now as common as vice and debauchery"—a warning that was seconded by Archbishop Tillotson, according to whom "atheism hath invaded our nation and prevailed to amazement."

References to the atheistic "disease" and to "atheistic monsters" remained common throughout the nineteenth century. Typical of this trend is a book published in 1878, *The Natural History of Atheism*, wherein the author warns of "the atheistic disease" that results from a "moral disorder of the reasonable creature." The author divides atheists into two categories: "atheistic incapables" and "atheistic monsters," both of which result from "the morbid atheistic pathology." This effort to slander atheism through metaphor is found even among modern writers. In 1971, the Catholic priest Vincent P. Miceli claimed that "every form of atheism, even the initially well intentioned, constricts, shrinks, enslaves the individual atheist within and against himself and, eventually, as atheism reaches plague proportions among men, goes on to enslave and murder society."[7]

THE SHORT AND EASY REFUTATION OF ATHEISM

Pick up a modern text on the philosophy of religion and you will likely read that atheism is the *belief* that God *does not exist*, and that an atheist is one who *affirms* the *nonexistence* of God. Then, working from these definitions, you will quickly be informed that atheism can never be justified. Why? Because even if we cannot prove the existence of God, this failure does not positively establish his nonexistence. Failure to prove a positive does not establish the negative. At most it would justify the suspension of judgment, in which the existence of God is neither affirmed nor denied. This suspension of judgment, commonly known as *agnosticism*, is typically offered as the only rational alternative to theism.

No one can lay claim to omniscience, but this is precisely what the atheist supposedly does when he says that God does not exist. How can the atheist possibly know this, since many things exist of which we are presently unaware and which elude our sensory powers? Even if the atheist is able to deny the existence of a particular god (e.g., the God of Christianity) owing to its contradictory attributes, this does not preclude the possibility that a god of some kind may still exist, even if we cannot define him adequately in human terms. Has the atheist explored every nook and cranny of the universe and exhausted every conceivable avenue in his search for God, only then to declare that God is nowhere to be found? Since this is an impossible task, atheism is rejected as irrational on its face, and the atheist is exposed for what he really is: a hypocritical friend of reason who criticizes theists for their supposed irrationalism, while professing to know something that cannot possibly be known, namely, that God does not exist.

It therefore seems as if we are left with one of two possibilities when confronted with someone who claims to be an atheist: Either the atheist understands what he professes to believe, in which case he is irrational or insincere; or the atheist doesn't understand the obvious irrationalism of his claim that God does not exist, in which case he is ignorant, stupid, or confused. In no instance, however, need the atheist be taken seriously.

So goes the short and easy refutation of atheism—a refutation simple enough for a child to understand but sophisticated enough to serve the needs of Hans Kung and a host of other theologians and theistic philosophers.

I suggest that this short and easy refutation of atheism, however popular and convenient it may be, is a bit too short and a bit too easy. Indeed, it is little more than unmitigated sophistry—an exercise in evasion and deceit that studiously ignores the kind of atheism that has been defended by virtually every prominent atheist over the past two centuries. The short and easy refutation achieves its victory by attacking a counterfeit form of atheism that has rarely been advocated by real atheists. It is no more justified than if an atheist were to include the belief in religious persecution as a defining characteristic of Christianity, thereby condemning all Christians as immoral and excluding from the ranks of Christianity anyone who believes in religious freedom. (Indeed, it is far easier to name prominent Christians who have defended persecution as an essential component of Christianity—e.g., Augustine, Thomas Aquinas, Martin Luther, and John Calvin—than to name prominent atheists who have defined atheism as a positive belief in the nonexistence of God.)

Nineteenth-century atheists repeatedly attacked the short and easy refutation by exposing its faulty definition of atheism (known as *positive* atheism, since it positively affirms the nonexistence of God). Consider the British atheist G. W. Foote, editor of the *Freethinker* and the author of many books and articles on atheism. Foote's atheism was scarcely of the timid variety; convicted of blasphemy and sent to prison, his case provoked a young John Stuart Mill to write a passionate defense of religious freedom. Yet Foote repeatedly insisted that atheism is properly defined as the *absence* (or lack) of theistic belief, and not as the *denial* of God's existence. In a typical exchange, Foote challenged a critic "to refer me to *one* Atheist who *denies* the existence of God." The atheist is a person who is *without* belief in a god; "that is all the 'A' before 'Theist' really means."

This was also the view of Charles Bradlaugh, the most influential atheist in Victorian England. In *The Freethinkers Textbook* (1876), after noting that the meaning of "atheism" had been "continuously misrepresented," Bradlaugh went on to say: "Atheism is *without* God. It does not assert *no* God." Similarly, in *Why I Do Not Believe in God* (1887) Annie Besant (who worked closely with Bradlaugh in the freethought movement prior to her descent into theosophy) defined atheism as "without God."

No historian has yet undertaken a thorough investigation of this negative definition, so we don't know when it came into common use, but we see traces of it as early as the seventeenth century. For example, John Locke, in *Essay Concerning Human Understanding* (1690), cited travel accounts that reported "whole nations" of atheists, "amongst whom there was to be found no notion of a God, no religion." The negative definition also appears in the first comprehensive defense of atheism, Baron d'Holbach's *The System of Nature* (1770). "All children are atheists," according to d'Holbach, because "they have no idea of God."

Unlike most of their modern counterparts, some previous Christians were fair-minded enough to read what atheists had actually said before attacking their position. One such person was Robert Flint, a highly respected scholar who wrote extensively on theology, history, and economics. Flint clearly understood that atheism, as defended for many decades by prominent atheists, is negative rather than positive in character. In *Agnosticism* (1903), Flint pointed out that the atheist "is not necessarily a man who says, There is no God." On the contrary, this "positive or dogmatic atheism, so far from being the only kind of atheism, is the rarest of all kinds. . . ." The atheist is simply a person "who does not believe that there is a God," and this absence of belief may stem from nothing more than "want of knowledge that there is a God." Flint concludes: "The word atheist is a thoroughly honest, unambiguous term. *It means one who does not believe in God, and it means neither more nor less.*" (Emphasis added.)

The same point had been made decades earlier by another Christian theologian, Richard Watson, who was well known for his attacks on Thomas Paine and other freethinkers. In *A Biblical and Theological Dictionary* (1831), Watson maintained that atheism literally means "*without* God": An atheist, "in the strict and proper sense of the word, is one who does not believe in the existence of a god, or who owns no being superior to nature."

Twentieth-century freethinkers have continued to defend the negative definition. In *A Rationalist Encyclopedia* (1950) Joseph McCabe, a former Jesuit priest who became a prominent atheist, defined atheism as "the absence of theistic belief." And Chapman Cohen, president of Britain's National Secular Society and author of many books on atheism, wrote: "If one believes in a god, one is a Theist. If one does not believe in a god, then one is an A-theist—he is without that belief. The distinction between atheism and theism is entirely, exclusively, that of whether one has or has not a belief in God."

If the foregoing passages (many more could be cited) seem to belabor the point, I have quoted them because some points need belaboring. No reasonable dialogue between theists and atheists is possible until the myth of positive atheism is put to rest once and for all. When the theist portrays atheism as necessarily irrational because no one can prove the nonexistence of God, he is attacking a position that has rarely been embraced by real atheists. The short and easy refutation of atheism is merely a mock refutation of a mock adversary.

PERSONAL ATHEISM

By *personal atheist*, I mean an atheist who was formerly a religious believer of some kind. Personal atheism is the outcome of a deliberative process—a mental transition from belief to nonbelief that I call *deconversion*.

The personal atheist, having experienced religion firsthand, may be able to empathize with the belief system that he now rejects. As a former Christian who deconverted in my teens, I can recall how it *felt* to believe in the Christian God and what the world looked like from a Christian point of view. It was comforting to believe that God was watching over me, that Jesus was listening to my prayers (though he usually said no), that my life had a divine purpose, that I was on the path to eternal happiness.

Such beliefs seemed to me incontrovertible, part of the warp and woof of my existence. I did not experience Christianity as a number of discrete beliefs, but as a *worldview* that unified my beliefs. My relationship with God did not manifest itself in different experiences, but was an interpretative framework that gave *meaning* to my experiences. I therefore felt no more need to prove the existence of God than to prove the existence of the ground on which I stood. For me to suppose that God did not exist would have been to imagine the unimaginable— a world turned inside out in which nothing made sense.

Although I now reject Christianity root and branch, I can

[25]

nonetheless empathize with the Christian point of view. This empathetic understanding, however, is often missing in the *natural atheist,* i.e., the atheist who has never been a religious believer and so remains in his original condition of nonbelief. Although both types are religious outsiders, the personal atheist was once an insider, so he is more likely than the natural atheist to understand his Christian adversaries.

Note that I said *empathetic* rather than *sympathetic.* Although the personal atheist may identify with the Christian point of view, this does not necessarily mean that he will be less critical than the natural atheist. Indeed, if anything, the opposite is more likely to be true: The personal atheist is often more critical of Christianity than his natural counterpart. There is a reason, after all, why the former Christian is a *former* Christian. There is a reason why he now rejects as irrational the same beliefs that he once accepted as infallibly certain.

The most passionate and forceful defenders of atheism are frequently those personal atheists who, prior to their deconversion, were enthusiastic champions of the faith. It will not do—notwithstanding that it is often done—to explain this phenomenon by psychological means, as if the former true-believing Christian merely shifted his dogmatic allegiance and became a true-believing atheist instead. Nor will it do to attribute the sometimes strident atheism of the deconverted Christian to an inner crisis that was precipitated by a loss of faith. Nor can we accept the traditional explanation that attributes deconversion to a willful and malicious rebellion against God.[8]

There are better ways to explain the strident atheism of former Christians. For one thing, no personal atheist can fail to notice a vast discrepancy between the expectation and reality of deconversion. He quickly learns that most everything he had been taught about atheism was misleading at best and fraudulent at worst. Depictions of atheism that he once accepted without question, such as referring to deconversion as a "loss of faith," now grate on his nerves. His deconversion, far from evoking in him a sense of loss, was experienced as an intellectual breath of fresh air. Atheism, by liberating him from the stern and steady gaze of an omnipresent voyeurist, gave him a sense of moral and intellectual privacy, a sphere of personal autonomy in which he need answer to no one other than himself. He was now free to think for himself—to question and criticize without moral restraint—to live and learn, succeed and fail, as an autonomous moral agent.

Atheism as it appears to the Christian is much different than atheism as it appears to the former Christian. Things look much different to the personal atheist after the process of deconversion is complete. The expected crisis and internal turmoil failed to materialize, and his deconversion ended with a whimper instead of a bang. The former Christian signed no pacts with the devil while traveling up the path to atheism—nor did he engage in licentious behavior, shake his fist at heaven in defiance of the Almighty, declare war on everything good and decent, sink to the depths of spiritual depravity, or pine after a lost deity.

The actual experience of deconversion, therefore, rarely conforms to Christian expectations. The deconverted atheist, having once been a Christian himself, knows this to be true, both from his own experience and from his interaction with other atheists. And it is this dual experience, I suggest, that chiefly explains the often militant character of personal atheism.

It is understandable why the personal atheist is sometimes hard on his former religion. This militant posture is the natural reaction to the deceit of antiatheistic propaganda. The personal atheist has no problem with the Christian who rejects the case for atheism after careful consideration. But this is a rare occurrence, as the personal atheist well knows. Rarely does the Christian regard atheism as credible, so he dismisses it outright as unworthy of further investigation. And it is this contempt for atheism that generates a countercontempt in the personal atheist, who knows that doubt will not land one in the spiritual abyss depicted in Christian propaganda.

NOTES

1. Given the wide diversity of religious opinions, I have chosen to discuss Christianity throughout this book in order to focus my arguments. But most of my arguments also pertain to any religion (e.g., Islam and some forms of Judaism) that contains the following elements: (1) a doctrine of personal immortality, (2) a promise of salvation for those with orthodox (i.e., correct) beliefs, and (3) a belief that at least some knowledge necessary for salvation requires faith in divine revelation, knowledge that cannot otherwise be justified through reason alone. These elements constitute what is generally called a "salvation religion" or a "personal religion," so I shall use these labels interchangeably.

2. *The Merriam-Webster New Book of World Histories* (Springfield, Mass.: Merriam-Webster, 1991), p. 26.

3. *The Writings of Justin Martyr and Athenagoras*, trans. M. Dods, G. Reith, and B. Pratten (Edinburgh: T. and T. Clark, 1867), p. 29.

4. Ibid., p. 389.

5. Michel de Montaigne, *An Apology for Raymond Sebond*, trans. and ed. M. A. Screech (London: Penguin Books, 1993), p. 2.

6. The antiatheistic passages in this section are taken from the following sources: Preserved Smith, *Origins of Modern Culture, 1543–1687* (New York: Collier Books, 1962); J. M. Robertson, *A Short History of Freethought: Ancient and Modern* (New York: Russell and Russell, 1957); George T. Buckley, *Atheism in the English Renaissance* (New York: Russell and Russell, 1965).

7. Vincent P. Miceli, *The Gods of Atheism* (New Rochelle, N.Y.: Arlington House, 1971), p. 19.

8. It is interesting to note how the prejudice against atheism is reflected in ordinary language. It is commonly said, for example, that the personal atheist has *lost* his faith, as if he no longer possesses something of value. As the atheist sees the matter, however, he has not "lost" anything except ignorance and error, and he has gained in understanding and knowledge. In addition, the label *vulgar atheism* is commonly applied to freethinkers who focus more on refuting the arguments of revealed theology (miracles, biblical prophecies, etc.) than on the more "sophisticated" arguments of natural theology (the First Cause Argument, the Design Argument, etc.) But there is nothing vulgar about taking Christians seriously enough to

deal with their most important arguments—for, as we shall later see, the vast majority of Christians consider the truths of revelation to be far more important than the truths of reason, since only the former are absolutely necessary for salvation. The charge of "vulgar atheism" is as pretentious as it is condescending, a bit of academic snobbery popular among professional intellectuals who would rather not dirty their hands with relevant details.

The Methodology of Atheism

THE BURDEN OF PROOF

Methodology is the study of method, and method (in Kant's words) is "procedure according to principle." By the "methodology of atheism," I mean a study of the *methods of argument* that have been used to defend atheism.

The first method is known as *onus probandi*, i.e., the onus (or burden) of proof. This principle states that the burden of proof falls on the person who affirms the truth of a proposition, such as "God exists." If the theist claims to know that God exists, then we have the cognitive right—indeed, the responsibility—to ask this person *how* he acquired this knowledge and *why* we should take him seriously. If the theist fails to meet his burden of proof, *atheism is left standing by default as the only rational alternative.*

Let us apply the *onus probandi* to a frivolous example. If a person insists that an invisible elf is sitting on my shoulder, but shows no interest in justifying this claim, then he has communicated to me one thing, and one thing only, that I did not previously know. He has informed me of what he happens to believe, and this is merely a psychological report without philosophical significance.

To claim knowledge without justification is to verbalize a psychological fact about oneself. It merely communicates to others that one has a particular mental attitude known as *belief*. And this report, though it may be of psychological interest to some, has no more philosophical significance than a report on how one happens to feel. It is only through a process of justification that a belief acquires philosophical significance and earns the respect of those who disagree with that belief.

If, when expressing a belief, the believer intends it to be taken as something more than a personal report on his state of mind—if, that is, he thinks his belief should influence the beliefs of *others*—then he must provide a *motive* for others to take him seriously. Why, after all, should others regard a report on the believer's state of mind as sufficiently important to influence their own thinking? What is there about the believer that makes his psychological report superior to the reports of countless others? Moreover, does the believer ever allow the beliefs of others to influence his own thinking—and, if so, under what conditions?

If the believer intends his expression of belief to be taken by others as something more than a psychological report, he must be prepared to justify his belief with arguments. When the believer argues—i.e., when he presents *reasons* to support his belief—he provides a reason for others to take his belief seriously. An argument, unlike a psychological report, is universal rather than particular. An argument, if valid for one person, is equally valid for another. Hence if the believer has good reasons for believing as he does, and if he presents these reasons to others, then he has bridged the gap of subjectivity between his own mind and the minds of other people.

It is through attempting to justify his personal beliefs with *imper-*

sonal arguments that the believer is able to convince others that the value of his beliefs is based on something more than the fact that *he* happens to believe them. A willingness to engage in the give and take of argument displays a commitment to cognitive egalitarianism—the proposition that all people should be treated as intellectual equals, and that no individual can legitimately claim a privileged immunity from the burden of proof.

The *onus probandi* is about as clear and incontestable as any philosophical procedure could possibly be. Indeed, it is indispensable to any intellectual exchange in which the participants are seriously committed to the pursuit of truth. For imagine what would ensue if the *onus probandi* were not accepted as a procedural rule.

Suppose that a person who believes in the existence of invisible elves (let us call him an "elfist") does not have the sole burden of proof, and that a person who does not believe in their existence (an "aelfist") has an equal responsibility to prove that invisible elves do *not* exist. "Granted," says the elfist, "I cannot offer even a scintilla of evidence to support my claim, so I do not expect the aelfist to believe as I do. Nevertheless, the aelfist cannot prove me wrong: He cannot prove that invisible elves do *not* exist. If the aelfist cannot see what I do, this is because he does not have the faith that is necessary if one is to perceive invisible elves. For these elves, sensitive critters that they are, will not reveal themselves to skeptics and disbelievers. You must have faith, you must first believe that they exist, before you can see them as I do. If the aelfist does not wish to make this commitment of faith, then that is his right, but it is not his right to dismiss my belief as unjustified merely because I cannot prove what I say. On the contrary, since the aelfist cannot prove that my elves do not exist, his disbelief is no more justified than my belief."

This kind of argument, which would be quite legitimate if not for the burden of proof, has a treacherous implication that may not be apparent at first glance. The elfist, by stipulating that one must first believe in elves before one can perceive them, has excluded as irrelevant any appeal to empirical evidence. This means that elfism cannot be falsified, even in principle, because failure to perceive these elves (who are, after all, invisible) can always be blamed on one's lack of faith. Thus without the burden of proof, a belief would become more reasonable as it became less vulnerable to falsification: *The fact that a belief could not be proven false under any circumstances would bestow upon it the same cognitive status as a belief that could be proven true.*

Consider: If another, more rationalistic elfist were to specify an empirical method whereby we could detect his elusive critters, then it would at least be possible (if this method were to fail) to *weaken* the case for elfism. The aelfist, even if he could not conclusively prove the nonexistence of elves, could at least undermine the ground on which the rational elfist claims to stand. Thus as the elfist becomes more rational—as he becomes more willing to present evidence for his belief—he also becomes more vulnerable to criticism. To provide evidence for a belief is to provide fodder for its critics; and with more evidence comes more opportunity for criticism. Conversely, with little evidence comes little opportunity for criticism, and a belief with no evidence becomes immune to all criticism.

If, therefore, we discard the *onus probandi*, if we divide the burden of proof equally among those who assent to an affirmative proposition and those who do not, then the justification for a belief will increase as the evidence for that belief decreases. And a belief that is supported by no evidence whatever, having been immunized against all criticism, will be the strongest possible belief, because it cannot possibly be disproved.

CONCEPTUAL ANALYSIS

A common atheistic method (one that dates back to the skeptics of ancient Greece) is to argue that the concept of God is literally *meaningless*—so to say that "God exists" is to say precisely nothing at all. I call this the atheistic method of conceptual analysis.

Is "God exists" a coherent, noncontradictory proposition? There is no way to answer this question unless we understand the meaning of the term *God*. We need a definition or description of God, a specification of his attributes that will enable us to assess the logical coherence of this concept. If the theist refuses to address this problem, if he insists that God refers to something that we cannot comprehend, then all discussion must immediately come to a stand, because we cannot reason about (or even have faith in) the existence of an empty concept. It would be like discussing the existence of a *Blictri* (a nonsense word that was popular during the eighteenth century). To assert the existence of a Blictri, while refusing to explain the meaning of this term, is to say precisely nothing at all.

If many people are more lenient when discussing the existence of a god than they would be when discussing the existence of a Blictri—demanding a definition of the former concept but not the latter—this is largely because the word "God" is already familiar to us. Consequently, when someone talks about God, he often expects us to "kinda know" what he means by the word. And, in a sense, this is true: Even the atheist does "kinda know" what his theistic adversary means by "God." He means a *kinda* being who, at the very least, is *kinda* smart and *kinda* powerful and *kinda* demanding. But if we "kinda know" what it means to speak of God, the same cannot be said for Blictri. We are totally unfamiliar with this word, so if someone were to assert the existence of a Blictri, we would have no idea of what he was talking about without a definition.

To "kinda know" what the theist means by "God" may be sufficient in some situations, such as during a casual conversation in which neither party is interested in changing the other person's mind. Not only with "God" but with other terms as well, we are often satisfied if we "kinda know" what someone means. Only an insufferable pedant would demand rigorous definitions for each and every word of a normal conversation.

But a philosophical exchange is not a normal conversation. Although philosophers disagree about many things, they generally agree that philosophy requires clarity above all else, and that to use key words with ambiguous or unclear meanings will invariably generate confusion. Studied imprecision is the last refuge of the philosophical scoundrel, so a philosopher cannot expect others to "kinda know" what he means when he speaks of God.

Of course, it is not always possible for a philosopher to define a key term at the outset of an investigation—to arrive at such a definition may, after all, be the purpose of his investigation—but definitions must always remain foremost in his mind. This sustained interest in clarity is a defining characteristic of the philosophic enterprise, one that sets it apart from the vagaries of ordinary discourse.

Philosophy, unlike mathematics and the natural sciences, is conducted in the natural language of everyday life. With a few exceptions (e.g., formal logic and probability theory), no philosophical discipline has recourse to the stipulative and operational definitions of an artificial language. The fact that the philosopher must use the same language as everyone else is at once a blessing and a curse.

It is blessing, first, because it makes philosophy accessible to nonspecialists, thereby extending its influence; and, second, because it introduces a literary component into philosophy, thereby making it possible for us to admire a great philosophical work for its aesthetic qualities. It is a curse because the philosopher must continuously wrestle with, and seek to overcome, the vagaries and ambiguities of natural language. What is for the poet a help is for the philosopher a hindrance.

It is because the philosopher speaks the language of everyday life that clarity is so essential to his enterprise. The same word can mean different things to different people, and these people often mistake the meaning of a word with connotations, feelings, and other incidental associations. Clarity is especially important for an argument in which *persuasion* is the primary goal of one or more disputants.

The typical exchange between a theist and an atheist is likely to be an argument in this sense, especially if the theist subscribes to a revealed religion, such as Christianity, that demands belief as a precondition of salvation. If, as the Christian maintains, the belief in God is fraught with momentous consequences, if what we believe about God will profoundly influence our lives (either here or in the hereafter), then we should indeed give the matter careful consideration. But this advice, if good for the atheist, is even better for the Christian—for it is he who has committed himself unreservedly to a belief system, and it is he who hopes to be rewarded for his devotion.

All of us have vague ideas—things we "kinda know" but cannot express clearly—but rarely do these vague ideas become the subject of an intense and sustained argument. If a traveler asks me for directions, and if I "kinda know" how to get from here to there, I would qualify my response accordingly. I might hesitate to give the traveler any advice at all, for fear that I might misdirect her to parts unknown. Or, if I did give directions, I would qualify them with a caveat that would convey my reservations. In any case, I would not express myself with complete assurance, since I only "kinda know" what I am talking about.

There is a significant parallel between this example and religious arguments. The traveler was soliciting advice about how she should *act*, not what she should think; the knowledge she sought was practical, not theoretical. The "knowledge" of Christian belief is also practical in this sense. Although Christianity does have a theoretical core, the issue of whether or not one believes this theory has momentous practical consequences. Christianity offers directions of how to get from the "here" of this life to the "there" of an afterlife, while avoiding the road that leads to hell.

Given these potential consequences, what are we to think of the believer who counts on others, including atheists, to "kinda know" what he means by "God"? If the believer expects others to be satisfied with a vague idea of "God," we must assume he has nothing better to offer, that he only "kinda knows" what he is talking about. And this means not only that the believer has committed his life to a vague idea, but that he seriously expects others to do so as well. In expressing complete assurance about something he "kinda knows," the believer is misleading others. When attempting to persuade others he should, at the very least, acknowledge the unclarity of his belief and express the appropriate reservations.

Theologians have long maintained we cannot define "God,"

because we cannot specify a genus, or general class, to which he belongs. God is said to be *sui generis*, i.e., in a class by himself. He is literally unique, a being unlike any other, so we have no basis for comparison on which we can base a definition. In more simple terms, God is said to be essentially *unknowable*.

I discussed this issue at some length in *Atheism: The Case Against God* (as have many other atheists), so I need not list here the many problems that attend the notion of an unknowable being. The key point is this: When the atheist is told that God is unknowable, he may interpret this claim in one of two ways. He may suppose, first, that the theist has acquired knowledge of a being that, by his own admission, cannot possibly be known; or, second, he may assume that the theist simply does not know what he is talking about. If the atheist regards the second assumption as far more likely, if he suspects the theist of uttering nonsense, this is partially because the first assumption is appallingly convenient. The theist, in affirming the existence of an unknowable being, places himself in a position similar to that the of the elfist: Both have an all-purpose excuse for exempting their claims from the burden of proof and the canons of critical scrutiny.

OCCAM'S RAZOR

In his *Summa Theologica*, Thomas Aquinas presents his famous "five ways" (i.e., proofs) for the existence of God. Before doing so, however, Aquinas mentions two arguments that might be used to prove that "God does not exist." One of these (the argument from evil) has received considerable attention, but the other has not. To quote Aquinas:

> What can be accomplished by a few principles is not effected by many. But it seems that everything we see in the world can be accounted for by other principles, supposing God did not exist. For all natural things can be reduced to one principle, which is nature, and all voluntary things can be reduced to one principle, which is human reason, or will. Therefore there is no need to suppose God's existence.[1]

Aquinas, of course, does not agree with this argument, but it is an intriguing argument nonetheless.[2] It is based on what has become known as "the principle of parsimony," or "Occam's Razor" (after William of Occam, an English theologian who lived during the fourteenth century, long after Aquinas). According to this principle, mental entities (e.g., concepts and explanations) should not be multiplied beyond necessity, i.e., beyond what is minimally required to explain the phenomenon in question.[3]

Aquinas, of course, does not agree with the argument we quoted earlier: Like other "objections" in his *Summa*, it is given life solely for the purpose of being killed by means of a counterargument. But it is an interesting argument nonetheless, because it implies that Occam's Razor, when used to argue that "there is no need to suppose God's existence," is relevant to the claim that "God does not exist." In other words, if there is no cognitive reason to posit the existence of God, if what needs to be explained can be explained by more economical means, then we may conclude that God does not exist.

Against this a counterargument immediately suggests itself—namely, that failure to justify the need for God as an explanatory principle cannot prove his nonexistence. Even if we concede that God is epistemologically superfluous, that what needs to be explained can be explained entirely by naturalistic methods, we are not entitled to conclude that God does not exist. The real existence of a being, after all, does not depend on whether our concept of that being is necessary for explanatory purposes.

It is interesting to note that Aquinas does not take this way out, even though it must have been as obvious to him as it is to us. Aquinas, in other words, does not retract his claim that the argument from Occam's Razor, if valid, would prove the *nonexistence* of God. Why Aquinas took this position I cannot say; I quote him merely as a prelude, not as a subject for interpretation. My purpose is to explore the possibility that an argument from Occam's Razor, if valid, can, prove the *nonexistence* of God.

A good place to begin is with the subject of Santa Claus. Ask the average adult whether or not whether Santa exists, and he will answer, "No; Santa is an imaginary being, a charming fable that we tell our children." I have never met an adult, including an adult theologian, who exhibits the least hesitation in asserting that Santa does not exist. But how do we *know* this for a fact?

Granted, we do not, like children, believe in Santa's existence; granted, we need not posit his existence in order to explain how children get presents on Christmas morning; granted, we have no evidence of his existence; granted, to believe in Santa would require that we accept other improbable beliefs (flying reindeer, elves, etc.)—we may grant all these points and more, but do they *prove* the *nonexistence* of Santa? After all, Santa may be hiding out near (or under) the North Pole, so maybe we can't find him because he doesn't wish to be found (rather like the invisible elves we discussed earlier). Hence the same argument that theologians apply to God can also be applied to Santa, viz., that failure to prove his existence does not prove his nonexistence.

Despite this philosophical nicety, few people would retract their claim to know that Santa does not exist. Even the most scrupulous philosopher would hesitate to declare himself a Santa agnostic who suspends judgment on the question of Santa's existence. But why? If positive atheism (i.e., the claim that God does not exist) is ruled out of court as theoretically unjustifiable, then how can it be any more reasonable to assert the nonexistence of Santa?

God does not exist. This claim can never be justified, we are told, because of man's limited knowledge. Man is neither omniscient nor infallible; there are many things he does not know (and never will know), and he is often mistaken about what he claims to know. And these innate deficiencies, we are further told, demand that we be metaphysically modest and remain open to the possibility of God's existence, even if this cannot be proven. It would be folly on our part to presume that we know everything, or to declare that something does not exist merely because we have no knowledge of it. In fine, the atheist, if he is a reasonable person, must acknowledge the *possibility* of God's existence, even if he doesn't believe in such a being at the present time.

And so we encounter the word "possible," one of the most ambiguous terms in that ambiguous discipline known as philosophy. What does it mean to say that God's existence is possible, even if there is no evidence whatever to suppose that he really exists? Immanuel Kant distinguished between two kinds of possibility, which he called *logical* and *material*, and I shall apply these concepts to the problem at hand.

Logical possibility pertains to the *internal coherence* of a proposition. A proposition is logically possible if it is not self-contradictory. Consider, for example, the proposition "There exists at least one married bachelor." It is logically impossible for this proposition to be true, because the predicate ("a married man") contradicts the subject ("a bachelor"). Moreover, to call this proposition logically impossible is to say that it is *incoherent*, that it has no meaning, that it literally makes no sense at all. We don't need to venture out into the world in search of a married bachelor, because we know in advance that married bachelors cannot possibly exist. The statement, "There exists at least one married bachelor," does not express anything that can be either true *or* false—so, strictly speaking, it is not a proposition at all but a meaningless utterance.

Logical possibility, as Kant emphasized, has no bearing on the question of whether something really exists. To say, for example, that the existence of life on another planet is logically possible is merely to say that this is a coherent proposition, i.e., that it has a *meaning* which we can understand. But this kind of possibility does not constitute evidence for the existence of alien life. Merely because a proposition is meaningful is no reason to suppose that it is true, for the latter supposition pertains not to logical possibility but to *material possibility*.

Material possibility has to do with the *truth* of a proposition rather than its meaning. To assert that a proposition is possibly true, in this sense, is to assert that we have at least *some evidence* to support our claim. Hence, to assert the *material* possibility of alien life is to say that we have some reason to suppose that life really does exist elsewhere in the universe. Unlike logical possibility, which depends on conceptual analysis, material possibility depends on the presentation and assessment of evidence.

It is unfortunate that the same word—"possibility"—is used in both senses, because the meanings of logical and material possibility are unrelated and easily confused. A statement must be deemed logically possible (i.e., meaningful) before we can even consider its material possibility (i.e., evidence for its truth). A meaningless statement asserts nothing—it has no cognitive status whatsoever—so we cannot even begin to assess its truth-value, because we have no idea of what we are assessing.

It has often been argued by atheists that the concept of God is self-contradictory—that the existence of evil, for example, is incompatible with a God who is omnibenevolent (and would therefore desire that no evil befall his creatures), omnipotent (and was therefore able to create a world without evil), and omniscient (and would therefore have foreseen the evil aspects of his creation). And if this is so, then the atheist is fully justified in affirming the nonexistence of God by appealing to a self-evident axiom of logic, known as the Law of Non-Contradiction, according to which something cannot be both A and non-A at the same time and in the same respect. The existence of God, in other words, is logically impossible because the concept of God is self-contradictory.[4]

The argument from Occam's Razor, as presented by Aquinas, does not appeal to the logical impossibly of God's existence; rather, it claims that God does not exist because the concept serves no explanatory function. Naturalism is at once a necessary and *sufficient* mode of explanation, so we have no need to invoke the existence of supernatural causes. As for the counterclaim that this argument, even if valid, it is insufficient to refute the *possibility* of God's existence—how we evaluate this objection will depend on how we interpret the crucial word "possibility." According to some atheists, if it is reasonable to assert that Santa does not exist, even if we cannot positively disprove the possibility that he exists, then it is equally reasonable to say the same thing about God. And if the latter is unreasonable, then why don't theologians abandon their dogmatic anti-

Santa sentiments and candidly admit that they simply *don't know* whether Santa exists or not, that they have suspended judgment on this matter and so have no opinion one way or the other?

Such are the pleasant inconsistencies of religious belief that make it possible to see the mote in the eyes of other people while remaining blissfully unaware of the beam in one's own.

NOTES

1. Thomas Aquinas, *Summa Theologica*, trans. Fathers of the English Dominican Province, Great Books of the Western World, vol. 19 (Chicago: Encyclopedia Britannica, 1952), p. 12.

2. Aquinas does not indicate who, if anyone, actually used this argument. My guess is that it may have been bandied about during theological debates at the University of Paris, where Aquinas taught for a number of years. The argument, resting as it does on naturalistic principle of explanation, has a distinctly Aristotelian ring about it, so it may have been proposed by more radical Aristotelians, such as Siger of Brabant, who were active in the Faculty of Arts (in effect, the undergraduate department) at the University of Paris. Siger and other "Latin Averroists"—so called because they were heavily influenced by Averroes (a Muslim expert on Aristotle) did not evade the anti-Christian implications of Aristotle's philosophy (such his denial of personal immortality), but cloaked them in a rather thin veil known as the doctrine of double truth. This doctrine, whether sincere or not, maintained that what is true for reason is not necessarily true for faith, and vice versa.

3. The true originator of Occam's Razor appears to have been Aristotle, who wrote the following in one of his works on logic: "We may assume the superiority *ceteris paribus* [i.e., other things remaining equal] of the demonstration which derives from fewer postulates or hypotheses—in short, from fewer premises. . . ." *Posterior Analytics*, trans. G. R. G. Mure, Great Books of the Western World, vol. 8 (Chicago: Encyclopedia Britannica, 1952), p. 118.

4. The argument that "God" is self-contradictory and therefore nonexistent has long been the basis for positive atheism, having been advanced by a number of atheists and skeptics in ancient Greece. This was pointed out by the English philosopher and theologian Ralph Cudworth who, in a mas-

sive critique of atheism, *True Intellectual System of the Universe* (1678), wrote that "because theists themselves acknowledge God to be incomprehensible, it may be from thence inferred [by some atheists], that he is a nonentity." The concept of God, according to these atheists, "is utterly inconceivable, because it is a "bundle of . . . impossibilities, huddled up together." This argument for positive atheism, however, is by no means inconsistent with the definition of negative atheism that I discussed in the first chapter. Positive atheism is a *subset* of negative atheism; after all, the belief that the concept of God is self-contradictory is a major reason why atheists *do not believe* in the existence of God. Many atheists have considered this to be an obvious point (though many theologians have found it difficult to understand). The nineteenth-century atheist Annie Besant is a case in point. While embracing the negative definition of atheism as the lack of theistic belief, Besant argued that "never yet has a God been defined in terms which were not palpably self-contradictory and absurd." A good deal of the confusion about this issue is owing to the fact that positive atheism and negative atheism are answers to two different questions, namely, "Does God exist?" and "Do you *believe* in the existence of God?" The positive atheist says no to former question, whereas the negative atheist says no to the latter. And since Christians typically stress the need for belief as a precondition of salvation, most atheists within Christian cultures have defined themselves in negative terms, as people who do *not* believe in God. Properly considered, therefore, positive atheism is simply a possible justification for the nonbelief of negative atheism rather than a competing definition.

Belief and Doubt

BELIEFS

I have many beliefs, far more than I could possibly list, but only a fraction of these are of interest to others. I happen to believe that George Carlin is a funny guy, that basketball is more entertaining than baseball, that cats make better pets than dogs, that I look better in red than in green—the list goes on and on, but few people would want me to continue.

Beliefs can express our personal preferences and casual opinions about unimportant matters. But this is not always the case: A belief can also convey a knowledge claim, a judgment as to the truth of a proposition. If I say, for example, that I believe in the existence of God, I am also claiming that the proposition "God exists" is true— that God does exist in fact.

Because this kind of belief has a cognitive content, because it embodies a claim to know on the part of the believer, I shall call it a *cognitive belief.* A cognitive belief is one in which the believer affirms the truth of a proposition. And since to affirm the truth of a proposition is to claim that one *knows* it to be true, a believer must be willing to *justify* his cognitive belief if he wishes others to take it (and him) seriously.

It is the assumption that a believer can justify his cognitive beliefs that commands the attention of other people. If I say that I believe in the existence of God while making no effort to justify this belief, I have merely reported on my subjective state of mind; and this psychological report, though it may be of interest to me and my friends, has no cognitive value. It is like saying, "I feel lucky today." If this is how I feel, good for me, but this feeling alone can oblige no one else to think or act differently than they would otherwise.

Merely expressing a belief, while making no effort to justify this belief, is to do nothing more than issue a psychological report, or personal notation, about one's state of mind. It may be true that I believe myself to be Napoleon, and this psychological observation may be of interest (or concern) to my friends and family, but my subjective belief per se has no cognitive value. The same applies if I happen to believe that I was Napoleon in a previous life. Or if I happen to believe that I am in telepathic communication with aliens from a distant galaxy. Or if I happen to believe that God is listening to my prayers. Or if I happen to believe that Jesus died for my sins.

Again, all such expressions of belief, when no effort is made to justify them, are nothing more than psychological reports of the believer's state of mind. And to a believer who expresses his unjustified beliefs we might say: "Fine, good for you, believe as you like—but of what interest are your personal feelings and attitudes to me?"

This, of course, is not the response that most of us want or expect when we express our cognitive beliefs; indeed, we would find it insulting. If it is true, as an eighteenth-century wit once said, that "everyone complains of his memory but no one of his judgment," this is because we view memory as an innate ability over which we have little or no control. But if a poor memory does not reflect on one's character, the same is not true of poor judgment. Judgment, unlike memory, is within our control. It is a skill that all of us must develop and use in our everyday lives, so we are apt to judge harshly a person whose judgment is consistently poor.

A person known for his poor judgment will find that his beliefs are rarely taken seriously by others. As Adam Smith observed:

> The desire of being believed, the desire of persuading, of leading and directing other people, seems to be one of the strongest of all our natural desires. . . . It is always mortifying not to be believed, and it is doubly so when we suspect that it is because we are supposed to be unworthy of belief. . . . The man who had the misfortune to imagine that nobody believed a single word he said, would feel himself the outcast of human society, would dread the very thought of going into it, or of presenting himself before it, and could scarce fail, I think, to die of despair.[1]

To express a cognitive belief, as we have seen, is also to affirm (at least implicitly) that the content of one's belief is true. And since to affirm the truth of a proposition is to judge its cognitive value, all such beliefs can reflect on our competency to judge.

There is an absurd but popular notion that one's fundamental beliefs are sacrosanct and therefore immune to criticism. Religious beliefs in particular are often spoken of in hushed and reverential tones, as if their lofty content automatically confers upon them the special privilege of unearned respect. A person is said to be admirable because he is a "deeply religious" person with "strong convictions." A person who has profound beliefs about God deserves our profound respect, however profoundly we may disagree with him.

All such claims are sheer balderdash. There is nothing admirable about a belief per se, whatever its object may be. To say that beliefs are a dime a dozen would be to overestimate their true value. A belief, subjectively considered, has no more cognitive value than a feeling, *viz.*, none at all. We are overstocked with beliefs; everyone has more than he needs, and everyone tends to think that his beliefs are especially important simply because they are *his.*

"*I* believe in a God of love"; "*I* believe that life has a divine purpose and that everything happens for a reason"; "*I* believe in a life after death"; "*I* believe . . . etc." Fill in the blanks any way you wish, but your belief does not command respect merely because *you* happen to believe it. What is relevant to others is not the fact *that* you believe this, or that *you* believe this, or that you *believe* this, or that you believe *this*—but rather *why* you believe as you do.

If you want your beliefs to be taken seriously by others, then you must present them as something more than personal notations on your state of mind. It is only by giving reasons that you can free your beliefs from the bonds of subjectivity and earn the respect that comes from objectivity. A belief becomes objective when it is justified with reasons that can be examined and evaluated by others.

If you don't want to subject your beliefs to this kind of critical review, then *you should keep them to yourself.* Or, at the very least, you should preface every expression of belief with the following proviso: "I will not attempt to justify what I am about to say, because you might evaluate my reasons differently than I do. You might, for example, criticize them as flawed or inadequate. Thus, since I don't want to be criticized, I won't present reasons in an effort to justify my belief. Having said this, here is what I believe. . . ."

This example is unrealistic, to say the least, because the proviso would undercut our desire to be taken seriously. Although this proviso might be appropriate in a psychological conversation, when our goal is to express how we feel about something, it would be inappropriate in any philosophical conversation or other dialogue in which we wish to *persuade* others to accept our point of view. Any such dialogue cannot proceed unless the participants are willing to *objectify* their beliefs through the presentation of evidence and arguments that can be evaluated by others.

There is far more at stake here than a philosophical nicety; this is a matter of showing respect for others. Suppose a Christian, who knows that I am an atheist, says to me: "I *know* with absolute certainty that God exists." In this case I would reasonably assume that the Christian is prepared to defend his knowledge claim, and that he would be neither surprised nor offended if I asked him for justification.

Let us now alter one detail in this example: The Christian, instead of claiming to *know* that God exists, tells me instead that he strongly *believes* in the existence of God. What am I to make of this profession? Why did the Christian bother to tell me about this belief in the first place? Since the Christian has expressed a *cognitive* belief, I see no essential difference between this profession of belief and the previous claim to *know* that God exists.

I, like most everyone else, do not care to hear unsolicited outbursts from total strangers about their personal feelings and convictions. Thus, unless I am willing to dismiss the Christian as a social barbarian, I must assume that his expression of belief was intended to be more than a psychological ejaculation. I must assume, in other words, that the Christian, in expressing his belief in the existence of God, is also claiming to have good reasons for this belief, reasons that can justify his implicit claim to know that God exists.

I will therefore demand that the Christian justify his belief in the existence of God with objective reasons, i.e., evidence and arguments that can evaluated by rational methods. And should the Christian be unwilling or unable to defend his belief, I will urge him to embrace the more reasonable alternative of atheism. And should he remain steadfastly indifferent to the issue of justification—should he say that he believes what he believes and that's all there is to it—then I will question either his judgment or his sincerity. For I would never have taken the Christian seriously in the first place, I would never have engaged in this dialogue, had he not deceived me into thinking that his belief in God was the belief of a reasonable person.

Thomas Paine put it well: To argue with a person who has renounced the use of reason is like administering medicine to the dead.

TWO ATHEISTS ON RELIGION AND DOUBT

The moral condemnation of doubt is a fundamental feature of revealed religion. The nineteenth-century atheist Ludwig Feuerbach had this to say about the religious prohibition of doubt:

> Religion annexes to its doctrines a curse and a blessing, damnation and salvation. Blessed is he that believeth, cursed is he that believeth not. Thus it appeals not to reason, but to feeling, to the desire of happiness, to the passions of hope and fear. It does not take the theoretic point of view; otherwise it must have been free to enunciate its doctrines without attaching to them practical consequences, without to a certain extent compelling belief in them; for when the case stands thus: I am lost if I do not believe,—the conscience is under a subtle kind of constraint; the fear of hell urges me to believe. Even supposing my belief to be in its origin free, fear inevitably intermingles itself; my conscience is always under constraint; doubt, the principle of theoretic freedom, appears to me a crime. And as in religion the highest idea, the highest existence is God, so the highest crime is doubt in God, or the doubt that God exists.[2]

Friedrich Nietzsche condemned Christianity as a decadent philosophy of life, because it appeals to the prospect of pleasure (heaven) and the fear of pain (hell) as primary motives for belief. The virtue of belief is rewarded with eternal felicity, whereas the vice of disbelief is punished with eternal torment, so the believer is encouraged to put aside his critical judgment and go for the brass ring instead. This intellectual hedonism—or "proof by pleasure," as Nietzsche calls it—requires the Christian to subordinate his critical judgment to his *desire* for happiness, as if that which will make one happy is necessarily true. But "when on earth was it established that *true* judgments give more enjoyment than false ones . . . ?" Experience teaches us that truth is sometimes unpleasant, so the honest truth seeker must value the judgment of his reason over what he would *like* to believe. Faith, therefore, "means not *wanting* to know what is true."[3]

Nietzsche points out that our beliefs, when valued for themselves instead of for the reasons that support them, become prisons for the intellect. Beliefs should function as means rather than ends: they should fashion and direct our passions in the pursuit of values. But the man of faith reverses this relationship by allowing his passions to determine his beliefs, and in so doing he becomes alienated from his reason and enslaved by his beliefs, which are no longer within his rational control. In short, the man of faith has destroyed within himself the spirit of impartiality. "The believer is not free to have a conscience at all over the question 'true' and 'false': to be honest on *this* point would mean his immediate destruction."[4]

DOUBT AS SIN

Doubt arises within a belief system, not outside of it. Only the believer can truly doubt; those who fall outside of a belief system are disbelievers, not doubters. I do not doubt the existence of Santa Claus; I *deny* his existence altogether. Only the child who believes in Santa can truly doubt his existence, and it is this doubt that paves the way to disbelief.

It is the moralization of doubt—the prohibition of doubt as sinful—that makes the Christian scheme of faith fundamentally dishonest at its core. I say "dishonest" because a Christian, having committed himself, through faith, to the tenets of his religion, is thereafter prohibited from doubting his fundamental beliefs. The Christian has pledged himself to resist all sinful temptations, including the temptation to doubt. The Christian who succumbs to this temptation, and who allows himself to doubt either the existence of God or the veracity of his revealed word, has done far more than commit a breach of religious etiquette, bereft of practical consequences. The Christian doubter, in presuming to question the dictates of his infallible God, is guilty of supreme insolence.

The doubter must challenge God to his face. He must say, in effect, "I believe in you, Lord, but I question whether you exist." And the Christian has good reason to fear how God will respond to this presumptuous challenge. Doubt is an affront to the very God in which the Christian believes, and this God does not take such matters lightly. Doubt can imperil the Christian's eternal soul.

God, omnipresent and omniscient, is privy to the Christian's every thought and feeling. There is no cognitive or emotional privacy in the Christian universe, no inner world into which one can retreat, no sovereign sphere of conscience in which one is accountable only to oneself, no room to question or criticize without fear of divine retribution. For the Christian God knows all and sees all. He is a jealous God who demands unconditional faith above all else.

To have faith means to trust in God without hesitation, so to doubt is to betray this trust and thereby jeopardize one's personal relationship with God. This is why it is extremely difficult for doubt to take root in the believer's mind. No doubt, however minor, can be concealed from an all-knowing and ever-present God; and no doubt, however honest, is free from the taint of sin. Thus the Christian, unable to doubt in private, unable to retreat into an inner sanctum of thought and deliberation, has no choice but to doubt in full view of God's omnipresent and vengeful eyes.

If the Christian is to embark on the road to atheism, this process of deconversion can only begin with doubt. The Christian must believe in God while somehow doubting that belief. But this can prove nearly impossible for the Christian who, while fully aware that God is monitoring his every thought, must call into question the very faith on which his salvation depends.

This is what makes Christianity fundamentally dishonest. The Christian, having entered into a belief system, finds that the door swings only one way, and that getting in was much easier than getting out. The Christian is effectively precluded from criticizing his own beliefs, for such criticism is always attended by the threat of divine retribution.

INFALLIBLE CERTITUDES

The Christian is certain of many things. He knows that God exists and that Jesus is the Son of God. He knows that God likes some people more than others and that he is on God's shortlist of favorites. He knows how the world came into being and how it will end. He knows that there is life after death and that he will end up in a better place than the atheist. He knows that life has a purpose and what that purpose is. He knows that good will ultimately prevail over evil. He knows why many people are miserable and what would make them happy. He knows which sexual acts are good and which are evil. He even knows that some scientific theories are right and others wrong.

Yes, the Christian knows all this and much more, and he knows what he knows with an absolute certainty untainted by doubt; for this knowledge comes via the Bible from God, and any revelation from this infallible being is necessarily true.

It may appear that the Christian has forever freed himself from the danger of doubt by building a massive wall of certainty between doubt and his doctrines. His beliefs, after all, are certified by the infallible authority of God, so what has he to fear from doubt? Of what possible threat are a few human doubts when compared to the fortress of revealed knowledge? Why does the Christian, secure in his citadel of certitudes, fret so much over even the slightest doubt?

To ask such questions is to answer them, at least in part. The Christian is quite right to feel apprehensive about his citadel of certitudes, as if it does not provide as much protection against doubt as may first appear. Indeed, his citadel, which supposedly rests on an infallible foundation, is a house of cards that could collapse upon the slightest tremor of doubt. The Christian is vulnerable to even the slightest and most insignificant doubt, because all of his beliefs rest on a single, narrow—and very unstable—point, viz., the appeal to infallible revelation. This is the foundation of his belief system, so if even one belief is called into question, if even a single, solitary doubt is permitted to invade this belief system at any point and for any reason, then the entire system can easily be thrown into a state of crisis. Why? Because if even one doubt is appropriate, if even one belief is made to seem less than infallible, then the same reasoning that justified this single doubt will apply to every other Christian belief as well.

This brings us back to a subject that I alluded to earlier, namely, the inner logic of deconversion. Doubt, as many people who have deconverted from Christianity to atheism can attest, will tend to progress rapidly in the mind of the believer, if it is not immediately crushed by fear, guilt, or some other prophylactic emotion. The gap between total belief and just one doubt, however minor, is far greater than the gap between one doubt and one hundred similar doubts—so the process of deconversion has already advanced to a considerable degree by the time one doubt has taken hold.

THE VARIETIES OF DOUBT

Perhaps the best way to approach the subject of doubt is to contrast it with other concepts. In other words, if we don't have doubt, what do we have instead? Doubt as opposed to *what*?

It might seem that "doubt" should be contrasted with "certainty"; we doubt that a proposition is true when we are not certain of its truth. But even if we accept this dichotomy, it does not suffice to explain the meaning of "doubt," because "certainty" is itself an ambiguous term that has (at least) two distinct meanings.

As with "argument" and similar terms, the word "certainty" has both psychological and logical meanings. The psychological (or subjective) meaning is reflected in statements like, "I am certain that p is true." The logical (or objective) meaning is present in statements like, "The truth of p is certain."

The difference between these two senses of "certain"—the subjective and the objective—can be illustrated in the following way. Suppose Jack says, "I am *certain* that at least one human being has been abducted by aliens from another planet." Jack is here expressing his strong *belief* in the existence of alien visitors, and the reality of this psychological state of mind does not depend on whether Jack's belief can be justified as objectively true. Even if Jack is wrong, even if aliens have never visited earth, the fact remains that Jack believes otherwise; he is *subjectively certain* that his belief is true.

Objective certainty, in contrast, refers not to a belief per se but to the *cognitive value* of that belief. A belief is objectively certain if, and only if, it has been sufficiently justified by rational methods. Objective certainty is the result of an epistemological judgment. To say, "The truth of p is certain," is to say that p has been tested for coherence, evidence, and so on, and has passed with flying colors.

It seems that "doubt" is most often contrasted with the *subjective* meaning of "certainty." To say, "I doubt p," is to express a mental attitude toward p, a *feeling* of hesitancy or reservation about the truth of p.[5] And this suggests that doubt is active rather than passive: To doubt is actively to question or challenge the truth of a belief.

This is what Thomas Hobbes had in mind when he described doubt as a chain of *alternate* opinions about the truth of a proposition.[6] I think p may be true, then I think p may be false, then I again think p may be true, and so forth: These alternating judgments, according to Hobbes, constitute the mental process known as "doubt."

This view suggests that we should differentiate between doubt and uncertainty. To be uncertain (in this context) is to believe with some degree of probability, while refusing to give one's full assent to the truth of a proposition. Such uncertainty may be purely negative in character. It may result from a lack of information about (or interest in) the subject at hand, in which case the uncertainty would not be accompanied by positive doubt. For example, I might be *uncertain* about the truth of Einstein's theory of relativity, since I lack the necessary information and skill to evaluate it for myself; but I would not normally be said to *doubt* its truth, since this would imply that I have *positive reasons* to question it.

Uncertainty is the absence of certainty, so an uncertain belief may be nothing more than a probable belief (which also indicates a lack of certainty) But to say that I regard *p* as *probably* true is not necessarily to say that I *doubt* the truth of *p*. Uncertainty is negative, whereas doubt is positive: Uncertainty is a mental *state* in which full assent is lacking, whereas doubt is a mental *process* in which the truth of a belief is actively called into question. Doubt therefore has an aggressive quality that pure uncertainty does not. To doubt is to actively question the truth of a proposition.

The foregoing analysis will aid our understanding of what it means to doubt a supposed revelation from God, and why this is said to constitute a grievous sin. In Christianity doubt stands opposed not to certainty per se, but to *faith*. To have faith, in a religious context, is to have absolute confidence in God and to trust his revelations unconditionally. Thus, for the Christian to be uncertain of a divine revelation is bad enough, but to doubt that revelation is incomparably worse, because the latter implies a readiness to criticize that the former does not. Uncertainty may be attributed to a temporary lapse of faith, a human foible that even God may understand and overlook. But actively to doubt the truth of a purported revelation is to challenge God himself, and this indicates a rebellious spirit, not a lack of self-confidence.

In short, for the Christian to doubt the truth of a purported revelation is potentially to challenge the authority of the infallible God in whom she believes. It is therefore religious doubt, not atheistic disbelief, that constitutes the greatest threat to orthodox beliefs, because doubt threatens to undermine a belief system from within. And this explains what might almost be called an invariable law of Christian history—namely, that *heretics* (unorthodox Christians) are far more despised and feared than *infidels* (nonbelievers, such as Jews, Muslims, and atheists).

We see what is perhaps the most significant difference between religion and philosophy in their respective attitudes toward doubt. Religion attempts to banish doubt, whereas philosophy tries to cultivate and refine it. This latter is by no means a simple task, so let's take a brief look at the philosophical uses of doubt.

Doubt may be divided into two broad categories: *spontaneous* and *methodic.*

Doubt is spontaneous when it arises, unplanned and sometimes unwanted, in the normal course of our lives. For instance, Jill may doubt the fidelity of her husband, Jack, owing to the many telltale clues she has inadvertently run across. Jill did not plan this doubt; she did not undertake a systematic investigation of Jack's activities in order to find evidence of his infidelity. On the contrary, prior to her accidental discoveries, she had never suspected him of anything. Hence Jill's doubt is spontaneous; it did not arise from foresight or design.

This is not the kind of doubt that characterizes philosophy. Of course, the philosopher is a human being who, like everyone else, will sometimes experience spontaneous doubt during the course of his life—but the doubt of the philosopher qua philosopher is methodic rather than spontaneous. In calling this doubt *methodic,* I mean that it is part of a systematic *method* used by the philosopher in his investigations. And this method—which Kant dubbed "procedure according to principle"—is the product of foresight and planning. Methodic doubt, in other words, is *purposeful* rather than spontaneous, systematic rather than incidental.

Methodic doubt stands in a category of its own; it is not what most people think of when they employ the word "doubt." Methodic doubt, for example, is fully compatible with subjective certainty. I may be fully convinced that there exists a world external to my consciousness, yet I may subject this belief to methodic doubt nonetheless. In my case, the purpose of this inquiry would not be to attain a higher degree of certainty than I already have; rather, I might question the existence of an external world in order to determine whether this is a reasonable question in the first place, and, if it is not, *why* it is not. Or, like Descartes, I might apply methodic doubt to my commonsense beliefs in order to identify the ultimate foundation of certainty. In any case, the philosopher will often apply methodic doubt to beliefs that would rarely, if ever, generate spontaneous doubt. And this use of methodic doubt does not *necessarily* mean that the philosopher has *any* subjective doubts about the belief that is being scrutinized. It may simply mean that the philosopher expects (or hopes) that something of value—a fresh insight, perhaps, or a new way of looking at an old problem—will emerge as a by-product of his methodic doubt.

It is primarily owing to methodic doubt that many people look askance at the philosopher, suspecting that he harbors nihilistic tendencies and desires. "Question everything! Let no belief, however sacred, escape the glare of critical scrutiny." This categorical imperative of philosophy raises the disturbing possibility that an omnivorous doubt will consume every belief in its path, leaving behind a swampland of skepticism where no belief can find solid ground on which to stand.

I cannot here discuss the absurdities of universal skepticism, except to note that it is *not* a logical outcome of methodic doubt. Indeed, methodic doubt can be (and frequently is) a prelude to certainty, since it is by examining the *grounds* of belief that certainty can best be justified. Recall my earlier statement that philosophy attempts to "cultivate *and refine*" the process of doubt. The philosopher refines doubt by using it purposefully and systematically, and this methodic doubt is the antithesis of the indiscriminate doubt that we find in universal skepticism.

If what I have said is true, if methodic doubt is fully compatible with certainty, then we may wonder why this kind of doubt has been condemned by so many Christians throughout history. After all, if methodic doubt can sometimes justify a greater degree of certainty for particular beliefs, then why should the true believer shy away from it? Is it not possible that his religious belief will also emerge a winner after having been subjected to the methodic doubt of philosophy?

In a word, the answer to this last question is "no"; in a few words, the answer is "not a chance." This is because Christian doctrines are supposedly based on revelations from God, and whatever God says is necessarily true. These doctrines, therefore, are already regarded by the Christian as *infallibly certain* prior to, and independent of, any further investigation. Thus, since it is impossible to improve upon an infallible belief by making it more certain than it already is, the

Christian has nothing to gain and everything to lose by subjecting his beliefs to the rigors of methodic doubt. Having already scaled the summit of cognitive perfection, the Christian has nowhere to go but down—and she has good reason to fear that this is precisely where philosophy will take her.

Whether a revealed religion lives or dies will depend, first and foremost, on its claim to possess infallible knowledge, and it is primarily owing to this claim that there will always exist a severe friction between religion and philosophy.

NOTES

1. Adam Smith, *The Theory of Moral* Sentiments, ed. D. D. Raphael and A. L. Macfie (Indianapolis: Liberty Classics, 1982), p. 336.

2. Ludwig Feuerbach, *The Essence of Christianity*, trans. George Eliot (New York: Harper Torchbooks, 1957), p. 186.

3. Friedrich Nietzsche, *The Anti-Christ*, trans. R.J. Hollingdale (London: Penguin Books, 1968), pp. 176–77.

4. Ibid., p. 183.

5. Of course, we may also say that the truth of p is *doubtful*, thereby using the term in an objective sense. The fundamental problem here is that the meanings of "doubt," "belief," etc. are determined by conventional usage, not by philosophical decree. The philosopher must rely on meanings that have already been established through conventional usage. And though these meanings are usually sufficient for the purpose of ordinary communication, they are often too vague and ambiguous for the philosopher, who must then *stipulate* what *he* means by a given word. It is therefore futile to search for the "true" meaning of a word like "doubt"; the most a philosopher can accomplish with linguistic analysis is to clarify and distinguish the various meanings and nuances of this word in the hope that this process will shed some light on philosophical problems.

6. Thomas Hobbes, *Leviathan*, ed. Michael Oakeshott (New York: Collier Books, 1962), p. 56.

Belief and Knowledge

Two Kinds of Belief

There are two major forms in which we express a belief, viz., "belief *that*" and "belief *in*." To say, "I believe *that* Jesus was born in Bethlehem," is to express one's assent to the truth of this *proposition*. To say, "I believe *in* Jesus," is to express one's commitment to the *person* of Jesus as a religious authority who should be trusted in all things.

This second kind of belief—belief *in* rather than belief *that*—often conveys one's devotion to someone or something of significant value. We see this kind of value-charged conviction in expressions like, "I believe in democracy" or "I believe in freedom." This kind of "belief in" always implies a corresponding "belief that" which articulates the reason for one's devotion. The libertarian believes *in* freedom, because he believes *that* freedom is essential to individual happiness and a prosperous society. The Christian believes *in* Jesus because he believes *that* Jesus is the Son of God who died on the cross to redeem the sins of humankind. In such cases, to "believe *in*" can express something more than one's assent to the truth of a proposition; it can also convey one's personal commitment to something of significant value.

The value-laden nature of personal beliefs helps to explain why we tend to be more jealous of our personal beliefs than our abstract knowledge claims, often defending them with more vigor and passion. When someone criticizes my personal beliefs (i.e., my "beliefs *in*"), she is doing far more than challenging my abstract claim to know, for this knowledge claim constitutes the foundation of my most important value commitments. And because my sense of "who I am" is inextricably linked to my fundamental values, I will defend the knowledge on which these values depend with great passion, as if I were fighting for my very existence—as indeed, in a psychological sense, I am.

DIFFERENT CONCEPTIONS OF BELIEF

According to some philosophers, the fundamental meaning of "belief" is best expressed as "belief in" rather than "belief that." Thomas Hobbes, for example, maintained that belief "beginneth at some saying of another, of whose ability to know the truth, and of whose honesty in not deceiving, he doubteth not. . . ."[1] Belief, in other words, is based on our trust, or "faith," in the credibility and veracity of another person. I believe *p* not because I can demonstrate its truth, but because an authority has assured me that *p* is true.

Other philosophers have followed the lead of Aristotle and other Greek philosophers who distinguished between knowledge (*episteme*) and opinion (*doxa*). John Locke, for example, equated "knowledge" with certainty and "belief" with probability. To know that *p* is true is to be *certain* of its truth, whereas to believe that *p* is true is to accept it with some degree of *probability*. Quoting Locke:

> *Probability* is likeliness to be true, the very notation of the Word signifying such a proposition, for which there be Arguments or Proofs, to make it pass or be received for true. The entertainment the Mind gives this sort of Propositions, is called *Belief*, *Assent*, or *Opinion*, which is the admitting or receiving any Proposition for true, upon Arguments or Proofs that are found to persuade us to receive it as true, without certain knowledge that it is so. And herein lies the *difference between Probability* and *Certainty*, *Faith* and *Knowledge*. . . .[2]

Knowledge, according to Locke, is based on *reason*, whereas belief derives from *judgment*. We believe *p* when, in the absence of a conclusive demonstration, we judge that the evidence in favor of *p* is sufficient to establish its truth with some degree of probability.

Locke's distinction between knowledge and belief (which, as I said, can be traced to the ancient Greeks) is sometimes reflected in our everyday use of these terms. For example, if I am asked about the date of a friend's birthday, I might say, "I *believe* it is February 10"— meaning this is *probably* the correct date, but I'm not certain. But if I say, "I *know* it is February 10," this suggests a high degree of *certainty*, as if I have no doubt whatever about the truth of my statement. Contrariwise, it might sound peculiar to say, "I *believe* that two plus two equals four," as if the truth of this proposition were a matter of opinion rather than knowledge. Less peculiar would be the statement, "I *know* that two plus two equals four."

But this distinction between belief and knowledge, however natural in some situations, might be objectionable in others, such as when discussing the religious beliefs of a Christian. Suppose a Christian tells me of his belief that Jesus is the Son of God, and I reply, "Since you speak of *belief* rather than *knowledge*, I must assume that you are not certain about whether Jesus was the Son of God, but regard this as merely probable." The Christian would rightfully object to this interpretation, because it does not represent what he wishes to convey. On the contrary, he will likely assign to this belief the highest degree of certitude, since he regards it as the revealed truth of an infallible God.

According to a third and more general meaning, "belief" is mental assent (to whatever degree) to the truth of a proposition. In this sense, to say, "I believe *p*," is to say that I affirm the truth of *p*. To say, for example, "I believe in the existence of God," is to say, "I affirm that the proposition 'God exists' is true."

It is this generic meaning of "belief"—which refers to a *psychological* act of assent—that I shall employ throughout this book. Thus, contrary to Locke, I shall not speak of knowledge in contrast to belief, but shall instead treat knowledge as a *type* of belief. Specifically, I shall follow the common philosophical practice of defining *knowledge* as a belief that is both *justified* and *true*.

The Elements of Knowledge

Knowledge, according to a standard definition, is justified and true belief. Justification and truth—these two elements are essential if a belief is to qualify as authentic knowledge. The following scenarios should help to explain why this is so.

Jack, a precocious six-year-old who wants to be a theologian when he grows up, has just been told by his older sister, Jill, that Santa Claus does not really exist. Little Jack is dismayed that his own sister—who had long shared his passionate belief in the existence of a being than which nothing jollier can be conceived—has joined the ranks of skeptics and blasphemers, so he resolves to save her from the torment of never receiving another present on Christmas morning.

"How can you possibly claim that Santa doesn't exist?" Jack says to Jill. "Just look at the evidence. First, our parents, neighbors, teachers, and other adults have assured us of the existence of Santa, and we have no reason to suppose they have lied to us. Plus, I get presents every Christmas that are personally signed, 'From Santa,' and he drinks the milk that we leave out for him. What are you—some kind of conspiracy nut who believes that the entire adult population is out to deceive little kids? Second, my letters to Santa (which I address to the 'North Pole') have never been returned by the post office, so what happens to them if they don't go to Santa? Do you expect me to believe that the United States government is part of this vast conspiracy of yours? And what about the news bulletins every Christmas Eve that track the movement of Santa's sled? Is the media also part of this global network of deceit? Am I to suppose that adults are so determined to lead kids astray that they would fake all this evidence? Thus, if I am to believe you, if I am to believe that Santa does not exist, I must reject the testimony of competent witnesses, ignore the evidence of my senses, and—worst of all—I must become a conspiracy nut who believes that parents, teachers, politicians, journalists, ministers, and countless other adults have nothing better to do than to participate in a nefarious scheme of deceit. All this strikes me as highly improbable, so I must logically conclude that Santa does in fact exist."

Given the evidence that is available to Jack, his belief in Santa, though mistaken, is quite reasonable. Indeed, when viewed within the context of knowledge that is available to a six-year-old boy, we may even say that Jack's belief is *justified.* But his belief, however justified, is *not true.* And because it is not true, Jack cannot be said to *know* that Santa exists. A belief, if it is to qualify as knowledge, must not only be justified, but must also be *true.*

Little Jack has another belief, one that is a bit more peculiar than his belief in Santa. For no particular reason, Jack passionately believes that the quantity of stars in the universe, if added together in a single sum, would constitute an *even* number. And Jill, who has decided that whatever her brother believes is probably wrong, embraces the opposite position: She believes that the sum of stars is an *odd* number.

Now in this case, either Jack or Jill—one or the other, but not both—has made the correct guess, since the number in question must either be even or odd. And since a true belief is one that corresponds to a fact of reality, we may say that either Jack or Jill—we don't know which—has a *true* belief. But regardless of who is right, we would *not* say that they have authentic *knowledge* of what they happen to believe, because their beliefs cannot be *justified*. Neither Jack nor Jill is in a *position to know* the total number of stars, so any belief about this matter, even if it happens to be true, does not constitute knowledge. If a belief is to qualify as knowledge it must be not only true but justified as well.

Knowledge is justified, true belief. Although this standard definition has been subjected to a good deal of technical criticism in recent decades, I believe it has survived relatively unscathed. Epistemology (the theory of knowledge) is a complex and controversial discipline. Every definition of "knowledge" has been so thoroughly analyzed that it is difficult to discuss this subject without getting lost in a picayune jungle of irrelevancies. Since this book is not a treatise on epistemology per se, but is rather the application of epistemological standards to the subject of atheism, I shall confine myself to a few remarks about the definition of "knowledge" as "justified, true belief."

JUSTIFICATION

It is essential that we distinguish the *psychological* concept of "belief" from the *cognitive* concept of "truth." Belief is the assent of the mind to the truth of a proposition, and to assent (or to affirm) requires an act of consciousness. (We could substitute another term, such as "disposition" or "attitude," for "act" or "activity." Subtle differences of meaning are unimportant for the present discussion, which is concerned only with the *psychological* orientation of belief.)

My beliefs, like my emotions, are *my* beliefs; they are psychological phenomena that cannot coexist in, or be transferred to, the mind of another person. A belief is the mental affirmation of an individual believer. A belief cannot exist outside of, independently of, or in addition to the consciousness of a particular individual.

A belief must have a content, or subject matter. To believe is to believe something; to assent is to assent to something; to affirm is to affirm something. Merely to say "I believe," without indicating (implicitly or explicitly) the object of one's belief, is to say nothing at all.

Thus where we have a belief, we must also have an object of belief. And in the case of a cognitive belief—i.e., a belief *that* such-and-such is true—this object is abstract rather than concrete, general rather than singular. To believe *that* such-and-such is the case is to affirm that *p* (a proposition) is true. This proposition is the abstract object of a cognitive belief.

It is owing to its abstract object that a belief can be something more than the subjective affirmation of a particular individual. It is the abstract object that makes a belief objective as well as subjective. My psychological world is private: No one else can share, or participate in, my subjective experiences—whether perceptual, emotional, or mental. Thus my belief, when viewed psychologically as my subjective assent to the truth of a proposition, is necessarily mine and mine alone.

When we say that two people have the *same* belief, we are speaking objectively rather than subjectively. My subjective assent cannot be your subjective assent, but we can both assent to the same abstract proposition. My belief, psychologically considered, cannot be your belief, but we can both believe in the same proposition. In other words, our mental acts of affirmation, though separate and distinct, can have the same abstract object. It is in this objective sense, when we affirm the same abstract truth, that we are said to have the same belief.

In addition to the subjective act of assent and the objective content of a belief, there is yet a third aspect that is in some respects the most important. This is the *cognitive value* of a belief, i.e., the justification or grounds of belief. To justify a belief is to assess its cognitive value and to pronounce it *worthy* of acceptance. To say, "My belief in *p* is justified," is to say (in part), "You *ought* to take my belief seriously, evaluate the evidence for *p*, and—if you agree that *p* has cognitive value—you *should* affirm it as true."

Justification is the intermediate link that joins together the subjective act of assent to the abstract object of belief, and thereby transforms belief into knowledge. For knowledge, as we have seen, is more than true belief; it is belief that is both true and justified. Justification is neither psychological assent nor the abstract object of belief; it is a *judgment* of cognitive value that determines whether we should (or should not) give our assent to the truth of a proposition.

This is what I mean when I say that justification serves as a bridge between the subjective and objective aspects of belief. In seeking justification we must make judgments of cognitive value— we must determine whether a belief is or is not worthy of our assent—and this process of evaluation has both subjective (psychological) and objective (abstract) components.

A belief cannot evaluate its own object: Only a thinking person (or other rational being) can assess the truth-value of a belief. In this sense, therefore, justification is a psychological process, one that can only occur in the mind of a particular individual. But this process of evaluation, if it is to serve its purpose, must employ abstract norms of cognition, and this gives to justification its objective character.

Justification, therefore, is neither wholly subjective nor wholly objective, but has both subjective and objective components. It is subjective inasmuch as only the individual can render judgments of cognitive value. It is objective inasmuch as this evaluation must be based on universal norms of cognition (logic, coherence, probability, evidence, etc.) that can be applied by others who may wish to evaluate the belief in question.

I shall use the term *contextual* to denote this dual nature of justification. Recall our example of precocious little Jack, who defends his belief in Santa Claus. To say that Jack's belief in Santa is *contextually justified* is to say that it has legitimate cognitive value *for Jack*, given his limited context of knowledge. Thus, although Jack's belief in Santa is false, it is also *reasonable*, because it is based on universal norms of cognition (credibility of witnesses, sensory evidence, etc.) that can be assessed by other people.

The abstract object of Jack's belief is the proposition "Santa exists," and it is in this objective sense that Jack may be said to have the same belief as other young children. But what is distinctive about Jack's belief, what sets it apart from the same belief of other six-year-olds, is its remarkably sophisticated level of justification. Jack defends the truth-value of his belief by appealing to abstract cognitive norms, so his false belief in Santa has better grounds than the beliefs of many adults. But Jack's belief, though contextually justified, is false nonetheless, so it does not constitute knowledge.

Justification is an assessment of cognitive value. To say that a belief is justified is to say that it has sufficient cognitive merit, or truth-value, to warrant the assent of a rational person, i.e., that it *should* be believed. And since justification is contextual, since objective norms must be applied to particular judgments of cognitive value, this means that two people with the same object of belief may have different grounds of assent. Two theists who share the same object of belief (e.g., the existence of God) may do so for different reasons—so if one theist is willing to justify his belief whereas the other is not, the belief of the former may be said to be more *rational* than that of the latter.

TRUTH

To summarize our discussion thus far:

- *Belief* is psychological assent to the truth of a proposition.
- *Knowledge* is belief that is at once justified and true.

[69]

- *Justification* is the evidence and/or arguments to which the believer appeals in support of her claim to know.
- *Truth* is the correspondence between a proposition and a fact. (A *fact* is that which *is*, i.e., that which exists independently of any perception, thought, belief, or knowledge claim.)

This last statement expresses what is commonly known as the correspondence theory of truth. A proposition is said to be true if, and only if, it corresponds to a fact.

The term *correspondence* is a somewhat unfortunate choice of words. For one thing, it is commonly associated with what philosophers call the "representationalist theory of ideas," which was defended by René Descartes, Locke, and some of their followers. According to this theory, we are directly aware not of a reality external to ourselves, but of our subjective "ideas," which are said to "represent" facts external to themselves. And this means that ideas as well as propositions can be either true or false, depending on whether or not they "correspond" to the facts they represent.

The problems with this theory are legion,[3] but they need not concern us here. In defining truth as correspondence to fact, I am referring not to *ideas* (concepts, mental images, etc.) but solely to *propositions.* Only a proposition can be true or false, because only a proposition (when expressed in the form of a belief) purports to *identify* a fact. The theist may have an idea of God, and this idea may be clear or muddled, coherent or confused, logically consistent or self-contradictory—but this idea, strictly speaking, can be neither true nor false. An idea neither affirms nor denies that something is a fact (to have an idea of God is not necessarily to affirm that God exists[4]), so it makes no sense to evaluate the truth of falsity of an idea per se.

Despite this and other attempts at clarification, it is unlikely that the correspondence theory of truth will ever be able to shed its ambiguities. Perhaps Ayn Rand had this problem in mind when she defined "truth" not as correspondence to fact, but as the *recognition* of fact. A true proposition, according to Rand, is one that correctly *identifies* a fact of reality.

Rand's formulation has considerable merit, because (whether she intended this or not) it calls our attention to the difference between primary judgments of fact and reflexive judgments of truth. Consider the proposition "The cat is on the mat." What do I mean to express when I utter this proposition (assuming, of course, that I believe it to be true)? Do I mean to say—as the term *correspondence* might suggest—that my proposition, "The cat is on the mat," somehow corresponds to a fact? Am I affirming the existence of a relationship (known as "correspondence") between my statement and the fact to which it refers?

Although this abstract relationship is implied by my statement, it seems peculiar to suppose that this is what I primarily have in mind when I say, "The cat is on the mat." What I mean to do, simply and directly, is to identify a fact—namely, the fact that the cat is indeed on the mat, rather than somewhere else.

My proposition is primarily intended to identify a fact, not to render an assessment of its own truth in terms of correspondence. This latter judgment—which philosophers call a *reflexive* judgment— is a secondary judgment that assesses the truth-value of my primary judgment. Thus, whereas my primary judgment is an assertion of fact ("The cat is on the mat"), my reflexive judgment is a judgment of this judgment—one that says, in effect, that the proposition "The cat is on the mat" corresponds to a fact and is therefore true.

I do not mean to criticize the correspondence theory per se; I wish only to distinguish between a primary judgment, which seeks to identify a fact, and a reflexive judgment, which affirms the truth of the primary judgment in terms of its correspondence to fact. Thus, although it is accurate to define "truth" in terms of correspondence, it is equally accurate to define "truth" in terms of identification. Which definition we employ in a particular case is contextual; it depends on the level of judgment—primary or reflexive—to which we are referring.

AYN RAND'S THEORY OF KNOWLEDGE

Ayn Rand's theory of knowledge challenges the conventional view that I am here defending. Rand does not agree that knowledge must be both justified *and* true; knowledge is merely justified belief and nothing more. Why? Because we have no way of ascertaining what is true except through justification, so to say that a belief, if it is to qualify as knowledge, must also be "true" is technically redundant. For truth, like justification, is contextual; it depends on the evidence that is available to us at a given time.

This position merits examination for two reasons: first, because it is an important element of Rand's contextualism, a theory of knowledge that is plausible and rich in implications; and, second, because it reveals a latent tendency toward epistemological relativism that sharply conflicts with Rand's spirited insistence that truth is "objective." (The philosopher Leonard Peikoff, a confidant of Rand's for many years, has extended Rand's contextualism beyond that which appears in Rand's published writings, so I shall rely on his treatment.)

Truth is defined by Ayn Rand as "the recognition of reality"—and this definition, according to Peikoff, is "in essence . . . the traditional correspondence theory of truth."[5] This is true to a point, but there is an interesting aspect to Rand's theory that distinguishes it from the approach I am defending here.

Rand, as we have seen, disagrees with the view that knowledge is true and justified belief. Her reason for treating truth and justification as virtually synonymous is a compelling one, namely, that we cannot know what is true except in the context of knowledge that is available to us at any given time. All judgments of truth by which we justify a belief are contextual, so to treat truth as if it were an abstract correspondence between a proposition and a fact, divorced from the particular judgments of concrete individuals, is implicitly to establish omniscience as a standard of human knowledge. As Peikoff puts it:

> There can be no "correspondence" or "recognition" without the mind that corresponds or recognizes. . . . The true is identified by

reference to a body of evidence; it is pronounced "true" because it can be integrated without contradiction into a total context.[6]

This is the foundation for Rand's contextual theory of certainty. Human knowledge is necessarily limited, which means that man has "a specific cognitive context" at every stage in the development of his knowledge. If, therefore, an idea can be traced to its foundation in sense data and is based on sufficient evidence, then that idea has been "validated." Again quoting Peikoff, "Logical processing of an idea within a specific context of knowledge is necessary *and sufficient* to establish the idea's truth."[7]

This statement, through reasonable on its face, leads to the rather peculiar conclusion—peculiar at least for those who stress the objectivity of knowledge—that there exist different truths for people who work from different contexts of knowledge. Consider one of Peikoff's examples: the belief of early medical researchers that four types of blood (A, B, AB, and O), while incompatible with each other, are each compatible with their own type. It was later discovered that this was not always the case: a recipient of blood from a donor with the same type occasionally responded negatively—a problem that was later explained by the RH factor, which is present in the blood of some individuals but not others.

The philosophical question raised by this story is this: Was the early belief—that each blood type is compatible with its own type—true or false? According to the conventional view (which I am defending), this belief, though justified given the information available to researchers at the time, was in fact *false*, because it did not take into account the RH factor, which was discovered later. But Peikoff disagrees. Given the knowledge available to the earlier researchers, their belief that type A bloods are compatible was justified. Thus, within that context, the proposition "A bloods are compatible" was *true*. As Peikoff says:

This proposition represented *real knowledge* when it was first reached, and it still does so; in fact, like all properly formulated

truths, this truth is immutable. Within the context initially specified, A bloods *are* and always will be compatible.[8]

This is a difficult passage to interpret reasonably, since it seems
so obviously wrong. If "within the context initially specified, A bloods
are and always will be compatible," then what was the original
problem that caused researchers eventually to discover the RH
factor, if not the fact that A bloods were sometimes *incompatible*? The
perception of a problem—that a blood type was not always compatible with the same type—necessarily preceded the search for a solution. Researchers had to become convinced that their current theory
was *false* (at least in some respects) or they would never have looked
for a better one. If Peikoff is correct, if the initial theory was
immutably true within the context of knowledge available to medical
researchers at that time, then there would have been no reason (and
no motive) for them to improve upon that theory.

If, contrary to Peikoff (and presumably to Rand), we distinguish
between truth and justification, then we can explain the preceding
example without difficulty. The initial belief about blood types was
justified, given the information available to early researchers, but it
was not *true*, as researchers themselves later discovered.

Why is this commonsense analysis objectionable to the Randian
contextualist? Because it allegedly divorces the notion of truth from
the knowing mind, exiling it to an ethereal world of Platonic
essences. But since there is no "truth" apart from the particular
recognition of a fact of reality, and since this presupposes a rational
being with a specific mode of cognition, our concept of truth, if it is
to have meaning, must be grounded in the fallible and limited nature
of human reason. Thus if we define "truth" as the abstract correspondence between a proposition and a fact, while neglecting the
cognitive process of recognition by which facts are identified, we
transform truth into an unattainable ideal that will forever lie beyond
our grasp.

This is a reasonable concern. Most forms of epistemological skepticism are based on the fallibility and limitations of human reason. It

has been claimed, for example, that we can never be certain of anything, because many beliefs from earlier ages, which were accepted with the highest degree of certitude, were subsequently proven to be false. And given our innate fallibility, our present beliefs may also be proven wrong by subsequent generations, which means that we should not claim certainty for any of them.

Though it is commendable that Rand and Peikoff wish to extirpate this kind of facile skepticism by pointing to its illicit reliance on infallibility as a criterion of certainty (a point that has been made by many other philosophers), this by no means requires that we reduce truth to sufficient justification, while dispensing altogether with the traditional notion of abstract correspondence. While we should not permit fallibility to be used as a pretext for skepticism, we should also avoid the opposite error of proclaiming as an "immutable truth" every justified belief that is subsequently revised or rejected.

There is a sense in which it redundant to define knowledge as "justified and true belief," because there is no royal road to truth apart from the justification we have to affirm the truth of a particular proposition. We cannot somehow circumvent our best available evidence in favor of a proposition and ascertain its truth directly, without the mediation of a cognitive process.

This applies even to self-evident truths, such as the Law of Identity (A is A) and other logical axioms. The traditional philosophical distinction between intuitive reason (which is able to grasp self-evident truth immediately) and discursive reason (which progresses in a chain of reasoning from premises to conclusion) is highly misleading at best. The axioms of logic, though first in the order of knowledge, are not first in the order of time. That is to say, although these axioms are logically presupposed by all other knowledge (in the sense that no valid knowledge can contradict them), they are not the first knowledge we acquire as infants. By the time we study logic (if we ever do), we already have a store of knowledge that we bring to bear in assessing its axioms, and in light of which we pronounce them "self-evident"—a term that would be meaningless if not set in opposition to truths that are *not* self-evident. Thus the axioms of logic, though self-evidently true, cannot be *identified* as such without a cognitive process. It is in this sense that *all* reasoning is discursive, and none is intuitive. No knowledge is given to man automatically, without mental labor.

What, then, is the point of retaining abstract truth in our definition of knowledge, if we cannot ascertain what is true apart from our contextually justified beliefs? The point is simply this: Truth and justified belief are not the same thing, so they need to be distinguished. Many justified beliefs—propositions that were perfectly reasonable to believe in a particular context—have been not only revised (as Peikoff seems to think) but also rejected completely.

The Copernican revolution in astronomy, which was followed by Johannes Kepler's rejection of circular orbits, is a clear example of this. Do we seriously wish to say that the medieval cosmology—an eclectic brew of Aristotelian physics, Neoplatonic metaphysics, and Ptolemaic astronomy—was (and is) "true," given the medieval context of knowledge and the best evidence that was then available? Do we seriously wish to say that the doctrine of circular planetary orbits was (and is) "true," given the fact it was supported by a long-established and coherent theory of metaphysics, was defended for centuries by the best scientific minds, and was quite adequate for explaining the best available astronomical data prior to the more precise observations of Tycho Brahe?

We might say that these and other scientific theories—which have not been merely revised, but completely *discarded*—were justified beliefs for medieval thinkers, given the apparent evidence in their favor and their overall coherence with the medieval worldview. But they were false nonetheless, absolutely and unequivocally, however justified they may have been at one time. They were not somehow "contextually" true, much less "immutably" so.

Of course, a ready reply to this argument is available to the defenders of Randian contextualism. It can be said (and often has been said) that the medieval cosmology was sustained by a rigid ecclesiastic orthodoxy during an age in which there was little if any authentic science. In this view, the scientific revolution was the triumph of honest inquiry, empiricism, and experimentation over the rigid dogmas of religious orthodoxy. Thus when confronted with the historical transition to modern science, the Randian contextualist might argue that the medieval cosmology does not qualify as even contextually true, because it was not based on logical cognition and authentic evidence. Modern science, therefore, was not a revision of medieval science, because the latter was not legitimate science at all.

This or any similar reply will not solve the incipient relativism of Randian contextualism, even if we accept the preceding characterization of the medieval cosmology at face value (which we should not). The Randian contextualist cannot pick and choose his contextual and immutable truths, depending on whether they approximate modern beliefs, for this would unfairly subject medieval thinkers to the same standards of infallibility and omniscience against which the Randians so vigorously (and rightfully) protest.

A contextual theory of knowledge, in my judgment, must strike a delicate balance between relativism and absolutism. And this is precisely why we should retain the traditional view that knowledge is justified *and* true belief. Justification is relative, whereas truth is absolute. That is to say, what counts as adequate justification for a belief may be relative to the available evidence and one's context of knowledge, whereas the truth of a belief is absolute. A proposition either corresponds to a fact or it does not, and this matter has nothing to do with the relative justification for a belief.

It is by blending the relativity of justification with the absolutism of truth that we arrive at a true contextual theory of knowledge. Justification without truth leads to a futile relativism, while truth without justification, by equating knowledge with infallibility, leads to a skepticism that is equally futile.

Although we have no royal roads to knowledge, although we cannot know what is true apart from what we are justified in believing to be true, this does not mean that we should dispense with the notion of absolute truth. This notion, if it is an abstract ideal, also functions as a concrete reminder of our fallibility. It stands, like Mordicai at the gate, as a reminder that no belief can claim a privileged immunity from critical evaluation; and that every reflective person, however justified his beliefs may be, is prey to the same errors of fallibility as everyone else.

NOTES

1. Thomas Hobbes, *Leviathan*, ed. Michael Oakeshott (New York: Collier Books, 1962), p. 57.

2. John Locke, *An Essay Concerning Human Understanding*, ed. Peter Nidditch (Oxford: Clarendon Press, 1975), p. 655.

3. For one thing, if our knowledge of objective reality is necessarily indirect, if all awareness must pass through the subjective filter of ideas, then we can never get "out there" to determine whether there is a true correspondence between our ideas and the facts they represent.

4. But this, as we shall later see, is precisely what the Ontological Argument seeks to prove, viz., that to understand the concept of God logically entails the existence of God.

5. Leonard Peikoff, *Objectivism: The Philosophy of Ayn Rand* (New York: Meridian, 1993), p. 165

6. Ibid.

7. Ibid., p. 171.

8. Ibid.; emphasis added.

Belief and Free Will

THE FOOL

R are is the theologian who, when discussing atheism, does not quote Psalms 14.1: "The fool says in his heart, 'There is no God.' They are corrupt, they do abominable deeds, there is none that does good."

Why does the Psalmist attribute atheism to the "heart"? Because, according to the standard interpretation, atheism originates in the will, not the intellect; it is the result of a foolish and arrogant pride in the power of reason to judge matters that are properly the concern of God. Or this at least is how this passage has been interpreted by hundreds of theologians. The existence of God, we are told, is so manifest (or self-evident, according to some theologians) that only a fool could possibly be an atheist. And this fool must deny

God in his heart rather than his head—i.e., he must *will* to disbelieve—because only an intellect that has been led astray by a perverse will could possibly deny such an obvious truth.

The will of the atheist (so goes the standard interpretation) has been vitiated by the sin of egoistic pride. The atheist values himself above God and chooses to follow his own feeble judgment rather than the infallible word of God. Atheism, therefore, is not merely a mistaken judgment. It is not the innocent error of a person who falls short in his quest for truth. The evidence for God's existence is abundant and irrefutable; his existence is obvious to all except those who are willfully blind. If the atheist does not see God, this is because he *cannot* see God; and if he cannot see God, this is because he *will* not see God. The atheist, blinded by his will, is unable to reason correctly in matters pertaining to God.

Thus the atheist, consumed by arrogance, denies God in his heart, and the influence of his corrupt will is so pervasive as to render him unable to do anything except "abominable deeds." Atheism is a rebellion of the will, a deliberate turning away from God, and since every action by the atheist must proceed from his sinful will, none of his actions is good.

Here, in four brief paragraphs, is the sum and substance of countless theological tomes, which elaborate upon the Psalmist in tiresome detail. And thus has an elegant (if false) aphorism become the basis for a dreary procession of *ad hominem* arguments in which the atheist is vilified, caricatured, and condemned.

Belief and Moral Responsibility

Is belief a matter of choice? Can we will to believe something without sufficient evidence, or in spite of evidence to the contrary? Can we choose *not* to believe something that has been logically demonstrated? And if we assent to a belief voluntarily, does it thereby become a legitimate subject of moral judgment? Does it make sense to speak of a belief per se as being either good or evil? Or, alternatively, is it reasonable to praise or blame a person for what he or she happens to believe? In other words, can we be held *morally* responsible for our beliefs?

These and similar questions pertaining to the ethics of belief, however theoretical they may appear, have been fraught with momentous practical implications throughout the history of Christendom, especially during the many centuries when religious persecution was the norm. If Augustine, Aquinas, Luther, and other theologians were to justify the punishment of heretics and other dissenters, they had to uphold the volitional nature of religious belief. For if we do not have control over what we believe, if the atheist does not *choose* to disbelieve in God, then on what ground can religious dissenters be held morally and legally responsible, and thereby punished, for their failure to accept Christian dogma?

Early proponents of religious toleration often maintained that belief is not a matter of free will, but is determined by our intellect, according as it is (or is not) persuaded by the available evidence. A typical example of this line of argument appears in the following passage, published in 1644 by the English individualist William Walwyn:

> Of what judgment soever a man is, he cannot choose but be of that judgment. . . . [N]ow where there is necessity there ought to be no punishment, for punishment is the recompense for voluntary actions, therefore no man ought to be punished for his judgment.[1]

This common argument also appears in John Locke's influential essay, "A Letter Concerning Toleration":

> [I]t is absurd that things should be enjoined by laws, which are not within men's power to perform; and to believe this or that to be true, does not depend on our will.[2]

Other proponents of toleration took a different view, maintaining instead that belief does have a volitional component. Christian belief, according to this argument, is meritorious precisely because it requires the voluntary assent of faith—so any attempt to use coercion can only nullify the merit that Christian belief would otherwise have. Coercion is incompatible with faith, which must be voluntary, so persecution has no legitimate role in the furtherance of religion.

This argument has a long ancestry, reaching back to the early Christian era. Consider, for example, this passage by Lactantius (240–320):

> [I]f you wish to defend religion by bloodshed, and by tortures, and by guilt, it will no longer be defended, but will be polluted and profaned. For nothing is so much a matter of free-will as religion; in which, if the mind of the worshipper is disinclined to it, religion is at once taken away, and ceases to exist.[3]

This and other calls for toleration were directed against the Roman persecution of Christians, before Christianity became the official state religion under the emperor Constantine. Subsequently, however, as Theodosius and other emperors enforced Christian orthodoxy by outlawing paganism and punishing dissenters, most theologians became avid defenders of persecution. As St. Hilary of Poitiers, a rare exception, wrote in 365:

> The Church terrifieth with threats of exile and dungeons; and she, who of old gained men's faith in spite of exile and prison, now brings them to believe in her by compulsion. . . . She, who was propagated by hunted priests, now hunts priests in her turn. . . .[4]

Although it is not my purpose to trace the relationship between religious persecution and the ethics of belief,[5] the reader should have some appreciation for the historical significance of this issue. Controversies in philosophy and theology, however theoretical and abstract they may seem, have sometimes become matters of life and death for countless numbers of people.

COGNITIVE DETERMINISM

According to the doctrine of cognitive determinism, what we do or do not believe is not a matter of free will but is determined by our intellect which, having analyzed and assessed the available evidence, judges whether a proposition has been sufficiently justified to qualify as true. And when the intellect makes this judgment, when it determines that a proposition is (probably or certainly) true, then belief follows automatically and immediately, without an intervening act of will.

Belief, in this view, is commanded by the intellect, not chosen by the will. Whether our judgment is good or bad, reasonable or unreasonable, it is how we assess the evidence for and against a proposition (*p*) that will determine whether or not we believe *p* to be true. For to believe is to assent, to assent is to affirm, and to affirm is *judge affirmatively*. In other words, to judge that *p* is justified is simultaneously to affirm that *p* is true—and from this affirmation there must necessarily follow the mental assent known as belief.

If we accept cognitive determinism, then we cannot say that the atheist chooses to disbelieve in the same sense that a thief chooses to steal. The thief, having weighed the pros and cons of various options, chooses to steal; but if there are no such options in the realm of belief, if our beliefs are *not* volitional, then the atheist, following the judgment of his intellect, cannot help but to disbelieve in God. He no more chooses to be an atheist than he chose to be born, so it would be manifestly unjust if God were to punish the atheist for something for which he is not responsible.

This conclusion is not necessitated by every form of cognitive determinism. John Locke, while denying the will any direct role in the determination of belief, still concedes that our choices can *indirectly* influence what we believe. For even if belief necessarily follows judgment, we must still choose how to exercise our judgment in a particular case. We may, for instance, refuse to consider pertinent evidence and, as a result of this willful ignorance, render a judgment that is inadequate or defective. Thus, although we are not directly responsible for what we believe, we are responsible nonetheless, because it is within our power to think or not to think, to consider or not to consider, when judging a particular issue.

Locke's theory—which assigns to free will a major role in determining not our beliefs per se, but the *quality* of our judgments on which those beliefs depend—does not fully support his argument (quoted above) that what we believe "does not depend on our will." For if it is true that I cannot will myself to believe something without sufficient evidence, it is also true that I may, through an act of will, consider evidence that I had previously ignored, and thereby alter the judgment on which my belief depends. And if this is possible, we can be said to exercise some control over belief—because we can choose to exercise better judgment and, in so doing, possibly alter the content or intensity of a given belief.

THOMAS AQUINAS

A detailed discussion of the ethics of belief appears in the thirteenth-century work *Summa Theologica*, by Thomas Aquinas. To believe, according to Aquinas, "is to think with assent"; belief "is an act of the intellect, according as the will moves it to assent."[6] Aquinas thus maintains that belief is at once cognitive and volitional: It is an act of both the *intellect* and the *will*.

Consider the difference between these two statements: "I believe in a god" and "I believe in God." The former (belief in a god) refers to the *object* of faith, to that being which one believes to exist, so it illustrates the cognitive side of belief. But the latter (belief in God) expresses one's trust, or faith, in the veracity of God, so it illustrates the volitional factor of belief. Belief *in* God comes about "in so far as the intellect is moved by the will."[7]

The volitional aspect of belief has always played an important role in Christian theology, for it enabled Aquinas (and many other theologians) to portray faith in God as a "meritorious act." We can be neither praised nor condemned for an act over which we have no control. Only volitional acts can properly be the subject of moral judgment; so if we have no control over what we believe, if our beliefs cannot be freely chosen, then the theologian cannot reasonably condemn atheism and other forms of disbelief as sinful.

Aquinas upholds two positions: first, "unbelief is a sin"; second, "every sin is voluntary."[8] It clearly follows, therefore, that whether or not one believes in God must be a matter of free will. It is this volitional element that distinguishes the truths of religion from the truths of science. Aquinas, like Aristotle, applies the term "science" to those truths that can be known with certainty —either intuitively (as when we grasp the truth of a self-evident proposition, e.g., "*A* is *A*") or through a process of deductive reasoning (as when we derive a true conclusion from a valid syllogism with true premises, e.g., "All men are mortal; Socrates is a man; *therefore*, Socrates is mortal").

Because scientific truths have been demonstrated by reason, we have no choice but to assent to their truth (assuming that we know of, and understand, the demonstration). As Aquinas puts it: "[T]he assent of science is not subject to free choice, because the knower is obliged to assent by the force of the demonstration." The only choice we have in this area is whether "to consider or not to consider."[9] We might, in other words, refuse to examine the proof for a scientific proposition and thereby remain willfully ignorant of its truth; but if we do examine and understand the proof for a scientific proposition, our mind will automatically assent to its truth without an intervening act of will.

As an example of what Aquinas means by a scientific truth, consider the proposition "Two plus two equals four." A person who is completely ignorant of mathematics will not know that this proposition is true, and he cannot acquire this knowledge unless he *chooses* to study the rules of addition. But if he achieves this level of understanding, he *must* thereafter assent to the truth of proposition "Two plus two equals four." He has no choice in the matter; he cannot will himself to believe otherwise (e.g., that two plus two equals five), because his will cannot overrule his intellect.

Aquinas (along with Aristotle, Locke, and many other philosophers) would regard it as improper to say, "I *believe* that two plus two equals four." We should say instead, "I *know* that two plus two equals four," because reason has demonstrated beyond doubt that this proposition is true. Belief pertains to those propositions that cannot be demonstrated with certainty. In such cases, when our intellect is not compelled by the force of a demonstration to accept a proposition as true, we have a choice as to whether or not we will believe that proposition.

This is what Aquinas means in saying that belief "is an act of the intellect, according as the will moves it to assent." Belief requires voluntary assent—an act of the will—and it is this power of choice that gives to belief a *moral character* that is absent in scientific knowledge, in which the will plays no direct role.

With the foregoing in mind, let us now examine what Aquinas has to say about the "sin of unbelief" which stands opposed to "faith."

There are two kinds of unbelief, according to Aquinas. The first kind of unbelief ("pure negation") is found in those people who have never heard of Christianity and therefore do not believe in it. This kind of unbelief, which is the child of ignorance, is not morally blameworthy: "If unbelievers of this kind are damned, it is on account of other sins."[10]

The second kind of unbelief flows from "opposition to the [Christian] faith, in which sense a man refuses to hear the faith, or despises it . . . and it is in this sense that unbelief is a sin." Indeed, "the sin of unbelief is greater than any sin that occurs in the perversion of morals."[11] The following discussion pertains only to this sinful species of unbelief.

Although unbelief resides in the intellect, it is caused by the will and is therefore a matter of choice. The dissent of the intellect is prompted by a will that is contemptuous of God's truth, a will that is vitiated by *pride.* One must understand the Christian view of pride in order to appreciate what Aquinas is getting at here. "Sin" literally means "missing the mark (or target)," so every sin entails a turning away from God—a missing of the divine mark, so to speak. That which leads us to God is necessarily good, and that which leads us away from God is necessarily evil.

Virtually every Catholic theologian agreed with Augustine that pride, not disobedience, was the real original sin. When Adam and Eve ate the forbidden fruit, their overt act of disobedience was preceded by the covert sin of pride. As Augustine wrote in his *City of God*:

It was in secret that the first human beings began to be evil; and the result was that they slipped into open disobedience. For they would not have arrived at the evil act if an evil will had not preceded it. Now, could anything but pride have been the start of the evil will? For "pride is the start of every kind of sin" [Ecclus. 10, 13]. And what is pride except a longing for a perverse kind of exaltation? For it is a perverse kind of exaltation to abandon the basis on which the mind should be firmly fixed, and to become, as it were, based on oneself, and so remain. This happens when a man is too pleased with himself: and a man is self-complacent when he deserts that changeless God in which, rather than in himself, he ought to have found his satisfaction. This desertion is voluntary. . . .[12]

Aquinas agrees that sin arises not from an error in judgment but from a perversion of the will, a will that has been corrupted by the pride of original sin. To say, therefore, that "the cause of unbelief is in the will" is to say that the unbeliever, motivated by pride, prefers to follow the dictates of his own reason rather than submit to the will of God. And this is why there is never a legitimate excuse for the unbeliever who, having become familiar with Christian belief, refuses his assent or, having accepted Christianity, dissents from one or more of its essential doctrines.

To appreciate the significance of Christian belief—as propounded by Augustine, Aquinas, and many other theologians—one must contrast it with the theory of Aristotle and other Greeks. Although Aquinas borrowed a good deal from Aristotle, his theory of belief turns Aristotle on his head. According to Aristotle, belief ("opinion") is inferior in certitude to knowledge ("science"). We are more certain of what we know than what we believe, and we should always strive to transform our beliefs into knowledge through logical demonstration.

Aquinas, by elevating faith above reason, reverses this order: Religious belief is afforded the highest degree of certainty, because it is based on the revealed word of an infallible God. Although Aquinas does invest reason with a degree of independence apart from faith, he leaves no doubt that, should these two spheres appear to conflict, faith should always have the final word. To assume otherwise, to assume that reason could ever overrule faith, would be to presume that one's own judgment is superior to God's—and this, as we have seen, is the sin of pride.

Moreover, by attributing unbelief to a sinful will, Aquinas stacked the cards against reason by assigning to faith a superior moral status. To believe requires choice—an act of will—so to believe in God requires the voluntary assent of faith, which is a meritorious act. Christian belief is praiseworthy because it requires that we give our voluntary assent to doctrines that we cannot prove and, in some cases (e.g., the Trinity), that we cannot even comprehend.

The implications of this doctrine are brought out by Aquinas in his answer to the peculiar question, "Whether in the Demons There is Faith." The medieval cosmos was inhabited not only by corporeal creatures, such as man, but by demons and angels as well. Thus, when Aquinas presented his views on knowledge, faith, sin, and so on, he often applied the topic at hand to these invisible creatures. Here the question had to do with whether demons can be said to have faith. Demons, after all, believe in God, the resurrection of Jesus, and other Christian dogmas, so, like human Christians, they seem to have faith. But faith, as we have seen, is a virtuous act, so if we are to attribute faith to demons, it seems we must also commend them for their virtue. And, what is worse, if the faith of demons is like the faith of Christians, then it would seem that demons are as virtuous as Christians in this respect.

Aquinas, while conceding that demons may be said to have faith in God, is unwilling to praise them on this account, because demons possess no virtues whatever. He is therefore compelled to differentiate two kinds of faith: one, the faith of demons, which is *not* virtuous, and another, the faith of Christians, which *is* virtuous.

Although I cannot profess to understand every detail of Aquinas's argument, his reasoning seems to be as follows: Belief, which is caused not by a command of the intellect but by an act of will, may arise from two different motives. The Christian believes because his will is directed to the good (i.e., God), so his faith is based on his love of God. The belief of demons, in contrast, is based not on the love of God, but on "many evident signs, by which they recognize that the teaching of the Church is from God. . . ." Hence "demons are, in a way, compelled to believe, by the evidence of signs, and so their will deserves no praise for their belief."[13]

Demons have witnessed more signs (miracles, prophecies, etc.) than humans, so their faith is supported by evidence that is more compelling than the faith of Christians, who must depend on their love of God. Demons, having witnessed many miraculous signs, have no choice but to believe in God and his teachings, and where there is no choice there can be no virtue.

Although this example may appear silly by modern standards, its message is deadly serious, and is as relevant today as it was in the thirteenth century. As incredible as it may seem, Aquinas is arguing that *the faith of demons, because it is based on the evidence of "signs," is more rational than the faith of Christians*. Thus the evidence available to demons is so strong as to leave them *no choice* but to believe, and it precisely *because of their rationality* that demons should *not* be praised as virtuous. The belief of Christians, in contrast, is morally superior because their faith is *not* based on evidence that is sufficient to compel their assent. Christians, motivated by their love of God, *choose* to believe without sufficient evidence, and it is this voluntary assent that renders them praiseworthy.

To restate the same point in different terms: Suppose that two Christians, Jack and Jill, share identical beliefs, but that Jack is far less able than Jill to defend his faith in God with rational arguments. Jack doesn't understand much of anything about his religion, but he loves God, so he will readily assent to anything that he believes to be the word of God. Jill, in contrast, is able to justify her faith with compelling arguments, so she has no choice but to believe as she does.

Now, which Christian, Jack or Jill, is more deserving of our praise? Who is more admirable—Jack, who wills himself to believe something without justification; or Jill, who can support her faith with compelling reasons? If we follow the twisted logic of Aquinas, Jack is far more virtuous than Jill. Indeed, to the extent that Jill is able to justify her faith, she deserves no praise at all—for the more she can justify, the more her belief will be determined by the command of her intellect rather than by the assent of her will. And since her intellect leaves her no choice but to believe as she does, her faith (like that of the demons) is utterly without merit.

Whatever we may think of this conclusion, Aquinas does raise some interesting and extremely significant issues about the ethics of belief. What is the relationship between volition and belief? Can we will ourselves to believe some things but not others? Or must the will always submit to the intellect, assenting to what it judges to be true on the basis of available evidence?

JOHN LOCKE

We have seen that, according to Aquinas, truths that have been logically demonstrated (i.e., the knowledge of "science") command the assent of the intellect, so our belief in them is not a matter of free choice. Aquinas adds a proviso, however: "But the actual consideration of what a man knows by science is subject to his free choice, for it is in his power to consider or not to consider."[14]

This is similar to Locke's argument that our knowledge "is *neither wholly necessary, nor wholly voluntary.*" Locke illustrates this point by comparing reason to the faculty of sight. If I look at some objects I cannot help but perceive various similarities and differences; I have no choice in the matter. But I do have a choice as to whether I will look in the first place. Moreover, I can also choose how carefully I will scrutinize the objects, i.e., whether I will survey them hastily or focus on them carefully. The same is true, says Locke, of our understanding:

> Just thus it is with our Understanding, all that is *voluntary* in our Knowledge, is the *employing*, or with-holding any of *our Faculties* from this or that sort of Objects, and a more, or less accurate survey of them: But they being employed, *our Will hath no Power to determine the Knowledge of the Mind* one way or the other; that is done only by the Objects themselves, as far as they are clearly discovered.[15]

Although Locke's distinction between certain knowledge and probable belief is similar to that of Aquinas, it is interesting to note that Locke, unlike Aquinas, does not regard belief as falling directly under our volitional control. We can choose whether or not we will consider all of the relevant evidence for a belief, but, once having made that decision, we are thereafter compelled to follow our judgment and assent to its decision. In matters of belief, a man *"can scarce refuse his Assent* to the side, on which the greater Probability appears." Hence *"Assent* [i.e., belief] is no more in our Power than Knowledge."[16] As Locke is quick to point out, however, we do exercise a kind of *indirect* choice over both our knowledge and our beliefs, because we can choose to think or not to think, to consider or not to consider:

> But though we cannot hinder our Knowledge, where the Agreement [between ideas] is once perceived; nor our Assent, where the Probability manifestly appears upon due Consideration of all the Measures of it: *Yet we can hinder both Knowledge and Assent, by stopping our Enquiry*, and not employing our Faculties in the search of any Truth. If it were not so, Ignorance, Error, or Infidelity could not in any Case be a Fault.[17]

Here we see Locke's concern that cognitive determinism might be used to absolve the religious disbeliever of moral responsibility. Locke addresses this concern by noting that, although we cannot directly choose whether or not to believe in God, the atheist is morally culpable nonetheless, because he has willfully refused to consider the matter of God's existence with sufficient care.

Thus do we return to a perennial theme of Christianity: that the atheist should be morally condemned for his disbelief. The existence of God is so obvious and easily ascertained that only a person who chooses to remain blind to the evidence could possibly be an atheist.

NOTES

1. William Walwyn, *The Compassionate Samaritane*, in *The Writings of William Walwyn*, ed. J. McMichael and B. Taft (Athens, Ga.: University of Chicago Press, 1989), p. 103. I have modernized spelling and punctuation.

2. *The Works of John Locke*, 12th ed. (London: n.p., 1824) vol. 5, pp. 23–24.

3. *The Divine Institutes*, trans. William Fletcher, in *The Works of Lactantius* (Edinburgh: T. and T. Clark, n.d.), p. 340.

4. Quoted in G. G. Coulton, *Inquisition and Liberty* (Boston: Beacon Press, 1959), p. 16.

5. For a discussion of this topic, see George H. Smith, "Philosophies of Toleration," in *Atheism, Ayn Rand, and Other Heresies* (Amherst, N.Y.: Prometheus Books, 1991), pp. 97–129.

6. Thomas Aquinas, *Summa Theologica*, Great Books of the Western World, vol. 20 (Chicago: Encyclopedia Britannica, 1952), pp. 391, 404.

7. Ibid., p. 392.

8. Ibid., pp. 427–28.

9. Ibid., p. 399.

10. Ibid., p. 427.

11. Ibid., pp. 427–28.

12. Augustine, *Concerning the City of God Against the Pagans*, trans. H. Bettenson (Harmondsworth: Penguin Books, 1972), pp. 571–72.

13. Aquinas, *Summa Theologica*, p. 411.

14. Ibid., p. 399.

15. John Locke, *An Essay Concerning Human Understanding*, ed. Peter N. Nidditch (Oxford: Oxford University Press, 1975), pp. 650–51.

16. Ibid., pp. 716–17.

17. Ibid., p. 717.

Why Philosophy?

History and the Inner Logic of Ideas

René Descartes once observed that no one can become a competent mathematician by merely memorizing the proofs that others have demonstrated: He must learn to solve problems on his own. Likewise, we can memorize the arguments of Plato and Aristotle, but we will never become philosophers unless we are able to assess arguments and analyze philosophical problems. We can read as many philosophers as we like, but if we fail to exercise independent judgment, our knowledge will be historical rather than philosophical.

Immanuel Kant made a similar point. The person who has learned a system of philosophy, however thoroughly he knows it, has no more than a "historical knowledge" of it: "He knows and judges only what has been given to him." Although this philosophy may have been justified by its originator and so may be "due to reason" in this sense, it does not arise "out of reason" for the person who accepts it uncritically, but is "merely historical."[1]

Kant distinguishes two types of philosophical knowledge: objective and subjective. A reasoned system of principles and arguments is objective philosophical knowledge; but if it is accepted secondhand, without comprehending the principles and their logical connections, then, subjectively considered, it is known as history, not philosophy.

To illustrate: The philosophy of Ayn Rand, by Kant's standard, qualifies as objective, because it is supported with arguments. (Of course, this does not necessarily mean that her arguments are valid.) But if an admirer of Ayn Rand accepts these arguments passively and uncritically, then he is functioning not as a philosopher but as a historian. He knows her ideas as he would know any historical data—as the particular thoughts of an individual named Ayn Rand—rather than as the universal principles of an authentic philosophy. And, as Kant puts it, such intellectual secondhanders remain in a state of "self-incurred tutelage" all their lives.[2]

Kant believes that philosophy cannot be learned, memorized, or taught. "We can only learn to philosophize, that is, to exercise the talent of reason, in accordance with its universal principles [while] reserving the right of reason to investigate, to confirm, or to reject these principles in their very sources."[3]

A somewhat different view was expressed by G. W. F. Hegel. He does not draw a bright line between the history of philosophy and philosophy per se, but has an organic conception of their relationship. According to Hegel, "the history of a subject is necessarily intimately connected with the conception which is formed of it."[4] This means that we can undertake historical investigations only with certain philosophical presuppositions which focus our attention on this rather than that, and which provide the general framework, or point of view, for interpreting and understanding the facts of history.

Historical investigation is an active process, not a passive one. The historian must actively engage the thoughts of past philosophers if he is to write a history of them. Or, as Hegel puts it, "the study of the history of Philosophy is an introduction to Philosophy itself."[5]

Hegel emphasizes the importance of understanding a philosophy as an integrated system of ideas. The great philosophers were system builders; and if we are to understand their systems, we must do more than understand their component parts separately. We must place ourselves within a system and view it internally, thereby comprehending its structure and internal logic—why it developed as it did, how this part relates to that, and so forth. Or, to put it in more Hegelian terms, we must comprehend the *spirit* of a philosophical system: its soul or animating principle, that which gives it life and movement, that which makes it worthwhile to ponder long after its originator has died.

Whereas Descartes and Kant might say that we can learn the history of philosophy without comprehending it (thus distinguishing history from philosophy), Hegel would say that we cannot truly grasp the history of philosophy without comprehending philosophy itself. A true history of philosophy must be internal, not merely external. To study the history of philosophy is itself a philosophic enterprise; and, conversely, to philosophize truly, we must know something of the historical problems and theories that have shaped one's own thinking and the nature of philosophy itself.

Hegel's argument has proved extremely influential, sometimes garnering unexpected support. Consider, for example, an excellent book, *The Unity of Philosophical Experience*, by the Thomistic philosopher and historian Etienne Gilson. Although we might not expect an Aristotelian to agree with much of what Hegel has to say, Gilson nonetheless begins his historical study of universals[6] by citing Hegel's preface to *The Phenomenology of Mind*. Hegel insists that knowing a philosophical system is something more than knowing its purpose and its result. The subjective purpose, or what the philosopher intended to do, is often vague and uncertain, and it may be nothing more than an unrealized intention. As for the result, Hegel compares this to "the corpse of the system which has left its guiding tendency behind it."[7] What is really important is to understand the "inner necessity of knowledge."

What Hegel was getting at is described by Gilson as the "inner history of ideas" and their "inner necessity." This inner logic of ideas refers to the fact that ideas tend to take on a life of their own, quite apart from the intentions or desires of their creators. Ideas, like actions, have unintended consequences. As Gilson so elegantly puts it:

> [I]n each instance of philosophical thinking, both the philosopher and his particular doctrine are ruled from above by an impersonal necessity. In the first place, philosophers are free to lay down their own sets of principles, but once this is done, they no longer think as they wish—they think as they can. In the second place, it seems to result from the facts under discussion, that any attempt on the part of a philosopher to shun the consequences of his own position is doomed to failure. What he himself declines to say will be said by his disciples, if he has any; if he has none, it may remain eternally unsaid, but it is there, and anybody going back to the same principles, be it several centuries later, will have to face the same conclusions. It seems, therefore, that though philosophical ideas can never be found separate from philosophers and their philosophies, they are, to some extent, independent of philosophers as well as of their philosophies. Philosophy consists in the concepts of philosophers, taken in the naked, impersonal necessity of both their contents and their relationships in the history of philosophy itself.[8]

It is by tracing this inner logic that we come to understand how a seemingly innocuous idea can develop over time into something far more radical. Unintended consequences have recurred throughout the history of philosophy.[9] The logical implications of a theory, even if not intended or foreseen by the theorist, will invariably be developed by others.

PROGRESS IN PHILOSOPHY

Sometimes the most interesting features of a philosopher are his errors, especially those that appear obvious to the modern reader.

How can it be, we ask ourselves, that a brilliant, first-rate mind could commit such flagrant blunders? Rather than dismiss such errors as the result of stupidity or mendaciousness, it is far more instructive to ask ourselves how these errors came about, and why they were not as apparent to the philosopher in question as they are to us. We can learn more from the errors of a genius than we can from the mundane truths of a lesser mind.

Consider a common complaint: that philosophy, unlike the special sciences, has not progressed over time, that modern philosophers are still debating the same unresolved problems that vexed the philosophers of ancient Greece. Surely there is something wrong with a discipline that moves perpetually in circles and never comes to rest with definite, widely accepted conclusions.

There are several things that can be said about this popular criticism. The success or failure of a discipline depends on how well it has achieved its primary goal, so we must first determine the purpose of philosophy before we can assess its progress. This purpose has traditionally been seen as *self-enlightenment*, i.e., as the intellectual and moral improvement of the individual philosopher. In other words, the goal of philosophy is *personal*, not social. Even if some of the basic problems in philosophy have been solved (and I think they have) this solution is useless for the person who has not personally thought through the problem for herself and arrived at a reasoned judgment.

In a sense, the individual must relive the history of philosophy in her own mind, going over the classic problems, analyzing them, and arriving at a solution. The microcosm of the individual mind, by reanimating past arguments and controversies, will reflect the macrocosm of philosophy's history. Only in this way is philosophy a living process rather than a dead subject matter.

This distinguishes philosophy from the natural sciences, such as physics and chemistry. These and other experimental sciences depend on specialization and the division of labor in a way that philosophy does not. No single physicist can hope personally to verify the experimental conclusions of all other physicists by repeating all of their experiments. Rather, he must rely on the standards of public verification that have been established within his own discipline; this is the function of scientific journals and conferences. These outlets allow peer review and debate, which the physicist must rely on when deciding which conclusions and theories he should accept as the basis for his own work. It is by thus building on the work of others that physical science tends to progress through the accumulation of new knowledge. (This does not mean, as is sometimes asserted, that a scientist must accept the work of other scientists on "faith." Rather, it is the purpose of standards within the scientific community to assure that a given scientist can trust the assertions of other scientists with a fairly high degree of probability, if not certainty.)

This is not the method of philosophy, however; philosophy is not the public pursuit of knowledge in this sense. Although the philosopher can (and should) learn from the work of other philosophers, both living and dead, she cannot accept an argument or a conclusion on the basis of peer review. No philosopher worthy of the name would endorse a position merely on the testimony of other philosophers, even if they constitute a large majority. The arguments and conclusions of others are regarded by the philosopher as suggestions and insights that may stimulate her own thinking. But ultimately the philosopher, if she is to utilize the work done by others, must retrace their arguments in her own mind and reach an independent judgment. This stress on independent judgment, based on the autonomy of reason, is and always has been the categorical imperative of pure philosophy.

As previously mentioned, philosophy is the most fundamental of cognitive disciplines, so it cannot look somewhere else for a definition of the philosophic enterprise. Philosophy is *autonomous*, i.e., self-legislating. It must establish its own identity by determining its proper subject matter, method, and perspective. Different conceptions of the scope and method of philosophy will naturally generate different conclusions. If philosophers cannot agree on what they are doing, it is unlikely they will agree on how to do it or when they are doing it well. This has led to the diversity of philosophic opinions, and this diversity has provided a good deal of fodder for the critics of philosophy. If philosophers cannot even agree on the purpose and standards of their discipline, then how can philosophy claim to be a valid discipline at all? If philosophers cannot even agree on the most basic issues, then how can it be said that philosophy serves a useful purpose?

Here we should recall that philosophy is first and foremost the personal quest for understanding. It is not, like the physical sciences, a public enterprise that depends for its progress on specialization and experimentation. Rather, philosophy is refined common sense. By this I mean that the philosopher deals with the common experience of humankind; he does not appeal to specialized experience, such as experiments undertaken in a laboratory. Philosophy is the systematic analysis of common experience.

If, as I have argued, philosophy is personal rather than public, then the success of philosophy must be measured in personal terms. Philosophic speculation, as conceived by the Greeks, is an end in itself, undertaken for the personal satisfaction and fulfillment of the philosopher. For many Greeks the purpose of philosophy is to develop the sage, or wise man—the person who lives a contemplative life. Although not everyone would agree with Aristotle that the contemplative life is ultimately the most satisfying kind of life, most of those who engage in philosophizing will agree that it yields personal benefits.

Philosophy is the quest for wisdom; it is a sustained and systematic effort to understand ourselves and the world in which we live. Many people claim that the pursuit of such knowledge has enriched their lives, and there is no reason to doubt such claims. Contrary to its critics, therefore, philosophy does tend to progress, but it does so at the *personal* level. Measured by this standard, philosophy has succeeded many thousands of times and will continue to do so in the future.

The counterclaim—the claim that philosophy represents a cognitive wheel that spins on its axis without moving anywhere—is based on a mistaken view of philosophy. If philosophy spins on its own axis, this is because the fundamental problems that confront human beings remain basically the same through time and across space. What is the nature of things? What can I know, and how do I know it? How should I live my life? These are among the perennial problems of human existence that confront every culture in every era. They are recurring problems that must be addressed anew, not only by every generation, but by every reflective person.

The vast majority of people are content to accept the answers that have been handed down to them by others, whether in the form of religious dogma, cultural norms, political decrees, or some other authoritative source. Philosophy, as it emerged in ancient Greece, was an effort to break free from the restrictive bonds of authority, and to think for oneself. Early philosophers did not abandon mythology and customary beliefs altogether, but they insisted that all knowledge claims, whatever their source, should be subject to criticism and rational scrutiny. If a Greek philosopher believed that we should abide by established customs, he gave reasons for this belief. Even so-called irrationalists in the history of philosophy have understood the need to present arguments for their viewpoint—to present a *reasoned* defense of irrationalism, so to speak.

If philosophy is primarily the personal pursuit of wisdom, it is also more than that; it does have a public aspect. In Eastern philosophy the pursuit of wisdom was often regarded as a solitary enterprise. The sage retreats within himself and, by clearing his mind of all external influences, achieves true wisdom. For many Eastern philosophers, to argue with others hinders our pursuit of wisdom, because it clutters the mind with needless baggage that obstructs our pure vision of the good, the divine, and so forth.

With some exceptions (such as mysticism), this solitary method has not been characteristic of Western philosophy. From its inception Western philosophy has stressed the interplay of like-minded persons in pursuit of truth. We see this clearly in the Socratic dialogues written by Plato. This was the original meaning of "dialectics"—i.e., a cooperative exchange of ideas in a common pursuit of knowledge.

This dialectical process, this ongoing exchange of ideas, can occur not only across space, with the living, but also through time, with the dead. A philosophy does not perish with its originator, but is given new life every time it encounters a new mind. This gives the history of philosophy (and ideas in general) an immediate relevance that is often missing in more conventional histories that deal with external events and actions.

The history of philosophy is an internal history of the human mind, a chronicle of various attempts to answer the perennial questions of human existence. And despite the individualizing influence of culture and personality on particular philosophers, we can identify with their thinking insofar as they were addressing the same universal issues that concern us as well. We can recreate in our own minds the chain of reasoning that occurred in their minds, and by so doing achieve a sympathetic understanding of their thoughts and insights.

THE SEVENTEENTH CENTURY

History is not a simple matter, and we can easily forget this whenever we section off a period of time and christen it with a proper name, such as "Renaissance" or "Reformation." But this kind of pigeonholing (or "periodization") is indispensable to the discipline of history. If it is true that we should never completely separate one era from others, as if what came before had no influence on what came after, it is also true that some periods stand out as times of rapid transition from the old to the new. As Herbert Butterfield has written:

> [W]e cannot hold history in our minds without any landmarks, or as an ocean without fixed points, and we may talk about this civilization and that as though they were ultimate units, provided we are not superstitious in our use of the word and we take care not to become the slaves of our terminology. Similarly, though everything comes by antecedents and mediations—and these may always be traced farther and farther back without the mind ever coming to rest—still, we can speak of certain epochs of transition, when the subterranean movements come above ground, and new things are palpably born, and the very face of the earth can be seen to be changing.[10]

During what period did the modern worldview—the secular perspective that many people now take for granted—take on its distinctive form? How we answer this question will depend on whom we ask. Popular candidates include the fifteenth-century Renaissance, the sixteenth-century Reformation, and the eighteenth-century Enlightenment. But there is a considerable gap here, namely, the seventeenth century. Sometimes called "the Age of Revolution"—owing to its rapidly changing perspectives in philosophy, science, religion, and politics—the seventeenth century may also be dubbed "the Heroic Age of Philosophy."

I say this because, between the time of René Descartes and Immanuel Kant (a span of approximately 150 years), virtually every major philosopher (and many scientists) worked outside of universities and other established institutions. This was the era of the independent intellectual—the heroic philosopher who challenged the status quo while receiving little or nothing for his efforts. And this was the stuff from which legends were made.

Francis Bacon, a former Lord Chancellor of England, was imprisoned and fined for judicial misconduct (taking bribes) during his tenure as a magistrate. He retired in disgrace and thereafter occupied himself with taking long walks and dictating his thoughts to a young Thomas Hobbes and other admirers. The result was several books that would profoundly influence the development of science and philosophy over the next two centuries.

René Descartes, who took some time off from his philosophical pursuits to invent analytic geomentry, became a wandering intellectual and professional soldier who, upon growing weary of military life, secluded himself in a cabin where he could meditate in peace and quiet. The result was a tract that would dramatically affect the course of Western philosophy.

The Dutch philosopher Hugo Grotius, who advocated toleration among individuals and peace among nations, escaped imprisonment and went on to become a founding father of international law.

Thomas Hobbes was born prematurely when his mother became frightened by rumors of an impending invasion by the Spanish

Armada. ("Fear and I," he said, "were born twins.") Hobbes gained employment as tutor to the son of Lord Cavendish, but he spent much of his time running errands and procuring money so this "wastrel" could gamble and otherwise enjoy the good life. Having discovered the joys of geometric reasoning late in life, Hobbes managed to convince himself (but no one else) that he had succeeded in squaring the circle. Somewhat more successful was his attempt to apply the geometric method to political philosophy (an effort that led Hobbes to crown himself the founder of political science). Hobbes began writing on political theory in his fifties. Although he hoped thereby to lend support to the tottering English monarchy, his arguments so infuriated the future King Charles II that Hobbes became hated by every political faction that had participated in the English civil wars.

Everyone was dazzled by the brilliance and scholarship of a young Jew named Baruch (later Benedict) Spinoza. But Spinoza's unorthodox religious opinions caused him to be anathematized by the elders of the Amsterdam synagogue, so he moved elsewhere and took up the profession of lens grinder. A fiercely independent thinker who turned down a university position for fear that it would compromise his integrity, Spinoza referred incessantly to God in his writings—while noting that, by "God," he meant "nature." And thus did this "God-intoxicated" philosopher achieve notoriety as the most famous atheist of the seventeenth century.

And then there was the sickly Blaise Pascal, a first-rate mathematician and experimental scientist who invented a working computer. After undergoing a profound religious experience, Pascal aligned himself with the French Jansenists (Catholic fundamentalists, in effect), and his satirical skewering of the powerful Jesuit order was read with delight by nearly everyone, except the Jesuits.

John Locke decided to become a physician because it was the only position at the University of Oxford that did not require him to take Anglican Holy Orders. Although his father had fought against the Stuarts during the English civil wars, Locke welcomed the restoration of the Stuart monarchy in 1660, hoping that it would also mean the restoration of social order. Locke's views quickly changed, however: He became a determined foe of absolute monarchy and a champion of the rights of resistance and revolution. After his personal and professional affiliation with Lord Shaftesbury (the leading opponent of the Stuarts) had led to his indictment for sedition, Locke fled to Holland, where he lived for six years under an assumed name. But even though the Glorious Revolution of 1688 enabled Locke to return to England a hero, to his dying day he would never admit that he had written the anonymously published *Two Treatises of Government*—a radical and immensely influential book that would become the ideological cornerstone of the American and French Revolutions.

Although this list omits a number of other philosophers (such as Gottfried Leibniz), and although it does not include Isaac Newton and other seventeenth-century scientists, it is an impressive list nonetheless. Indeed, with the exception of Greek philosophy during the fifth and fourth centuries B.C.E., there is nothing that even comes close. And if we compare this to a list of the most influential names of the sixteenth century, such as Thomas More, Desiderius Erasmus, Martin Luther, and John Calvin, we can clearly see a markedly different orientation. Seventeenth-century philosophers, whatever their theological interests may have been, displayed a secular spirit and interest in science that had not been seen for nearly two thousand years. The seventeenth century was a gateway to the modern world.

NOTES

1. Immanuel Kant, *The Critique of Pure Reason*, trans Norman Kemp Smith (New York: St. Martin's Press, 1965), p. 656.
2. Immanuel Kant, "What is Enlightenment?" in *Kant on History*, trans. and ed. Lewis White Beck (Indianapolis: Bobbs-Merrill, 1963), p. 3.
3. Kant, *Critique of Pure Reason*, p. 657.
4. G. W. F. Hegel, *Lectures on the History of Philosophy*, trans. E. S. Haldane (Lincoln: University of Nebraska Press, 1995), p. xliv.
5. Ibid., p. 5.
6. Etienne Gilson, *The Unity of Philosophical Experience* (New York:

Charles Scribner's Sons, 1965). The "Problem of Universals," one of the oldest and most enduring themes in the history of philosophy, is concerned with the nature of concepts, or general ideas. When, for instance, we speak of "man" (the human species, not the male gender), we are referring not to any particular individual but to humans in general. Hence, in this context, "man" is a universal. But what does this entail? Where precisely is the element of universality located? The traditional answers to this question are often divided into four categories: (1) According to the Extreme Realism of Plato, universals exist apart from our minds and the external world of concrete objects. They exist in an independent realm of pure forms. (The term "idea," which was coined by Plato, originally referred to these ethereal and rather mysterious Platonic Forms.) (2) According to the Moderate Realism of Aristotle (who studied under Plato for nearly two decades), universals exist independently of the mind, but not in an autonomous realm. They are embedded, so to speak, within concrete individuals (as "essences") and then abstracted by human reason during the act of cognition. (3) According to Conceptualism (such as we find in William of Occam and John Locke), universals refer to concepts and therefore exist only in the mind. (4) According to Nominalism (whose most influential champion was George Berkeley), universals are a fiction. Abstract ideas do not exist—we cannot, for example think of "horseness" apart from the specific qualities of size, shape, etc.—so universal are simply general terms that we use to signify similar objects.

    7. Quoted in ibid., p. 3

    8. Ibid., p. 302.

    9. Hegel viewed the history of philosophy (and of thought in general) as the deterministic development of the world spirit, or universal mind, wherein each stage of development is a necessary outcome of the previous stage and a necessary foundation for the next stage. Hence the history of philosophy is also its logical unfolding. The historical progress of philosophical thought is a necessary development in which one category of thought pushes forward to another through a dialectical process. Unfortunately for Hegel, however, the history of philosophy has not actually followed this kind of logical progression; and, as many critics have pointed out, Hegel committed some serious distortions in his effort to interpret history according to a predetermined theory of development. For an insightful critique of "historicism," as Hegel's approach is often called, see two works by Karl Popper: *The Poverty of Historicism* (New York: Harper Torchbooks, 1961) and *The Open*

Society and Its Enemies, vol. 2 (London: Routledge & Kegan Paul, 1966). Cf. Ludwig von Mises, *Theory and History: An Interpretation of Social and Economic Evolution* (New Rochelle, N.Y.: Arlington House, 1969).

10. Herbert Butterfield, *The Origins of Modern Science, 1300–1800*, rev. ed. (New York: Free Press, 1965), p. 192.

The Career of Reason

FRANCIS BACON

It is difficult to imagine the course that modern philosophy might have taken if René Descartes and Francis Bacon had never existed. Both are widely recognized as key figures in the development of modern philosophy, although for somewhat different reasons. Descartes is given credit as the founding father of the philosophical trend known as rationalism, whereas Bacon, if he does not receive similar credit as the father of empiricism (an honor usually reserved for John Locke), has at least attained the status of its godfather.[1]

Unfortunately, modern philosophers have tended to pay less attention to Bacon than to Descartes, despite their comparable influence on European thought. There are a number of reasons for this, of which I shall mention three. First, Descartes was more of a pure philosopher than Bacon, who, like a pre-Enlightenment *philosophe* ("man of letters"), often preferred to survey a wide range of topics rather than focus on a single subject. Second, Bacon's version of the scientific method has often been understood as a rejection of theory in favor of pure induction, and this simplistic misinterpretation has made it seem as if his works do not merit close attention.[2] Third, although Bacon was a brilliant stylist (those nineteenth-century scholars who questioned whether Shakespeare really existed invariably placed Bacon on their shortlist of possible authors), his rich Elizabethan prose can prove tough going for modern readers, so many rely on secondary accounts rather than read Bacon for themselves.

If the writings of Bacon are an acquired taste, this is a taste that, in my judgment, is well worth acquiring. But one must dig beneath Bacon's celebrated aphorisms—e.g., "Knowledge is power"—and study him carefully. There is a good reason why empiricists, such as Hobbes, Locke, Hume, Voltaire, and Jean D'Alembert, preferred Bacon over Descartes and regarded his contributions as more lasting and significant. Bacon was a thoroughly secular thinker in a way that Descartes was not, and his brilliant analysis of the psychology of reasoning remains unmatched to this day.

Although Bacon was accused of being a secret atheist, his belief in Christianity, though extremely liberal by the standards of his day, appears to have been sincere. He flatly rejects a literal interpretation of the Bible in favor of doctrinal pluralism, maintaining that biblical passages should serve as "infinite springs and streams of doctrines." Because biblical writers typically expressed themselves through metaphor, Scripture should not be used as a source of scientific knowledge, nor should it serve as a basis to criticize the conclusions of science. The spheres of religion and science should be kept completely separate, neither being allowed to impinge on the domain of the other. The various "mysteries" of Christian revelation, such as the Trinity, are incomprehensible to reason and therefore must be accepted entirely on faith. When theology is permitted to transgress beyond its proper sphere, "every development of philosophy, every new frontier and direction, is regarded by religion with unworthy suspicion and violent contempt."[3] Thus, as Peter Urbach notes, Bacon "banished the Bible as a source of information for the scientist."[4]

In driving a wedge between philosophy and theology by insisting that we "give to faith only that which is faith's," Bacon gave his blessing to a secular tendency that, like a slow-acting poison, would eventually prove fatal to the tenets of orthodox Christianity. As Franklin Baumer, commenting on the rise of seventeenth-century secularism,[5] writes:

> Secularism, unlike free thought, posed no threat to particular theological tenets. What it did was to outflank theology by staking out autonomous spheres of thought. The tendency was, more and more, to limit theology to the comparatively restricted sphere of faith and morals.[6]

Bacon's scientific secularism, while it did not challenge Christianity per se, exiled God to the nether regions of faith and theology, thereby denying to him any direct role in the acquisition of natural knowledge. "God," according to Bacon, "worketh nothing in nature but by second causes." To speak of God as the first cause is a matter of theology, not science, and reasonable men "do not unwisely mingle or confound these learnings together."[7] So consistent was Bacon's secularism that he rudely dismissed any reference to miracles in accounts of natural history: "[A]s for the narrations touching the prodigies and miracles of religions, they are either not true, or not natural; and therefore impertinent for the story of nature."[8]

Given these attitudes, it is fair to say that Bacon had more influence on the rise of secularism than Descartes, who assigned to God a key role in his philosophical system. Far more significant, however, is the fact that Bacon and Descartes differed substantially in their views of human reason (or "understanding," as Bacon, Locke, and others in their tradition often called it). In a nutshell, we may say that, for Descartes, reason is an infallible faculty of cognition, an instrument that cannot fail in its quest for absolute certainty if used properly. For Bacon, in contrast, reason is inherently fallible; it is prone to error in even in the best of circumstances, so we must stand perpetually on guard, willing to correct or revise our present beliefs.

Michael Moran has nicely summarized this crucial difference between Bacon and Descartes as follows:

> [D]espite their superficial similarities of aim in producing new methods of enquiry, in both philosophy and science, there is in fact a crucial disagreement between Bacon and Descartes, a disagreement which was to be of great significance in the subsequent history of metaphysics. As a guide to the true understanding of nature, Bacon distrusts not so much the senses . . . but the human mind itself. And really, for him, the role of "reason" is just as suspect as the role of "imagination" in metaphysics. . . . Both reason and imagination are seen to be equally culpable, equally productive of spurious anthropomorphic fantasies which stand in way of genuine knowledge.[9]

Although Bacon and Descartes both rejected the epistemological skepticism of Montaigne and other fideists (according to whom we must rely on faith to attain a certainty that reason is unable to provide), their approaches to this problem were significantly different. Bacon, unlike Descartes, does not attempt to overthrow skepticism with a definitive theoretical refutation; he does not employ the Cartesian method of systematic doubt in an effort to establish an infallible criterion of knowledge, such as the intuitive grasp of clear and distinct ideas. Rather than employ this kind of shortcut, Bacon plots a course to certainty that must be traveled step-by-step, and he insists that we must sometimes traverse the same ground over and over again in order to check our bearings. Certainty does not reveal itself to reason in a flash of insight, but is instead an elusive ideal that reason may attain to a greater or lesser extent, depending on the circumstances.

As Bacon sees the matter, the skeptical argument that we can never achieve certainty amounts to little more than a pretentious bit of futile and self-defeating dogmatism. The skeptic, having proclaimed that infallible certainty is unattainable, never tries to attain it, because he knows that man is a fallible being for whom error looms as an ever-present possibility. To this objection Bacon responds, in effect, "So what? If you define 'certainty' in a way that requires infallibility, then the skeptical argument, though valid on its own terms, has no relevance whatever to fallible human beings." Thus, rather than blocking the path to knowledge with an arbitrary and unrealistic definition of "certainty," we should recognize at the outset that the quest for knowledge is beset with difficulties, and then, through a process of trial and error, we should see whether these difficulties can be overcome.

> Our method and that of the skeptics agree in some respects at first setting out, but differ most widely, and are completely opposed to each other in their conclusions; for they roundly assert that nothing can be known; we, that but a small part of nature can be known, by the present method; their next step, however, is to destroy the authority of the senses and understanding, whilst we invent and supply them with assistance.[10]

As part of his attack on skepticism, Bacon distinguishes between two kinds of doubt, viz., "particular and total." Particular doubt—i.e., doubt that arises in a specific context in regard to a particular knowledge claim—is useful both as a spur to inquiry and as an antidote to the proliferation of error (as when a false conclusion is inferred from a premise which has not been sufficiently justified). Total doubt, in contrast, is the universal doubt of skepticism, and this is what Bacon regards as a rather cowardly surrender to the difficulties of attaining knowledge.

Skeptics often pointed to the diversity of philosophic opinions as proof that knowledge is unattainable, but Bacon was unconvinced. Nature is infinitely more complex than the mind of man, so the same essential truth may be expressed in different ways by different thinkers. Scientific knowledge, cumulative and open-ended, progresses as one scientist improves upon the contributions of his predecessors. The human intellect is not an infallible instrument—far from it—but to say that an instrument can sometimes fail is not to say that it must necessarily fail in every case. Just as the human hand could not construct architectural wonders without the aid of external tools, so the human intellect cannot attain certainty without the aid of objective methods to test and validate our knowledge claims.

> The unassisted hand and the understanding left to itself possess but little power. Effects are produced by the means of instruments and helps, which the understanding requires no less than the hand; and as instruments either promote or regulate the motion of the hand, so those that are applied to the mind prompt or protect the understanding.[11]

The skeptic who denies that we can ever attain certainty is like a person who, after observing the limited power of the naked hand, declares that man will never be able to build a cathedral. The skeptic, trapped in a sophistical web of his own making, perpetually whines about the obstacles to knowledge. Bacon suggests that the time of the philosopher would be better spent in devising methods—cognitive instruments, in effect—that would enable us to overcome those selfsame obstacles.

Thus, if Bacon's stress on the inherent fallibility of reason does not land him in skepticism, this is because he rejects infallibility as a criterion of certainty. Certainty is something we achieve through sustained mental effort, a laborious and systematic process of trial and error, not something that is revealed to us in a flash of infallible insight. This is not to say that reason cannot arrive at its own certainties, such as the laws of logical inference, but these are a means rather than an end. These are cognitive instruments that must be coordinated, refined, and fashioned by the philosopher-scientist so as to serve as a reliable method in his investigation of nature.

According to Bacon, therefore, certainty is achieved piecemeal through the investigation of particular knowledge claims, not wholesale though a process of deductive reasoning based on clear and distinct ideas. Our ideas, if they are to generate useful knowledge, must be framed according to our experience of nature; and this experience, if it is to be reliable, must be subjected to objective methods of verification.

The foregoing must be kept in mind if we are to appreciate Bacon's celebrated discussion of the various idols, or "fallacies of the mind of man," that hinder our quest for knowledge. Bacon was the first great pathologist of human reason, and his mode of analysis—a mixture of psychology, sociology, and epistemology—was used by later philosophers to explain why reasonable people with good intentions can, and often do, hold incompatible beliefs. It was thus largely owing to Bacon that religious dissent, which had previously been condemned as the deliberate (and therefore sinful) rejection of divine truth, came to be regarded instead as the innocent by-product of human fallibility. And this doctrine of the natural diversity of opinion was destined to play a key role in the struggle for religious toleration.

Bacon's basic point is quite simple and, from the perspective of a Cartesian rationalist, quite disturbing. There is no natural harmony or correspondence between the world of ideas and the world of nature. If, as the Cartesian maintains, our sense organs are inherently untrustworthy and liable to lead us astray, the same is true of reason itself.

The human intellect has its own distinctive characteristics, a nature apart from that which it seeks to know. Understanding is not a passive process in which the intellect merely reflects the external world of nature. Rather, the intellect actively contributes to the cognitive process, leaving indelible marks on its final product. Thus, "the human mind resembles those uneven mirrors which impart their own properties to different objects, from which rays are emitted and distort and disfigure them."[12] These natural distortions are what Bacon calls idols, or false notions, of the human understanding.

Bacon's divides his idols into four principal categories: (1) Idols of the Tribe "are inherent in human nature and the very tribe or race of man"; (2) Idols of the Cave pertain to the individual, for "everybody (in addition to the errors common to the race of man) has his own individual den or cavern, which intercepts and corrupts the light of nature . . ."; (3) Idols of the Market are "formed from the commerce and association of men with each other . . .";; and (4) Idols of the Theater "have crept into men's minds from the various dogmas of peculiar systems of philosophy . . . as so many plays brought out and performed, creating fictitious and theatrical worlds."[13] (Since there is a good deal of overlap among these catergories, I shall simply discuss some of Bacon's more interesting points without attempting to classify them.)

The human understanding, according to Bacon, does not operate in isolation, apart from the will and affections. Our desires and feelings influence how we think. We are more likely to believe something that we wish were true, the comfortable and the familiar, rather than something difficult, disturbing, or unconventional. We also tend to develop a vested interest in our beliefs, defending a pet theory because we created it, worked hard on it, or simply because of its familiarity.

Bacon notes that people who think differently will often exhibit different biases. People with strong powers of observation, for example, may attribute too much importance to minor differences among things, whereas other people may overemphasize their similarities. In any case, examining our own beliefs objectively is extremely difficult, given the many subjective factors that affect our understanding. But Bacon does offer a valuable piece of advice, namely, that we should be particularly suspicious of those theories that give us the most satisfaction, subjecting them to rigorous scrutiny and criticism.

Among the Idols of the Tribe (i.e., erroneous tendencies which, because they flow from the nature of the intellect, are common to every person), two are especially interesting. The first is the natural tendency of the human understanding to suppose "a greater degree of order and equality in things than it really finds."[14] We are uncomfortable with something that appears unique, something that we cannot fit neatly into a pattern, so we will invent an imaginary order through the use of parallels, analogies, and the like.

After adopting a pleasing or popular theory, we tend to notice only that evidence which seems to support it, while ignoring all counterevidence, however cogent and abundant, that might conflict with our theory. And even when we do become aware of counterevidence, we will be extremely reluctant to admit that our theory has been falsified; instead, we will modify and reinterpret our theory, rationalize and explain away the troublesome evidence, or find some other way to save our theory from the perils of criticism.

According to Bacon, our tendency to bypass negative evidence is due to more than bias and mental inertia.

> [I]t is the peculiar and perpetual error of the human understanding to be more moved and excited by affirmatives than negatives, whereas it ought duly and regularly to be impartial; nay, in establishing any true axiom, the negative instance is the most powerful.[15]

Bacon is here pointing out that an inductive generalization can be falsified (or at least seriously called into question) by the discovery of one negative instance that contradicts the generalization. For example, let us suppose that, having seen only white swans during my life, I postulate that "all swans are white." And let us further suppose that I search for additional evidence in an effort to test my postulate. What kind of evidence would be most useful? Suppose I located two more white swans, then twenty more, then two hundred more, and so forth. These additional white swans are affirmative instances in Bacon's sense, because they affirm, or strengthen, my theory that all swans are white. But consider the impact that one black swan would have on my theory. To discover just one such negative instance, just one swan that is *not* white, would serve to falsify the proposition "*All* swans are white."

When testing the proposition "All swans are white," the discovery of one black swan would be far more significant than finding more white swans. Thus, if I am seriously interested in testing my theory, I should earnestly try to find at least one black swan, rather than adding to my list of white swans. In other words, I should search for negative evidence that would falsify (or at least weaken) my theory, rather than seeking comfort in additional evidence that appears to support my theory.

Perhaps the most radical aspect of Bacon's approach is his unequivocal rejection of final causation as a legitimate mode of explanation. To appeal to a final cause is to explain a phenomenon in terms of its supposed purpose; and though Bacon's critique of this method was primarily directed at the Aristotelians of his day—known as "scholastics" (i.e., "schoolmen") because of their dominant presence in European universities—it had far broader implications for the Christian worldview. To banish final causation from the realm of explanation is, in effect, to banish all references to a divine purpose as a rival to the theories of philosophy and science. God, in the hands of Bacon, becomes an absentee architect of creation—a first cause who, having created the universe, thereafter leaves it alone to operate according to the secondary causes of natural law.

Indeed, depending on how we read Bacon, he may even have rejected the notion of a first cause altogether, thereby leaving precious little room for the theist to maneuver. This interpretation is based on Bacon's insistence that we cannot reasonably demand an explanation for existence, because something must first exist before it can function as a cause of something else. So why do so many people seek to go beyond the brute fact of existence and posit God as a first cause? Because, says Bacon, the human mind is active and restless; it is engaged in a perpetual quest for intelligibility, for ultimate explanations that will satisfy its desire to understand. But when reason is unable to satisfy this metaphysical urge, as is often the case, the imagination steps in with fanciful explanations of its own.

This is what happens when the mind moves up the ladder of cause and effect and posits God as the ultimate cause of everything else. But this is a fancy of the imagination, not a judgment of the understanding. Reason tells us that "the greatest generalities in nature," such as the fact of existence, must be accepted "just as they are found," and that such facts are "not causable." Existence, in other words, is a causal primary, the ultimate foundation on which all explanations depend, an irreducible fact beyond which the mind cannot go. But this is not what the mind wants to hear; it cannot find satisfaction in being told that its metaphysical journey must end, abruptly and unceremoniously, at the impenetrable wall of existence. Thus does the imagination satisfy this metaphysical desire at the expense of reason, and thus does another idol take its toll.

JOHN LOCKE

All knowledge, according to John Locke, is ultimately derived from two sources of experience. The first is perception of the external world (*sensation*), and the second is introspection of the mind and its operations (*reflection*). Sensation and reflection "are the fountains of knowledge, from whence all the ideas we have, or can naturally have, do spring." And here we have the essential tenet of Locke's empiricism, a perspective that would eventually wreak havoc on all appeals to a supernatural source of knowledge.

If everything that we can possibly know must have its origin in experience, whether external or internal, then any given knowledge claim must be traceable to this source, if the person making that claim wishes others to take him seriously. Of course, there is a sense in which even the most dedicated supernaturalist can appeal to experience: He may say, for example, that he knows that God spoke to him because he had a personal experience to that effect. But this is merely to use the same word, "experience," with a different meaning, for this is not at all what Locke was getting at.

In stating that all knowledge originates in sensation or reflection, Locke was attempting to level the epistemological playing field, so to speak, by excluding all appeals to special privilege in the realm of knowledge. Normal human beings are roughly equal in their sensory and intellectual faculties, so if one person is able to experience something, then others should be able to experience it as well. Or, if this is not always strictly possible, others should at least be able to *understand* the experience in question and to *evaluate* its credibility, because no person may legitimately claim to possess a special faculty of perception that others lack.

Suppose, for example, that Jack claims to have experienced a personal revelation directly from God, and that God supposedly bestowed upon Jack the title "Sovereign Emperor of Planet Earth." Now if Jack is credulous enough to believe his own story, there may be little chance that we can change his mind. But what are *we* to make of this story? The point is not whether we will believe Jack's account, for we obviously will not; rather, the point is whether we should even take Jack seriously enough to examine his claim in detail, or whether we should dismiss it outright as utterly lacking in credibility. If the latter is far more likely, this is because Jack is appealing to a privileged "experience" that supposedly derives from something other than sensation or reflection—those universal sources of experience that provide a common basis for the evaluation of knowledge claims. In making a claim that cannot be replicated or substantiated by others, Jack is also claiming a special exemption for his belief (one, incidentally, that he himself would be unwilling to concede to others with similar claims). In thus removing his belief from the realm of social evaluation, Jack is also removing *himself* from the realm of social credibility.[16]

Locke's theory of cognitive egalitarianism—the demand that all knowledge claims should be grounded in the common world of human experience—had potentially disastrous implications for the claims of revealed theology, such as the argument from religious experience. Locke understood and pursued some of these avenues of inquiry, but others he did not. But, whereas it can sometimes take decades or even centuries for the inner logic of ideas to generate unintended consequences, in Locke's case these consequences became obvious to many of his contemporaries as soon as they read *An Essay Concerning Human Understanding*. Deists in particular, such as John Toland and Anthony Collins, adopted the basic tenets of Locke's epistemology and then used these formidable weapons with great success in their frontal assault on Christian revelation. This is why the deists praised Locke as one of their own, indeed, as their founding father, even though he did not share their repudiation of Christianity.

It is not my purpose to analyze Locke's theory of knowledge, which is fraught with technical problems and curious inconsistencies.[17] Rather, in keeping with the previous discussion of Francis Bacon, I shall focus on some general points about human fallibility and the psychology of reasoning.

Although Locke was essentially an empiricist, his work also exhibits the Cartesian interest in the ability of intuitive reason to apprehend the truth of "clear and distinct ideas" with infallible certainty. And it was this concession to rationalism that led Locke to forge a fairly useless distinction between *reason* and *judgment*. Reason, according to Locke, gives us *certain knowledge*, whereas judgment provides us with *probable beliefs.*

We needn't here explore this misleading and unnecessary dichotomy between knowledge and belief, except to note that it is the offspring of a dysfunctional marriage between rationalism and empiricism. Reason, for the rationalist, is an infallible instrument of cognition, so the truths of reason (e.g., the laws of logic and mathematics) can be known with absolute certainty. It is only this kind of truth, according to the rationalist, that qualifies as authentic knowledge. And any truth that falls short of infallibility, any truth that is *probable* rather than certain, is mere *belief* rather than knowledge.

Although Locke (unlike Bacon) accepted this rationalist premise, he managed to avoid the epistemological dead end to which it normally leads. Rationalists, having established an infallible foundation for knowledge, would typically attempt to elevate various "beliefs" to the status of "knowledge" by linking them through deductive reasoning to that foundation. But when these efforts failed, as they inevitably did, the door was left open for the skeptical argument that certainty is unattainable by fallible human beings, that what we *think* we know is for the most part not authentic knowledge at all, but mere opinion.

In this context, the epistemological skeptic is little more than a pessimistic rationalist; skepticism is rationalism gone bad. For consider: The rationalist and the skeptic agree that knowledge requires certainty, and they further agree that certainty is assessed by a standard of infallibility. The two sides merely disagree about whether, or to what extent, this demand for infallibility can be satisfied. The rationalist is optimistic, the skeptic is pessimistic—and when optimism gives way to pessimism the result is a degenerate form of rationalism known as skepticism.[18]

Locke, as I said, managed to avoid this exercise in futility, but he did so at the price of consistency. In accepting the rationalist premise that infallibility is the proper criterion of knowledge and certainty, Locke imported a foreign element into his empiricist methodology and thereby generated a number of technical difficulties.[19] Nonetheless, Locke was first and foremost an empiricist who clearly understood, and repeatedly emphasized, the fallibility and limitations of human understanding: "All Men are liable to Errour, and most Men are in many Points, by Passion or Interest, under Temptation to it."[20] It was this sensitivity to fallibilism that led Locke to explore the psychology of reasoning[21] in a manner reminiscent of Francis Bacon.

Nowadays it might strike us as peculiar if a philosopher were to include lengthy discussions of psychology in a work on epistemology. Epistemology (the theory of knowledge) investigates the nature of concepts, truth, validity, and the like; and its interest in reasoning is principally *normative* rather than descriptive. That is to say, epistemology *prescribes* how we ought to think if we wish to reason well. It does not describe how we do think in fact—that is the business of cognitive psychology—but how we should think in theory.

We sometimes take intellectual specialization for granted, as if what appears obvious to us should have been equally obvious to someone living several centuries ago. Or if we profess to understand that the "obvious" will vary according to the intellectual and cultural context of a given thinker, this concession will sometimes be tinged with a sense of superiority, as if our perspective is significantly better than earlier perspectives. We have, after all, made considerable progress in the fields of science and technology, so it seems reasonable to suppose that we have made philosophical progress as well. Hence, while professing to understand why Bacon, Locke, and their contemporaries often failed to differentiate philosophy from psychology and other disciplines, we are apt to feel that the modern method of specialization is significantly better than the interdisciplinary method of an earlier time.

This issue is more complex than it may first appear, for philosophy is not a specialized discipline in the same sense as the physical sciences. Moreover, even if we suppose that philosophy has a distinctive subject matter, this does not mean that a philosopher cannot deal with the subject matter of other disciplines from a *philosophic point of view*. (We can undertake a philosophical analysis of baseball without suggesting that baseball is a philosophical subject per se.)

If we could travel back in time and inform John Locke that much of what he wrote about should properly be classified as psychology rather than philosophy, he would probably shrug his shoulders and say, "So what? I am interested in the fundamental problems of the human condition; that is what I write about, and that is what I call philosophy. If you wish to tack on some extra labels—if you wish to say that I also write about psychology, sociology, cultural anthropology, and the like—then go right ahead. If you can contribute to my quest for knowledge then I am in your debt; but if you cannot, if what you call psychology cannot improve on the insights of what I call philosophy, then you are merely asking me to participate in a linguistic minuet that, after providing some exercise, will leave us at precisely the same point from which we began."

To draw abstract lines of demarcation between disciplines is one thing, but to build walls of separation is another thing entirely. Lines provide us with a map of cognitive territories, and this map can serve as a navigational guide as we pass from one territory into another. But walls will obstruct this journey altogether, forcing us to remain within the narrow confines of our cognitive homeland.

Even granting all this, we may still wonder why Locke had so much to say about the psychology of reasoning. The key, I think, lies in the fallibilism that is so characteristic of the empiricist tradition. Although both empiricists and rationalists were interested in the sources of human error, they dealt with this problem in somewhat different ways.

For rationalists, reason is essentially an infallible instrument;

error originates in the senses, so it is by severing reason from the changing and deceptive world of appearances that certain knowledge is achieved. For empiricists, on the other hand, reason has its own inherent problems quite apart from the senses, so we must explore the psychology of reasoning if we wish to understand what these problems are and how they can be corrected.

This difference is reflected in the tendency (and it is only a tendency, not a hard-and-fast rule) of rationalists and empiricists to employ different methods in their quest for certainty. For Descartes and other rationalists, "only certainty can engender certainty."[22] In other words, the certainty of a given truth must either be apprehended immediately (by intuitive reason) or it must be based on, and derived from, other truths whose certainty has already been established by the same methods. This means that our quest for certainty is a *direct* search. We know that certainty is out there, waiting to be discovered; we know what it looks like and how to find it; so, with this information in hand, it is only a matter of using the correct methods in order to complete our quest.

The same quest for certainty takes the empiricist along a different path. Because fallible reason may err at any point, the empiricist must follow an *indirect* route to certainty, one that approaches it step-by-step through the elimination of error. There is no way to guard against the sources of error en masse (since reason itself is fallible), so we must deal with the possibility of error on a case-by-case basis, while attempting to minimize or overcome its ever-present influence. Hence it is through the progressive elimination of error rather than through the intuitive apprehension of truth that certainty can best be achieved.

I previously noted that a theory of fallibility and the sensitivity to error which it engenders were closely related to Locke's interest in religious toleration. This connection is evident in Locke's "Letter Concerning Toleration," but we also find it in his *Essay*:

> The necessity of believing, without Knowledge, nay, often upon very slight grounds, in this fleeting state of Action and Blindness we are

in, should make us more busy and careful to inform our selves, than constrain others. At least those, who have not thoroughly examined to the bottom all their own Tenets, must confess, they are unfit to prescribe to others; and are unreasonable in imposing that as a Truth in other Men's Belief, which they themselves have not searched into, nor weighed the Arguments of Probability, on which they should receive or reject it. Those who have fairly and truly examined, and are thereby got past doubt in all the Doctrines they profess, and govern themselves by, would have juster pretence to require others to follow them: But these are so few in number, and find so little to be magisterial in their Opinions, that nothing insolent and imperious is to be expected from them: And there is reason to think, that if men were better instructed themselves, they would be less imposing on others.[23]

This kind of argument has led to a common misunderstanding in historical accounts of religious toleration. It has become something of a truism among historians to claim that religious persecution was facilitated by the belief that certainty is an attainable ideal, so those Christians who believed themselves privy to divine revelation also felt they had a right (indeed, a duty) to impose their beliefs on others. And it was only when Locke and other empiricists repudiated certainty in favor of probability that toleration came to be accepted as the only sensible way to deal with religious differences.

This is a misleading way of looking at the matter. The significant contribution of empiricism was not the eradication of certainty, but the eradication of *infallibility* as a *criterion* of certainty. And this shift from infallibilism to fallibilism had profound consequences not only for toleration, but also for the subordination of faith to reason and theology to philosophy.

Divine revelation, since it originates with an infallible God, had long been upheld as the epitome of certain knowledge, an ideal that could never be equaled by reason alone without the assistance of faith. Locke agreed—and who would not?—that any direct communication from an infallible (and nondeceitful) God is beyond reasonable doubt (since *infallible*, by definition, means "*incapable* of error.")

But Locke also understood that all knowledge claims, whatever their supposed source, must ultimately pass through the fallible medium of our understanding, so we should subject all knowledge claims to the same canons of critical scrutiny.

For example, suppose that Jack believes that God spoke to him in a dream, and he insists that *we* should accept the content of his revelation without criticism, as infallibly certain, because any communication from an infallible being cannot be wrong. In response, Locke (and Hobbes before him) pointed out that *we* are under no obligation to accept this claim, because *we have received it not from God, but from a fallible human being named Jack*. To say that God has spoken to a man in a dream, wrote Hobbes,

> is no more than to say he dreamed that God spake to him; which is not of force to win belief from any man, that knows dreams are for the most part natural, and may proceed from former thoughts: as such dreams as that, from self-deceit, and foolish arrogance, and false opinion of a man's own godliness, or other virtue , by which he thinks he hath merited the favour of extraordinary revelation. To say he hath seen a vision, or heard a voice, is to say, that he hath dreamed between sleeping and waking: for in such manner a man doth many times take his dream for a vision, as not well observed his own slumbering. To say he speaks by supernatural inspiration, is to say he finds an ardent desire to speak, or some strong opinion of himself, for which he can allege no natural and sufficient reason. So that though God Almighty can speak to a man by dreams, vision, voice, and inspiration; yet he obliges no man to believe he hath so done to him that pretends it; who, being a man, may err, and, which is more, may lie.[24]

If Jack believes that God spoke to him, and if we are unable to change his mind, he will doubtless accept the content of his revelation as infallibly certain. But he cannot reasonably expect the same from others, because we receive the information from a fallible source who has no more authority in matters of knowledge than anyone else. Whatever Jack tells us, therefore, is a knowledge claim like any other, one that must meet the test of critical evaluation before we will take it seriously.

This line of reasoning runs throughout Locke's discussion of faith and religious experience, with the result that fallible reason is made the final arbiter over infallible revelation. There is no escape from fallibility, no shortcut to certainty. And since it is our ever-present liability to err that generates the need for critical standards to distinguish some beliefs from others—i.e., those that are worthy of our consideration (and ultimately our acceptance) from those that are not—no belief can legitimately claim to be exempt from the universal criteria of rational evaluation. Thus (to return to an earlier point), there is for Locke no such thing as privileged knowledge, even in the realm of revelation.

The foregoing material should help us to understand what Locke had in mind when he described the *Essay* as following the "historical, plain method."[25] History is concerned with the individual and concrete, not the general and abstract. Thus Locke does not intend to engage in metaphysical speculation about the "essence" of the human mind, but instead will take the mind as he finds it, complete with imperfections, conflicting tendencies, and diverse opinions; and he will explore the foundation of *particular* knowledge claims from this perspective. In other words, rather than posit infallibility as an ideal of human knowledge and then bemoan man's inability to scale this summit of epistemological perfection, Locke will accept reason (or the "understanding," to use his term) for what it is—a fallible and often unreliable means of cognition—and he will proceed on this basis to investigate the origin of knowledge in sense experience as a way to sort the wheat from the chaff. Such sorting is *always* necessary, regardless of the belief in question, because no belief is exempt from the pitfalls of fallibilism.

What are the primary sources of human error? Locke, like Bacon before him, spends a good deal of time discussing the "imperfection" and "abuse" of language; and he also focuses on the various reasons for mistaken judgment, whereby we give our assent to that which is not true. I shall now summarize some of what Locke has to say in these two areas.

Language has two basic functions, according to Locke: The first is to facilitate our own thinking, and the second is to communicate our thoughts to others. In most cases these goals are served quite well by natural language—i.e., language that has evolved spontaneously over time to serve many purposes, rather than having been designed for a single purpose—but a problem arises when this informal means of communication is applied to the more exacting demands of philosophy. The "civil use" of language, whereby words "serve for the upholding common Commerce about the ordinary Affairs and Conveniences of civil life," is "very distinct" from the "philosophical use" of language, whereby words "convey the precise Notions of Things, and . . . express, in general Propositions, certain and undoubted truths. . . ."[26]

The basic "imperfection" of language is that there exists no necessary or natural relationship between a particular word (or "sound," as Locke says) and the concept (or "idea") that it signifies. It is solely owing to custom and convention that English-speaking people use the word "man" to mean "rational animal," just as different sounds are used in other languages to denote the same thing. Thus: "Words having naturally no signification, the *Idea* which each stands for, must be learned and retained by those, who would exchange Thoughts, and hold intelligible Discourse with others, in any Language. . . ."[27]

Consider the word *God*.[28] If a person claims to know that God exists, and if he argues that I should believe likewise, then we must assume, first, that the theist has a fixed and determinate concept in his own mind to which he attaches the sound "God"; and, second, that I can successfully understand what he means by the word, thereby assuring that we are talking about the same thing. But there exist natural barriers to this kind of mutual understanding, according to Locke, especially when we take the rigorous demands of philosophy into account.

Consider the fact that single words often signify *complex* ideas that have been abstracted and combined from a number of more simple ideas. This means that we must understand these component parts separately, as well as how they have been integrated into a single concept, if we are to use such words with precision.[29] And since the most abstract ideas, such as "God," are invariably the most complex, precision is more difficult to attain here than anywhere else. Yet, more often than not, it is with words like "God" that this precision is sorely lacking.

Lastly, we should note that Locke, like many of his contemporaries, is a determined foe of custom and tradition as grounds for belief. People hold a great number of absurd and conflicting opinions which cannot all possibly be true. Yet such propositions, however irrational they may be, are accepted as sacred truths by people who display good judgment in other matters. Such people would sooner sacrifice anything, including their lives, rather than doubt or question these sacred beliefs.

How does this come about? How it that ideas that are learned uncritically in childhood become vested with the dignity of fundamental *principles*?

Most people desire some foundation or principle for their beliefs, a fundamental belief by which they can judge other matters of truth and falsehood, right and wrong. But the vast majority of people, occupied with the labors of daily life, have neither the time, taste, nor talent for philosophic reflection, so they tend to accept their beliefs upon *trust.* They believe what was taught to them in early childhood, especially in matters of religion and morality. Unaware of how or when these early beliefs were acquired, people come to accept them as absolutely certain, as if they were natural or self-evident. Custom, says Locke, is "a greater power than nature," so it is hardly surprising that few people seriously question their own tenets—"especially when one of their principles is, that principles ought not to be questioned."

Locke is keenly aware of the psychology of inertia and vested interests in matters of belief. Rare is the person who, by shaking his past thoughts and actions to their foundations, will risk having to confess that much of his previous life was based upon error and falsehood. Rare is the person who is willing to endure the reproach and condemnation that awaits anyone who deviates from the respectable opinions of his neighbors or country. "And where is the man to be found that can patiently prepare himself to bear the name of whimsical, skeptical, or atheist; which he is sure to meet with, who does in the least scruple any of the common opinions?" And these customary beliefs will instill even more fear, making them nearly impossible to question, when they are venerated as the sacred commands of God. Thus is the character of divinity stamped upon absurdities and errors —as people, unable or unwilling to grasp the true principles of knowledge, embrace the beliefs of others with uncritical reverence.

NOTES

1. It is at this point that the historian of philosophy is expected to display his sophistication by pointing out that the traditional scheme of rationalism versus empiricism is by no means a clear-cut distinction, since many philosophers (e.g., John Locke) who were influenced by both Descartes and Bacon exhibited both tendencies to one degree or another. This is doubtless true—no historian that I know of has ever denied it—but it is scarcely to the point. The traditional division between rationalism and empiricism is an example of what Max Weber called "ideal types," i.e., abstract models of essential characteristics that omit particular variations for the purpose of analysis and as an aid to historical understanding. To draw an abstract line of demarcation between rationalism and empiricism is quite legitimate in this sense, even if that line tends to become blurred in individual cases. After all, to say that Locke incorporated some features of both approaches provides a valuable insight into some of the internal tensions and inconsistencies of his philosophy, and this kind of insight would not be possible unless we had previously distinguished between the ideal types of rationalism and empiricism.

2. Sir Karl Popper and his followers have been among the most severe (and misleading) of Bacon's critics. See, for example, Popper's essay, "On the Sources of Knowledge and of Ignorance," in *Conjectures and Refutations: The Growth of Scientific Knowledge*, rev. ed. (London: Routledge and Kegan Paul, 1965), pp. 12–18; and Hans Albert, *Treatise on Critical Reason*, trans.

Mary Rorty (Princeton: Princeton University Press, 1985), pp. 30–38. For a much-needed corrective of the Popperian misunderstanding of Bacon, see Peter Urbach, *Francis Bacon's Philosophy of Science: An Account and a Reappraisal* (La Salle, Ill.: Open Court, 1987). What makes Urbach's account especially interesting is his listing of the many similarities between and Popper and Bacon, as we see in the parallel passages on pp. 86ff.

3. Quoted in Urbach, *Francis Bacon's Philosophy of Science*, p. 102.

4. Ibid., p. 103.

5. The term *secularism* was coined in the nineteenth century by the English freethinker George Jacob Holyoake, who hoped it would serve as a socially respectable substitute for *atheism*. And so it has.

6. Franklin Baumer, *Modern European Thought: Continuity and Change in Ideas, 1600–1950* (New York: Macmillan, 1977), p. 66.

7. Francis Bacon, *The Proficience and Advancement of Learning, Divine and Humane*, Great Books of the Western World (1605; reprint, Chicago: Encyclopedia Britannica, 1952), p. 4.

8. Ibid., p. 33.

9. Michael Moran, "Metaphysical Imagination," in *Dictionary of the History of Ideas: Studies of Selected Pivotal Ideas* (New York: Charles Scribner's Sons, 1973), vol. 3, p. 215.

10. Francis Bacon, *Novum Organum*, Great Books of the Western World, (Chicago: Encyclopedia Britannica, 1952), p. 109.

11. Ibid., p. 107.

12. Ibid., p. 109.

13. Ibid., pp. 109–10.

14. Ibid., 110.

15. Ibid.

16. It is within this context that we should read the lengthy critique of innate ideas in Locke's *Essay Concerning Human Understanding*. Because the once influential theory of innate ideas (i.e., ideas that we are supposedly born with, potentially if not actually) was rejected long ago by most philosophers, Locke's treatment of this subject may strike the modern reader as a bit arcane. But its central message remains as relevant in our day as it was in Locke's, to wit: All knowledge claims are equal, because all knowledge is born in sensation and reflection, and it is this common origin in experience that makes the public verification of knowledge claims possible. Locke believed that the theory of innate ideas was an effort to exempt some beliefs from this precept of cognitive egalitarianism.

17. For a superb technical discussion of Locke's epistemology, see the two-volume work by Michael Ayers, *Locke: Epistemology and Ontology* (London: Routledge, 1991).

18. I hope it is clear by now that *epistemological* skepticism is by no means the same thing as *religious* skepticism.

19. Locke will sometimes smooth over the technical bumps in his theory with commonsense qualifications. For example, while conceding that probable beliefs do not meet the strict standards required for knowledge, Locke also notes that the probability of some beliefs is sufficiently high to qualify them as "certain" for practical purposes. Locke is here alluding the traditional distinction between "metaphysical" (or theoretical) certainty and "moral" (or practical) certainty. A proposition is metaphysically certain if it is beyond the *theoretical* possibility of doubt, whereas a proposition is morally certain if it can be relied upon as a practical guide to action.

20. Bacon, *Novum Organum*, p. 718.

21. To avoid unnecessary confusion, I am now returning to the conventional meaning of "reason" to signify the cognitive faculty of human beings. Locke's conception of "reason," as we have seen, was more restricted than this, since he wished to contrast it with "judgment." Locke customarily referred to man's cognitive faculty as the "understanding" rather than "reason," but to adopt this specialized terminology would serve no purpose for the present discussion.

22. Émile Bréhier, *The History of Philosophy: The Seventeenth Century*, trans. Wade Baskin (Chicago: Chicago University Press, 1966), p. 66.

23. John Locke, *An Essay Concerning Human Understanding*, ed. Peter Nidditch (Oxford: Clarendon Press, 1975), pp. 660–61.

24. Thomas Hobbes, *Leviathan*, ed. Michael Oakeshott (New York: Collier Books, 1962), pp. 272–73.

25. Locke, *Essay*, p. 44.

26. Ibid., p. 476.

27. Ibid., p. 477.

28. Locke does not actually use this example, but since his points about language were quickly and eagerly applied by deists and freethinkers to the subject of God, I shall use this example as a means of indicating the impact of Locke's treatment (as well as the similar treatments of Bacon and Hobbes) on theological controversies.

29. Locke's approach, which was to decompose complex ideas into

simple ideas and then trace the latter to their origin in experience (either sensation or reflection), has been called *the psycho-genetic method* (or, more simply, *the genetic method*) because of its stress on the *psychological genesis*, or origin, of ideas. This "plain, historical method" (as Locke called it) was widely criticized by later philosophers (especially post-Kantians) as an illicit mixture of epistemology and psychology. The origin of an idea, we are told, is an issue distinct from the validity or truth-value of that idea; and Locke's genetic method, we are further told, fails to take this crucial distinction into account. But I think this criticism is a bit unfair to Locke, who nowhere (that I know of) expressly articulates the view commonly attributed to him. And I also think that philosophers who accept this criticism tend to do so either because they rely more on secondary accounts than the original text, or because they read the text with preconceptions of what they expect to find, thereby fastening upon any passage that that seems to support their preconceptions and glossing over any that may contradict it. In any case, the common complaint that philosophers before Kant failed to grasp the difference between epistemology and psychology—between the justification of a belief and its origin in sense experience—is an egregious and pretentious assumption that, if true, would mean that Locke and other empiricists were ignorant of a basic distinction that is taught in first-semester courses on logic. My interpretation of Locke (which is admittedly a sympathetic one) may be summarized as follows: The genetic method is primarily a method of conceptual analysis and clarification, a means whereby we can make our ideas clear by giving to them fixed and determinate meanings. Thus any complex idea that cannot be broken into its constituent parts and ultimately traced to experience is bound to be unclear or, at worst, incoherent. Thus, according to this view, Locke's genetic method was concerned first and foremost with *meaning*—and this is related to *justification* inasmuch as the meaning of a proposition must be made clear before we can know what kind of evidence would be relevant to establishing its truth.

Theology and Metaphysics

THE SCIENCE OF GOD

Theology, or the "science of God," is customarily divided into two categories: natural and revealed. Natural theology seeks knowledge of God solely through reason, whereas revealed theology requires faith in the veracity of divine revelation.

According to Thomas Aquinas, natural theology—a metaphysical investigation of the nature and existence of God—is a branch of philosophy, whereas revealed theology, or the "science of sacred doctrine," is a separate and distinct discipline. Why is this latter discipline necessary? Because our salvation requires knowledge that exceeds the grasp of reason, and such knowledge can come only from God. Moreover, even in cases where reason is adequate, such knowledge would be available only to a few philosophers who have invested the necessary time and effort. Revelation is therefore necessary so that salvation will be available to everyone.

Revealed theology, according to Aquinas, is a legitimate science; its truths, which are backed by an infallible authority, can be justified with absolute certainty. Although the appeal to authority is a weak argument when based on the testimony of human beings—our faith in the veracity of other people often perpetuates error—this is not true when the authority in question is God. God neither errs nor deceives, so his testimony provides us with a degree of certainty to which fallible reason cannot aspire. Revealed theology is therefore the supreme science, one that is immune to the error and uncertainty of the philosophical sciences.

It is clear that Aquinas does not regard religious faith as in any sense irrational; indeed, nothing could be more rational than to have faith (i.e., complete confidence) in the word of an infallible and trustworthy being. But it would be a mistake to suppose that Aquinas grants to reason a status equal to that of faith. Reason is independent in the sense that it has its own sphere of knowledge (philosophy), and it is autonomous in the sense that faith is not required to justify this knowledge, but reason is not sovereign even within its own sphere. The certainty of reason is inferior to the certainty of faith, so the former must submit to the latter in the event of conflict. Reason cannot achieve the same degree of certainty as faith, so the science of sacred doctrine, the truths revealed by God, is the sovereign judge of all other knowledge: "Whatsoever is found in other sciences contrary to any truth of this science, must be condemned as false."[1]

Articles of faith, such as we find in the Bible, are grounded in the infallible authority of God and cannot be demonstrated by reason. This means that the Christian cannot convert the unbeliever by appealing solely to natural theology. Although the arguments of natural theology (e.g., the First Cause Argument) can prove the existence of God, according to Aquinas, rational theism cannot justify the specific doctrines of Christianity. Disagreements among Christians can be resolved (at least in theory) by citing Scripture, because both parties accept the Bible as the ultimate arbiter in matters of faith.

But this method will not work with atheists and other unbelievers who reject Christianity altogether. Natural theology can justify theism, but it cannot justify *Christian* theism. Reason can neutralize the atheist by refuting his arguments against Christianity (which must be wrong, since they contradict the infallible word of God), but reason cannot prove that Christianity is true, unless the atheist first believes in the authority of divine revelation.[2]

TWO KINDS OF ARGUMENT

An invalid argument may persuade me, while a valid argument may fail to persuade me. This distinction between proof and persuasion, between the reasons that *justify* a belief and the motives that *cause* a belief, is essential to the enterprise of philosophy. The philosopher is concerned with the logic of demonstration, not with the psychology of persuasion.

We thus see that *argument*, like many similar terms, has two distinct meanings: one *logical*, the other *psychological*. The logic of an argument pertains to its abstract and universal characteristics that do not vary from person to person. The validity of an argument has nothing to do with how many people find it convincing; a valid argument for one person is valid for everyone else. The psychology of an argument, on the other hand, pertains to its effectiveness in causing a person to believe, and this will vary from case to case.

The philosopher should focus not on whether an argument is persuasive but on whether it is sound. He should concern himself with knowledge rather than belief, since the latter has nothing intrinsically to do with rational justification. But what of the Christian theologian? If articles of faith are at once essential to salvation and immune to proof, then how can the atheist be dissuaded from his folly?

This brings us to a fundamental tension between philosophy and Christian theology (as well as other revealed religions in which belief is a precondition of salvation). This tension is reflected in the different attitudes of atheists and those Christians who wish to convert them. As the atheist sees the matter, he should believe in Christianity only if his adversary can present a reasonable case, arguments that appeal to reason rather than faith. But this is an impossible task, according to most Christians; there must occur a "leap of faith" before the atheist will understand the wisdom of belief and submit to the authority of God.

This is a crucial leap indeed, at least for the Christian, since the atheist who refuses to budge is doomed to suffer the eternal torments of hell (or possibly face other unpleasant consequences). The atheist, however, has a different perspective. Believing in neither God nor in an afterlife, the atheist does not believe that his disbelief will have catastrophic consequences, so he subjects the arguments for Christianity to the same logical norms that he applies to every other argument. There should be no double standard: If the Christian may call on faith to support his arguments, then the atheist may do likewise by maintaining that people should have faith in the existence of a natural universe without God.

The leap of faith is a strategic impasse that confronts every Christian in search of converts; and, as he sees the matter, there is no wrong way to become a Christian. It is the end that is important, not the means; it does not matter *why* you believe, so long as you *believe*. For the philosopher, in contrast, the paramount issue is the justification of belief, not the fact of belief itself.

Thus do the philosopher and the theologian exemplify the two different meanings of "argument." The logic of validity is the principal concern of the philosopher, whereas the psychology of persuasion is the principal concern of the theologian. Of course, these approaches are not necessarily incompatible: The philosopher, after all, may sometimes find that reason is the best method of winning others to his point of view. But the theologian cannot rely on this happy coincidence. He must bypass reason in pursuit of a greater good, viz., a state of eternal bliss that is attainable only to those who have been saved through faith. When salvation is at stake, when failure to covert the atheist may land him in hell, the Christian becomes a spiritual Machiavellian for whom the end justifies the means.

The key point here is captured in Augustine's celebrated remark that we must believe in order to understand; i.e., we must first have faith in God before we can have knowledge of divinely revealed truths. How we assess this maxim again depends on our point of view. What for the theologian is a commendable act of faith is for the philosopher a violation of intellectual integrity. This tension is as old as Christianity itself, as we see in the following passage from Celsus, a critic of Christianity who lived during the second century.

> More and more the myths put about by these Christians are better known than the doctrines of the philosophers. Who has not heard the fable of Jesus' birth from a virgin or the stories of his crucifixion and resurrection? . . . But the point is this, and the Christians would do well to heed it: One ought first to follow reason as a guide before accepting any belief, since anyone who believes without testing a doctrine is certain to be deceived. . . . Just as the charlatans of the cults take advantage of a simpleton's lack of education to lead him around by the nose, so too with the Christian teachers: they do not want to give or receive reasons for what they believe. Their favorite expressions are "Do not ask questions, just believe!" and: "Your faith will save you!" "The wisdom of the world," they say, "is evil; to be simple is to be good." If only they would undertake to answer my question—which I do not ask as one who is trying to understand their beliefs (there being little to understand!). But they refuse to answer, and indeed discourage asking questions of any sort.[3]

What was condemned by Celsus as a philosophical vice was praised by the Christians of his era as a theological virtue. A rather extreme illustration of this is found in the voluminous writings of Tertullian (c. 160–225), an apologist who wrote:"[T]he Son of God died; it is by all means to be believed because it is absurd. And he was buried and rose again; the fact is certain, because it is impossible."[4]

This curious passage contains a serious point, one that is by no means as bizarre as it may first appear. Tertullian was responding to Marcion, a Christian heretic who rejected belief in the literal resurrection of Jesus owing to its irrationality. This absurd belief is "unworthy of God," according to Marcion, so we should interpret the resurrection in spiritual rather than in physical terms. Tertullian responds to this objection by pointing out that this kind of critical approach will leave nothing left standing of Christianity. If we follow reason in this case, then why not follow it in all others as well? And if we adopt this rationalistic method, then what will prevent us from repudiating Christianity itself? To say, therefore, that the physical resurrection of Jesus "is certain because it is absurd," is merely to say that this story differs not at all from other Christian beliefs. All such beliefs are justified by an unconditional faith in the infallible word of God, and to assess these beliefs by the canons of reason is to destroy Christianity root and branch.

The moral here is that revealed theology is far more important to Christianity (and other salvation religions) than is natural theology. The classical arguments of natural theology can, at most, justify belief in the deistic god of nature, a creator who does not intervene in human affairs. But, as Pascal pointed out, deism is "almost as remote from the Christian religion as atheism."[5] The deist and the atheist have much in common: Both reject revealed theology, both value knowledge over belief, neither is willing to subordinate reason to faith, and neither is willing to exempt some beliefs from the rigor of critical scrutiny. There are historical similarities as well. Early criticisms of the Bible, miracles, and other forms of Christian revelation owed far more to popular deistic writers than to their atheistic fellow travelers, who were relatively scarce during the seventeenth and eighteenth centuries. And few could equal the deistic enthusiasm for scientific progress and unrestrained freedom of thought.

As for the contention that reason can prove the existence of God—even this core belief of deism tended to strengthen the alliance with atheism. According to the deists, if reason can demonstrate this highly significant truth, then we should not dismiss it as incompetent in any sphere of knowledge, including religion. For the deist, as for the atheist, reason is the sovereign judge of every belief.

The metaphysical God of the philosophers, as Pascal noted, differs radically from the personal God of Abraham, Isaac, and Jacob.

This observation expresses Pascal's belief in the incomparable significance of revealed theology, a value that natural theology cannot approximate. Pascal's hostility to natural theology did not stem from a conviction that all arguments for the existence of God are worthless; on the contrary, he was convinced that belief in God can be supported (though not rigorously proven) by rational methods. But the appropriate arguments for Christianity are those of revealed theology (e.g., the appeal to miracles and biblical prophecy), because only through these do we come to understand the redemptive powers of faith in God and belief in Jesus as the Christ.

It is interesting to note that Pascal does not condemn the arguments of natural theology on philosophical grounds. He criticizes them not for invalidity or for failing to achieve their intended purpose, but for achieving a purpose that is at odds with the purpose of Christianity. An abstract knowledge of God is "useless and sterile" without a personal belief in Jesus Christ; and this explains the "remarkable fact that no canonical author has ever used nature to prove God. They all try to make people believe in him."[6]

According to Pascal, those Christians who appeal primarily to natural theology in their attempt to convert unbelievers are reversing cause and effect. A belief in Christ is the basis for a true understanding of God, not vice versa. This is because (as we noted in our discussion of Augustine, who influenced Pascal tremendously) the Christian gives priority to those beliefs that are necessary for salvation, while demoting the need to justify these beliefs to a secondary consideration. God demands *that* we believe in him but seems unconcerned with the *why*.

For the Christian, therefore, revealed theology is preferable by far to natural theology, because it is only through the former that he has any chance of converting atheists. Quoting Pascal:

The metaphysical proofs for the existence of God are so remote from human reasoning [i.e., how people *actually* think about God] and so involved that they make little impact, and, even if they did help some people, it would only be for the moment during which they watched the demonstration, because an hour later they would be afraid they had made a mistake.[7]

METAPHYSICS

Scan the "metaphysics" section of your local bookstore and you will likely find titles on everything from crystals and pyramids to theosophy and the paranormal. Many books with nothing in common except an esoteric subject matter that cannot readily be classified as philosophy, psychology, or any other traditional discipline are exiled to an intellectual wasteland called *metaphysics*.

We should therefore pity the modern philosopher who lays claim to metaphysical knowledge, for he must do battle on two fronts, both popular and professional. Although the philosophical discipline of metaphysics bears no resemblance to its popular and bastardized namesake—a label for weird beliefs on the fringes of credibility—the philosopher is likely to suffer from guilt by association. He must declare his allegiance to reason in an effort to distance himself from the occult and mystical connotations of popular metaphysics; he must explain that metaphysics, as understood by the philosopher, is not a refuge for credulous and careless minds but requires a sustained commitment to critical thinking.

The modern metaphysician faces another problem that is far more serious. Even if he manages to gain public respectability he will still encounter suspicion from many of his peers, those philosophers and other intellectuals who hold metaphysics in low esteem. Metaphysics, according to its critics, is undisciplined speculation that cannot be tested by empirical means, so it can neither be verified nor falsified. Or, even worse, it is a meaningless enterprise that relies on arbitrary definitions and ambiguous terminology.

The term *metaphysics* was coined in the first century B.C.E. by librarians in Alexandria who, while cataloging the writings of Aristotle, had to come up with a name for his untitled work on first principles. Their solution, to call it *Metaphysics*, was at once logical and unimaginative: It simply referred to the fact that this book was listed immediately *after* the book on *physics.*

The label *metaphysics* emerged from this humble beginning to become the most influential and controversial branch of Western philosophy. Hailed for centuries by medieval philosophers as the Queen of the Sciences, a discipline which yielded fundamental knowledge of the universe, metaphysics became a target of sustained criticism during the seventeenth and eighteenth centuries as John Locke, David Hume, and other empiricists undermined its traditional foundations.

No trend in modern philosophy is more significant than the shift of emphasis from the metaphysical theory of being to the epistemological theory of knowledge. Alexander Pope's dictum that the proper study of mankind is man was echoed by David Hume's contention that a "science of man" is the foundation of all other sciences, because all knowledge, including our knowledge of nature, is a product of the human mind. Thus, as John Locke had previously argued, philosophers should investigate the origin and limitations of human knowledge before venturing into the murky world of metaphysical systems.

Locke's empiricism and high regard for Newtonian physics made him contemptuous of traditional metaphysics. "You and I have had enough of this kind of fiddling," he wrote to a friend; "we are unlikely to learn anything in metaphysical works on God and spirits." And, in his *Essay Concerning Human Understanding*, Locke declares that the "master-builders" of his era were not metaphysicians but scientists, such as "the incomparable Mr. Newton," whose work had been hindered by the "uncouth, affected, or unintelligible terms" of metaphysics. Metaphysicians attempted to pass off "vague and insignificant forms of speech" as profound insights and deep learning, when in fact they were nothing more than "the covers of ignorance, and hindrance of true knowledge."[8]

This is fairly complex issue, as we see in the fact that Locke himself would later be hailed by Enlightenment thinkers as the father of *modern* metaphysics. Modern and traditional metaphysics had something in common, in that both viewed metaphysics as what Aristotle had called the *science of first principles*. But modernists looked for these first principles in the human mind, not in "being" external to the mind, because there can be no knowledge without a cognitive process that produces this knowledge. Moreover, this modernist metaphysics included more than we now understand by the term *epistemology* (which was coined in the nineteenth century). Modernist metaphysics included both epistemology *and* psychology, insofar as the latter was concerned with the origin and formation of ideas.

In a famous passage, Locke described his philosophic role as a modest one—"as an underlaborer in clearing the ground a little, and removing some of the rubbish that lies in the way to knowledge."[9] (This refers, of course, to metaphysical rubbish.) This profession of modesty, however, was a bit disingenuous. Locke was calling for a revolution in philosophy, and he knew it.

ARTHUR SCHOPENHAUER

Arthur Schopenhauer was one of the most interesting atheists of the nineteenth century. A fan of Eastern philosophy, he praised the philosophical insights of Buddhism and Hinduism as far superior to those of Christianity and Judaism.[10] An admirer of Kant who did not hesitate to criticize his master, he joined in the popular German search for the elusive "thing-in-itself"—that noumenal realm of being as such that played a far greater role in post-Kantian philosophy than it did in Kant's own work, and which Schopenhauer located in the primordial "will," or striving for existence, that permeates the entire universe. Then there was Schopenhauer's unmitigated contempt for Hegel (the most influential continental philosopher of the time), upon whom he heaped scorn and ridicule in terms that that have rarely seen the like in the annals of philosophy.

Our interest in Schopenhauer does not lie in his pessimism (for which he is best remembered), but in his views on metaphysics, theology, and popular religion. Man, according to Schopenhauer, is a metaphysical animal owing to his reason, which gives him the ability to reflect on his destiny in a manner that other animals cannot. Although some animals other than man have the ability to think, such thinking is tied to the concrete particulars of perceptual experience. Only man has the power of *abstract* thought, and it is this that enables us to transcend the dictates of the will and ponder issues that are not linked to the immediate problems of survival.

Most people are unwilling or unable to undertake the laborious (and often thankless) task of philosophical reflection; and in such cases reason remains a servant of the will, a pragmatic means for the satisfaction of desire, rather than an autonomous instrument that sets its own course and seeks knowledge for its own sake. Nevertheless, most people cannot help but wonder about the world, especially the reasons for evil and the possibility of an afterlife, and it was from these universal concerns that religion emerged as an explanation for the unknown and a balm for the discomfort of uncertainty. As Schopenhauer puts it:

> [W]ith this reflection and astonishment arises the *need for metaphysics* that is peculiar to man alone; accordingly, he is an *animal metaphysicum*. At the beginning of his consciousness, he naturally takes himself . . . as something that is a matter of course. This, however, does not last long, but very early, and simultaneously with the first reflection, appears that wonder which is some day to become the mother of metaphysics. In accordance with this, Aristotle says in the introduction to his *Metaphysics*: "For on account of wonder and astonishment men now philosophize, as they began to do in the first place."[11]

Metaphysical knowledge, for Schopenhauer as for Kant, is knowledge that lies beyond the *possibility of experience*, i.e., knowledge that cannot be acquired through sense experience. Most people lack the taste, talent, or leisure for this kind of speculative enterprise, and this fact, when combined with many cultural variables, has generated a diverse array of religious doctrines about God, man's place in the universe, and life after death. These religious systems—which Schopenhauer dubs "popular metaphysics"—typically rely for their verification on the external evidence of signs, miracles, and other form of revelation. "Their argument are mainly threats of eternal, and indeed also temporal evils, directed against unbelievers, and even against mere doubters."[12]

In contrast to the popular metaphysics of religion stands the metaphysics of philosophy, which, because it requires reflection, leisure, culture, and skillful judgment, is accessible only to a miniscule number of people. Philosophical metaphysics "has its verification and credentials *in itself* ": Unlike popular metaphysics, it appeals not to the revealed truth of an external authority but to the critical judgment of each individual, who must weigh the arguments for and against a theory before embracing it. Hence philosophical metaphysics may be called a "doctrine of conviction," whereas popular metaphysics may be called a "doctrine of faith."

Contrary to the common interpretation of Schopenhauer as a defender of irrationalism, owing to his emphasis on the blind force of the primordial will,[13] he held reason in high esteem. But he was no child of the Enlightenment; on the contrary, he was pessimistic about the influence of reason and philosophy on popular culture. The discipline of philosophy will always be restricted to a very small minority not because this is the way things should be, but simply because this is the way things are. The isolation of philosophy will be with us so long as human nature remains human. Hence, if Schopenhauer was something of an elitist in matters of philosophy, this was an elitism born of necessity, not preference.

Schopenhauer could not accept the Enlightenment ideal of intellectual progress, according to which the masses would be led from the darkness of religion to the light of philosophy through popular education, the debunking of superstition, and the dethroning of "priests" and other religious authorities. The deck is stacked against philosophical knowledge in favor of religious belief, partially because the former is attainable only by adults, whereas the latter can be, and typically is, taught to young children who passively assimilate what they are told without protest or criticism. Thus, by the time people become old enough to appreciate philosophy, they are already encumbered with a good many metaphysical beliefs that they are unwilling to question, thereby making it impossible for philosophy to gain a foothold.

The promise of an afterlife is undoubtedly the greatest advantage that religion has over philosophy, and it is the chief reason why most people refuse to give serious consideration to atheism. Indeed, Schopenhauer speculates that people would quickly abandon their belief in God and "be eager for atheism," if it could be shown that disbelief rather than theism is necessary to achieve immortality. The belief in God would be cast aside with scarcely a second thought if atheism were better able to alleviate the fear of death.

What has been the prevailing historical relationship between the metaphysical systems of philosophy and religion? It has been fraught with tension, conflict, and violence, according to Schopenhauer. Every metaphysical system faces competitors, but philosophy wages war with "word and pen," whereas religion has frequently resorted to "fire and sword." Religion, because of its popular appeal, has been the dominant cultural force, and if it sometimes tolerated the dissenting voices of philosophy, this was often owing to their small numbers and lack of influence. At other times (such as during the late Middle Ages), religion has attempted to conscript philosophy into its service, but such attempts have usually backfired and proven detrimental to religion in the long run. For whenever philosophy is given room to breathe it will invariably seek revenge against religion (by stealth, if not openly) by gradually expanding its sphere of jurisdiction. And the dangerous nature of philosophy is increased by the fact that it encourages the development of science, a secret ally which, even if not openly opposed to religion, will unexpectedly do it great harm.

We now come to Schopenhauer's hostility to "that strange hybrid, or centaur, the so-called philosophy of religion."[14] This attitude toward natural theology is based on Schopenhauer's conviction that philosophy and religion communicate through different kinds of language. Philosophy is concerned with the literal expression of truth, whereas religion conveys whatever truth it may contain allegorically through fables, mysteries, and doctrines that would be impossible or incomprehensible if construed literally. Thus the strict interpretative method of philosophy cannot be applied to the allegorical method of religion without corrupting both disciplines in the process.

It is interesting to note that natural theology as viewed by the atheist Schopenhauer is essentially a mirror image of natural theology as viewed by the Christian Pascal. Schopenhauer wanted to keep philosophy and religion separate for the sake of philosophy, whereas Pascal was concerned with preserving the internal integrity of the Christian faith. Indeed, Pascal would have found little to disagree with in the following remarks by Schopenhauer:

> [W]hy should a religion require the suffrage of a philosophy? Indeed, it has everything on its side, revelation, documents, miracles, prophecies, government protection, the highest dignity and eminence, as is due to truth, the consent and reverence of all, a thousand temples in which it is preached and practiced, hosts of sworn priests, and, more than all this, the invaluable prerogative of being allowed to imprint its doctrines on the mind at the tender age of childhood, whereby they become almost innate ideas. With such an abundance of means at its disposal, still to desire the assent of wretched philosophers it would have to be more covetous . . . than appears compatible with a good conscience.[15]

NOTES

1. Thomas Aquinas, *Summa Theologica*, trans. Fathers of the English Dominican Province, Great Books of the Western World, vol. 19 (Chicago: Encyclopedia Britannica, 1952), p. 6.

2. Many Christians disagree with the views expressed by Thomas Aquinas about natural and revealed theology. (Some eminent theologians, for example, have maintained that reason is unable to prove the existence of God.) I have focused on Aquinas because he represents a wing of Christian rationalism that, though sometimes dismissed as outdated, deserves

serious consideration. Aquinas pushed the camel's nose of reason under the tent of Christianity about as far as it can go without causing it to collapse, and even a little reason goes a long way. This makes Aquinas a worthy adversary for the atheist who would rather do battle with giants rather than dwarfs.

3. Celsus, *On the True Doctrine: A Discourse Against the Christians*, trans. R. Joseph Hoffmann (New York: Oxford University Press, 1987), p. 54. Although there were numerous early critiques of Christianity, only that of Celsus is extant, and it is incomplete. It is not as if Christian censors failed to destroy this critique along with all the others; rather, we have what we have because Origen of Alexandria quoted Celsus at length in the course of rebutting his arguments.

4. Tertullian in *The Ante-Nicene Fathers*, ed. A. Roberts and J. Donaldson (New York: Charles Scribner, 1905), vol. 3, p. 525

5. Blaise Pascal, *Pensées*, trans. A. J. Krailsheimer (London: Penguin Books, 1966), p. 168.

6. Ibid.

7. Ibid.

8. John Locke, *An Essay Concerning Human Understanding*, ed. Peter Nidditch (Oxford: Clarendon Press, 1975), p. 89.

9. Ibid.

10. Schopenhauer detested the Koran, however, which he called a "wretched book." Contrary to an unwritten rule of contemporary philosophy, Schopenhauer often used polemical and acerbic language; and this, combined with his brilliantly lucid and witty style—a rarity among German philosophers—makes him a pleasure to read, whatever one may think of his arguments. Perhaps most unusual is Schopenhauer's kind treatment of Aristotle, whom he frequently cites, during a time when that great philosopher was largely neglected or maligned by philosophers other than Thomists (Catholic followers of Thomas Aquinas) and a few others. Schopenhauer was thus an *eclectic* in the best sense: discriminating in his use of other philosophers (however unfashionable they may have been) and subservient to none, while constructing a philosophical system that was distinctively his own. Another one of Schopenhauer's favorite targets (which was probably fueled by Hegel's immense influence in German universities) was the professional teacher of philosophy: "Those who live *by* philosophy are not only, as a rule and with rarest exceptions, quite different from those who live *for* philos-

ophy, but very often they are even the opponents of the latter, their secret and implacable enemies" (*The World As Will and Representation*, trans. E. F. J. Payne [New York: Dover Publications, 1958], vol. 2, p. 163).

11. Ibid., p. 160.

12. Ibid., pp. 164–65.

13. Schopenhauer's concept of the will influenced Sigmund Freud's concept of the Id, and this emphasis on the irrational (or, more precisely *non-rational*) component of human nature has caused both men to be unfairly branded as champions of irrationalism. But philosophers have long recognized this dark side of human nature, as we see in the writings of Plato, Aristotle, the Stoics, etc. Moreover, Spinoza—an unqualified rationalist by anyone's standard—devoted a large section of his *Ethics* to the same subject. (This discussion, "Of Human Bondage or the Strength of the Emotions," provided Somerset Maugham with the title for his famous novel.) When philosophers have emphasized human irrationality, they have usually done so in the hope that a better understanding of, and appreciation for, this feature of human nature will better enable reason to do its work of bringing the passions under control, which is essential for living a good life. Where philosophers tend to differ is in their estimate of how much we can realistically expect reason to accomplish in bringing about change for the better. For example, although Voltaire exerted a tremendous influence on the French Enlightenment, he knew history too well—calling it a chronicle of follies, vices, and crimes—to be overly optimistic about the future influence of reason on humankind. Although Schopenhauer believed that the will (i.e., the instinct for self-preservation at any cost) is the dominant factor in human behavior, he also maintained that man's capacity for abstract thought can liberate him from bondage of the will and thereby open up to him a transcendental world of pure knowledge and beauty. This is scarcely the ideal of an irrationalist, however pessimistic Schopenhauer may have been about the cultural prospects of philosophy.

14. Schopenhauer, *The World as Will and Representation*, p. 168.

15. Ibid., p. 166.

Metaphysical Muddles

The Ontological Argument

INTRODUCTION

O ntology, which has been traditionally conceived as a branch of metaphysics, is the study of being as such, apart from any particular type or form of being. The Ontological Argument attempts to prove the existence of God from an analysis of the idea of a perfect being, a being than which nothing greater can be conceived. It is by understanding the nature, or essence, of God that we come to know that God must necessarily exist. We needn't search the outside world for signs or evidence of divine workmanship; rather we need only look within our own minds and reflect upon our idea of God in order to prove his existence.

The endurance of the Ontological Argument is one of the most mysterious of theological mysteries. First presented in the eleventh century by St. Anselm of Canterbury, it failed to impress most philosophers and theologians until it was revived (and revised) by René Descartes in the seventeenth century. This was a curious incident indeed. Descartes, a virtual poster boy for modern philosophy and the scientific revolution, resurrected an argument that so reeked of an archaic Neoplatonism that it was even rejected by most medieval theologians, who were otherwise disposed to smile upon proofs for the existence of God.

There are two major reasons why the Ontological Argument is relevant to a study of atheism: (1) As developed by Anselm, the Ontological Argument was expressly intended to expose atheism (or at least positive atheism) as a self-contradictory, incoherent position. Thus the Ontological Argument is to the theist what the Method of Conceptual Analysis is to the atheist—namely, a fatal blow to the heart of the opposition that will annihilate its credibility. (2) Discussions of the Ontological Argument brought the principal attributes of God, such as perfection and necessity, into critical focus; and this contributed greatly to the atheistic arsenal of arguments.

ANSELM

St. Anselm (1033–1109), a native of Italy who became the Archbishop of Canterbury, had the soul of a mystic and the mind of a philosopher. He longed to see God face-to-face, to experience him directly, but this was impossible for a human nature that had been corrupted by original sin. We have lost the ability to see God (i.e., to experience him, in effect, as we would another person) so we cannot possibly hope to *understand* the divine nature. But we have a strong desire to see God nonetheless, and this is why Anselm agreed with Augustine that belief must precede understanding: "For I do not seek to understand that I may believe, but I believe in order to understand. For this also I believe—that unless I believed, I should not understand."[1]

This is the background against which Anselm presented his version of the Ontological Argument. This argument is the closest that reason can ever come to understanding the nature of God. It is by meditating on the concept of God, according to Anselm, that we come to understand that God must *necessarily* exist. There is much about God that we cannot know, but we do know that his essence and his existence are one and the same thing—that *what* God is cannot be separated from the fact *that* God is—and this is enough to banish all doubt about his existence. For we know that God is the most perfect being imaginable, and this tells us that God must necessarily exist—for if he did not exist, he would not be the most perfect being imaginable. Thus, beginning with the premise that God is "a being than which nothing greater can be conceived," we are led to the conclusion that God exists.

A major purpose of Anselm's argument is to demonstrate the logical absurdity of (positive) atheism. The atheist, according to Anselm, denies the existence of God; and this he cannot logically do unless he possesses a concept of God. To deny the existence of *x* is meaningless unless we first understand the meaning of *x.* Thus, in claiming that God does not exist, the atheist implicitly concedes that he understands what it means to speak of God. The idea of God must exist as an object of the understanding in the mind of the atheist. The atheist, though he denies that God exists *objectively*, as a being external to consciousness, must at least concede that he exists *subjectively*, as a concept in the mind of man.

This premise is crucial to Anselm's argument, because it establishes a common ground between the atheist and the theist. The atheist denies what the theist affirms, but both affirm that the idea of God exists subjectively as an object of the understanding. And this subjective idea is sufficient to prove that God exists as an objective being external to consciousness. The atheist need only analyze his concept of God in order to see that God must necessarily exist. In asserting that God does not exist, the atheist immerses himself in a logical contradiction—for his assertion is incompatible with the subjective idea of God, as it exists in the mind of the atheist himself.

If the atheistic position seems reasonable to many people, this is so, says Anselm, because we ordinarily distinguish between that which exists in the understanding (as a concept) and that which exists in reality (as a being). The painter, before he puts brush to canvas, may have a mental picture of what he wishes to paint, in which case this picture is an object of his understanding. But the painter does not understand the painting to exist until he actually paints it, after which the painting exists both in his understanding and in reality. Similarly, we may suppose it possible for the atheist to understand the concept of God while denying his existence, but, according to Anselm, this is logically impossible. To understand the concept of God is necessarily to understand that God exists. The former logically implies the latter, so the denial of the atheist is self-contradictory, incoherent, and self-refuting.

Even if we accept the premise that the atheist has an idea of God, how does Anselm get from the *here* of God qua subjective idea to the *there* of God qua objective being? Anselm's argument may be summarized as follows.

The idea of God refers to the most perfect of beings, "a being than which nothing greater can be conceived." This means that God must exist not only in the mind but also in reality. Why? Because a real being is necessarily "greater" than a mere concept of that being. If God exists only as an idea, it cannot be the case that God is a being of which nothing greater can be conceived—because an existent God is necessarily greater (i.e., is more real) than a mere idea of God. If we suppose that God exists only in the understanding, then we implicitly contradict our concept of God, for such a being is not the greatest that can be conceived. It is greater to exist in reality than to exist merely in the mind, so to understand that God is the greatest of conceivable beings is also to understand that God must necessarily exist.

After presenting this part of his argument, Anselm proceeds to argue that the nonexistence of God is inconceivable. (Some commentators treat these parts as two distinct arguments, but I think they constitute two steps of one argument.) Having established the *existence* of God from the idea of a supremely perfect being, Anselm now extends his discussion to the *nature* of God.

According to Anselm, it is impossible to conceive of the nonexistence of God. This contention is also based on the notion of God as a being than which nothing greater can be conceived. We can conceive of a logically necessary being—i.e., a being whose nonexistence is inconceivable—and such a being is greater than a being whose nonexistence is conceivable. Hence it is "an irreconcilable contradiction" to say that God's nonexistence is conceivable; because if this were so, God would not in fact be the greatest conceivable being.

Thus, after establishing the existence of God in the first phase of his argument, Anselm next argues that God's nonexistence is inconceivable. In other words, to deny the existence of God is not merely false: it is self-contradictory. Just as the concept of a supremely perfect being logically implies the existence of such a being, so the existence of God logically implies that his existence cannot be coherently denied.

Anselm's refutation of atheism is now complete. The atheist, if he is to deny the existence of God, must first have a concept of God (or there would be nothing to deny). He claims to understand that the idea of God signifies the greatest being that can be conceived, while denying the existence of this being. But these two positions are logically incompatible, for truly to understand that God is the greatest conceivable being is also to understand that God must exist. The theist, therefore, need not refute the atheist, because the atheist refutes himself as soon as he denies the existence of God.

How can the atheist commit such an obvious blunder? There is only one plausible answer, according to Anselm: The atheist is both "dull and a fool."

> So, then, no one who understands what God is can conceive that God does not exist; although he says these words in his heart, either without any, or with some foreign, signification. For, God is that than which a greater cannot be conceived. And he who thoroughly understands this, assuredly understands that this being so truly exists, that not even in concept can it be non-existent. Therefore, he who understands that God so exists, cannot conceive that he does not exist.[2]

The antiatheistic focus of the Ontological Argument makes it especially pertinent to our discussion, for it contends that atheism is self-contradictory, incoherent, and therefore without any credibility whatever. If Anselm is right, then atheism is literally *unthinkable*, and anyone who claims to be an atheist should not be taken seriously. Only a fool, after all, would attempt to defend a logical absurdity, and there is no point in arguing with a fool.

If this is your first encounter with the Ontological Argument, you will likely agree with Schopenhauer that it is "nothing but a cunning and subtle game with concepts, without any power of conviction."[3] Be this as it may, if many people find it difficult to identify precisely what is wrong with this peculiar argument, this is mainly because they find it exceedingly difficult to understand. And this is largely because the Ontological Argument is based on antiquated notions like "degrees of perfection" and "the most real being" that are foreign to our way of thinking.

Before Europeans rediscovered the works of Aristotle in the late twelfth century, many Christian theologians had embraced the conceptual realism of Plato and later Neoplatonists (such as Plotinus). Realism, as it applies to the controversy over the nature of concepts (or universals), maintains that a being is more or less real—and hence more or less perfect—according to the extent of its universality. The highest degree of reality, according to conceptual realism, exists as pure form without matter. Thus, just as Plato had maintained that our ability to conceive of a perfect triangle means that the idea of "triangle" must exist somewhere in a transcendent world of pure forms, so Anslem maintained that our (supposed) ability to conceive of a perfect being means that God must really exist. (Or, to put it in more modern terms, the more abstract something is, the more real it is.) To quote from the brilliant account of Wilhelm Windelbandt:

> [T]hrough the whole development which this line of thought had already taken in antiquity, we find that the worth-predicate of *per-fection* was inseparably fused with the conception of being. The degrees of being are those of perfection; the more anything *is*, the

more perfect it is, and *vice versa*, the more perfect anything is, the more it *is*. The conception of the highest being is, therefore, also that of an absolute perfection; that is, of a perfection such that it cannot be thought higher and greater. . . . In accordance with these presuppositions, Anselm is perfectly correct in his conclusion that, from the mere conception of God as most perfect and most real being, it must be possible to infer his existence.[4]

Windelbandt notes that the Ontological Argument, despite its flaws, "is yet valuable as the characteristic feature of medieval Realism, of which it forms the most consistent expression." This raises the interesting question of how some contemporary philosophers can continue to defend the Ontological Argument while rejecting the conceptual realism on which it depends. At the very least, this historical perspective helps us to understand how this argument, which strikes many people today as sophistical, might have appeared more credible in centuries past.

AQUINAS

The Ontological Argument is commonly said to be an *a priori* proof, because it supposedly appeals to reason independently of experience. Unlike the First Cause Argument, the Design Argument, and other *a posteriori* proofs that begin with empirical premises (observations about causation, order, etc.), we are told that the Ontological Argument begins with nothing more than the concept of God; and then, through an *analysis* of this concept, it progresses to the conclusion that God must necessarily exist.

Although this traditional classification may apply to some versions of the Ontological Argument, it does not apply to Anselm's original version. As we have seen, Anselm begins not with the mere concept of God but with the concept of God as it exists *as an object of understanding in the human mind.* Anselm asserts that the concept of God exists even in the mind of the atheist who denies the existence of God, and it is this assertion that enables him to conclude that the existence of God cannot be denied without self-contradiction. This is clearly an empirical assertion, since it depends on the truth of a *psychological* observation about human consciousness.

Do we possess the idea of God as a perfect being? Do we understand what it means to identify God's essence with his existence? Whatever the other problems with Anselm's argument may be (and they are legion), his argument cannot even get off the ground unless we answer "yes" to these *factual* questions. Hence, contrary to the standard interpretation, Anselm's argument is based on an empirical premise, on an alleged fact about our idea of God.

This point was recognized by Thomas Aquinas, who penned a brief but incisive critique of the Ontological Argument in the thirteenth century. Aquinas considers this argument under the question of whether the existence of God is self-evident. A proposition is self-evident when a predicate is included within the meaning of its subject. Consider the proposition "Man is an animal." This is self-evidently true (provided we understand the meaning of both terms), because the predicate "animal" is included within our definition of "man."

Is "God exists" a self-evident proposition? Aquinas maintains that this question may be interpreted in two ways. A proposition may be absolutely or contextually self-evident. A proposition, though self-evident in itself, will not be contextually self-evident to those who do not understand the meaning of the relevant concepts. And this is what we find with the proposition "God exists." God's essence is identical to his existence, so if we could understand *what* God is, we would also know *that* God exists without further deliberation. But the nature of God cannot be grasped by the human intellect, so the existence of God is *not* contextually self-evident to human beings.

The validity of the Ontological Argument does not hinge on the theoretical issue of whether a full understanding of God's nature would carry within itself a knowledge of his existence, for this follows automatically from the statement that God's essence is existence. The key question is factual, not theoretical. Can our limited intellect truly grasp what it means to say that God's essence is existence? No, says Aquinas, so we cannot base a demonstration for the existence of God on nothing more than an analysis of God's nature.[5]

We thus see that Aquinas criticizes Anselm by attacking the empirical premise from which his argument proceeds. Given our inability to understand the nature of God, atheism cannot be summarily dismissed as an incoherent position. That there exists a being than which nothing greater can be conceived is precisely "what is not admitted by those who hold that God does not exist." If the atheist fails to understand the true nature of God, this stems from a defect of the human intellect and so is true of everyone, theist and atheist alike. And if the existence of God seems self-evident to many people, this is because they have believed in God for many years: "as a result, what the mind is steeped in from childhood it clings to very firmly, as something known naturally and self-evidently."[6]

DESCARTES AND GASSENDI

René Descartes presented his own version of the Ontological Argument in his *Meditations on the First Philosophy*, and it was from this highly influential source that the argument found its way into modern philosophy. Descartes claimed that his argument was altogether new, rather than a revision of Anselm's argument. Indeed, Descartes rejected Anselm's argument as invalid, having detected "a manifest error in the form of the argument." Anselm (according to Descartes) maintains that "when the meaning of the word God is understood, it is understood that God exists in fact as well as in the understanding." But this does not follow: "[B]ecause a word implies something, that is no reason for this being true." Even if it is true that to exist in fact is more perfect than to exist as an idea, we cannot conclude from this that God must necessarily exist. We cannot spin real existence from the thread of word usage.

In contrast to Anselm's formulation, Descartes puts his own version of the Ontological Argument as follows:

> That which we clearly and distinctly understand to belong to the true and immutable nature of anything, its essence, or form, can be truly affirmed of that thing; but, after we have with sufficient accuracy investigated the nature of God, we clearly and distinctly understand that to exist belongs to His true and immutable nature; therefore we can with truth affirm of God that He exists.[7]

Descartes regards this argument as superior to that of Anselm, because it is grounded in our clear and distinct idea of a perfect being who *must* possess existence as one of his attributes. And since, according to Descartes, a clear and distinct idea is necessarily true, it logically follows from the fact that we possess an innate idea of a perfect being that God exists.

This summary contains gaps that can be filled in only with an account of Descartes's theory of knowledge, e.g., his theory of essences and innate ideas, and his contention that "clear and distinct ideas" are the ultimate criterion of certainty. But it is not my intention to present a crash course in Cartesian theory of knowledge, a complex and often implausible theory that would strike most readers as more problematic than the Ontological Argument itself. Suffice it to say that Descartes, whatever his disagreements with Anselm may have been, worked from a similar set of assumptions—most notably, that there are various degrees of reality, that God's essence cannot be distinguished from his existence, and that perfection and existence are metaphysical properties of being. When these assumptions were effectively criticized or overthrown, the Ontological Argument, in whatever form it was expressed, appeared to most philosophers to lose whatever credibility it may have previously possessed.

Rather than undertake a technical analysis of Descartes's version of the Ontological Argument (which, in my judgment, is generally inferior to that of Anselm), I shall focus instead on some criticisms that were voiced by contemporaries of Descartes. Exploring these criticisms will highlight some important philosophical developments, such as the emergence of modern empiricism, the rejection of metaphysical "essences," and a growing skepticism about the meaning and coherence of the divine attributes.

The first objection to the Ontological Argument was expressed by a priest who believed that the refutation of Thomas Aquinas (discussed above) applied as much to Descartes's version of the argument as it did to Anselm's. This critic concluded:

> Though it be conceded that an entity of the highest perfection implies its existence by its very name, yet it does not follow that the very existence is anything actual in the real world, but merely that the concept of existence is inseparably united with the concept of highest being. Hence you cannot infer that the existence of God is anything actual, unless you assume that that highest being actually exists; for then it will actually contain all its perfections, together with the perfection of real existence.[8]

We see here a common complaint, namely, that the Ontological Argument is guilty of begging the question, of assuming as true the very proposition ("God exists") that it purports to demonstrate. According to this criticism, if existence is a perfection, then God will be truly perfect only if he actually exists. In other words, we must first know that God exists *before* we can conclude that God must *necessarily* exist. At best, therefore, the Ontological Argument can arrive at nothing more than a hypothetical conclusion: *If* God exists, *then* he is a necessary being (because existence will be inseparable from his essence). Or: *If* God exists, *then* we cannot logically conceive of him as nonexistent. All such inferences, however, *presuppose* the existence of God.

If God does not exist, if there is no entity that corresponds to our idea of a perfect being, then "God" has no real nature to which we can assign real attributes, necessary or otherwise. If "God" exists only as an idea in the mind, if he is merely a figment of our imagination, then his essence is as imaginary as his existence—and what we are able to imagine imposes no necessity on the real world. In other words, we cannot get from the *here* of ideas, which may be imaginary, to the *there*

of real existence by merely stipulating that God's existence is inseparable from his essence. Something must exist before it can have an
essence, and we cannot conjure up this essence through an act of the
imagination.

A similar criticism was developed at considerable length by
Pierre Gassendi, a French philosopher who was as famous in his day
as Descartes.[9] Rather than repeat the standard refutation of the
Ontological Argument, Gassendi undertakes an investigation of its
epistemological presuppositions. He detects in the Ontological Argument remnants of Platonic realism, according to which essences
exist in their own right, apart from concrete individuals. Gassendi's
own epistemological theory is known as *conceptualism*, because it
maintains that "essences" exist only in the form of *concepts* that have
been abstracted from objects with similar characteristics, objects
that become known to us through sense experience.

Gassendi rejects the Cartesian argument that "God" is an innate
idea, maintaining instead that our idea of God (such as it is) is an
abstraction that can ultimately be traced to our sensory perceptions.
Every attribute that we ascribe to God—"perfection," "infinite," and the
like—can be accounted for by this empirical method, so we have no
legitimate reason to call upon the alternative hypothesis of innate ideas.

This contention alone was enough to demolish the Ontological
Argument, which is why Descartes protested so vigorously when
Gassendi (and others) challenged his theory of innate ideas.
According to Descartes, our senses are a primary source of deception
and error—so to say that our knowledge of God's essence (his infinite
perfection) has no better foundation than fallible experience is to
demolish the absolute certainty and necessity on which the Ontological Argument depends.

Some of Gassendi's points hark back to the earlier criticism of
Aquinas. As a good Aristotelian empiricist, Aquinas insists that all of
our concepts—and hence all of our knowledge—rest upon a fundamental distinction between essence and existence, between *what*
something is and the fact *that* something exists. Therefore, to say
that God's essence cannot be differentiated from his existence is to

say that God's essence is *unknowable* to man. This is why the Ontological Argument can never get off the ground. According to Aquinas,
we have no true understanding of what it *means* to identify God's
essence with his existence, so this vague idea cannot possibly serve
as the premise of a valid argument.

We cannot have a clear and distinct idea of God's essence if this
idea is abstracted from sense experience because, in forming concepts in this fashion, we must invariably distinguish between the
essence of something and the fact that it exists—which we supposedly cannot do in the case of God. This explains why Descartes first
had to establish that "God" is an innate idea *before* he could proceed
with his Ontological Argument. The realm of innate ideas is the
realm of necessary and eternal truths—absolutely certain knowledge
that is not vulnerable to the inherent fallibility of the senses—so
Descartes repeatedly draws a parallel between the necessary truths
of geometry and the necessary existence of God. Gassendi knew what
he was about when he attacked the Ontological Argument by under-
cutting the Cartesian theory of innate ideas on which it depends.

The Ontological Argument, as we have seen, is incompatible with
empiricism. It cannot be reconciled with the claim that our ideas are
ultimately derived from experience, for this supposition will lead
directly to the conclusion that our idea of God, in which essence and
existence are merged, is anything but "clear and distinct." On the
contrary, as Gassendi put it: "God is most certainly beyond the widest
grasp, and when our mind addresses itself to the contemplation of
God, it not only gets befogged but comes to a standstill."[10]

No version of the Ontological Argument can hope to succeed if it
must begin with a "befogged" idea of God. We thus see that, here as
elsewhere, how we evaluate the credibility of a complex argument for
the existence of God will largely depend on the theory of knowledge
from which we work.

A conceptualist epistemology is the background for Gassendi's
critique of the Ontological Argument. Descartes claims that we
cannot separate God's essence from his existence, any more than we
can separate our idea of "triangle" from the fact that the sum of its

angles is equal to two right angles. But this is a misleading comparison for two reasons.

First, the essence of a triangle (its definition) is simply "a sort of mental rule" by which we decide whether we should call something a "triangle." But this definition does not mean that "such a triangle is something real and a true nature over and above the understanding."[11] The essence of "triangle" is simply a concept that has been abstracted from our experience of shapes, and we assign the properties of the ideal triangle to material triangles when the need arises.

Second, the relationship between our idea of "triangle" and the sum of its angles is a comparison of "essence with essence," or "property with property." The Ontological Argument, on the other hand, compares "existence with property."[12] It would be correct to say that God's omnipotence is to the essence of God as two right angles are to the essence of a triangle, but in neither case does this relationship prove that the "essence" must really exist. We can name as many properties as we please, and we can designate this or that property as essential to the nature of an entity—but if we restrict ourselves to an idea as it exists in the mind, we can never legitimately infer that the corresponding entity exists in reality as well.

The main problem with Descartes's argument is that he treats existence as if were a divine attribute (or "perfection"). But, according to Gassendi, "existence is a perfection neither in God nor in anything else; it is rather that in the absence of which there is no perfection."[13] That which does not exist has neither perfection nor imperfection; the nonexistent is nothing, and nothing has no attributes whatever. Existence is not an attribute of something, but is a necessary presupposition of all attributes. This is why we do not speak of "existence" as if it were an attribute of the perfect triangle. We can speak of the angles of the perfect triangle as equal to 180 degrees without implying that the perfect triangle is anything more than an idea. And we do not regard our idea of a triangle as any less "perfect" because it does not correspond to any material triangle. Gassendi continues:

> Wherefore, as in enumerating the perfections of a triangle you do not mention existence, nor hence conclude that the triangle exists, so, in enumerating the perfections of God, you ought not to have put existence among them, in order to draw the conclusion that God exists, unless you wanted to beg the question.[14]

It is responding to Descartes's contention that we can distinguish essence from existence in everything except God that Gassendi makes one of his most telling criticisms. We can *never* separate essence from existence except in thought, because essences do not exist outside the mind at all; they are concepts created by the intellect, not metaphysical properties. No essence can be said to exist unless its corresponding entity also exists; if the entity does not exist, then neither does its essence. Essence, in other words, presupposes existence, and this is true regardless of whether we are talking about horses, triangles, or God.

The distinction between essence and existence is epistemological, not metaphysical. The essence of an entity is not a distinct property that can literally be separated from its other properties; rather, its essence is a *concept* that has been abstracted from entities with similar properties, and is then reapplied to a specific individual for the purpose of demonstration. Consider the syllogism "All men are rational; Plato is a man; therefore, Plato is rational." The major premise states the essence, or defining characteristic, of man (rationality), but this essence does not exist in itself, apart from its manifestation in particular human beings. Rather, having *observed* many people with this common characteristic, and having concluded that rationality is a distinctive attribute of human beings, we form the universal concept "rationality" and denominate it the "essence" of man. Then, in concluding that *Plato is rational*, we are, in effect, reassigning this universal characteristic to Plato through the process of logical demonstration.

This theory is fatal to Descartes's Ontological Argument, for it places all essences on the same level by insisting that what is true of one essence must also be true of others. When it is claimed that God's essence cannot be separated from his existence, Gassendi notes that this is true of everything, not only God. We cannot, for example, separate Plato's essence from his existence, because for a nonexistent Plato, a nonbeing without attributes, there is no group of characteristics from which we can select one as more essential than others.

Gassendi arrives at the same conclusion as other critics of the Ontological Argument, namely, that this argument begs the question, because we can establish that God's essence is existence only if we first establish that God really exists. If God exists, then, upon investigating his nature, we may discover that his existence is necessary. Short of this, however, to define "God" in such a way that he must necessarily exist is nothing more than an exercise in circular reasoning.

Consider once again the idea of a perfect triangle. We can say that *if* the perfect triangle exists, *then* it must have the essential properties *x, y, z,* and so on; but this is far different from positing the *existence* of a perfect triangle. Whether or not such a triangle exists has nothing to do with those essential characteristics in virtue of which we dub it "perfect." If no material triangle is perfect, then, strictly speaking, the essential characteristics of the perfect triangle do not exist at all (except as an idea in the mind). Likewise, a nonexistent God—however "perfect" we imagine him to be—possesses no attributes whatsoever, including the (supposed) attribute of existence. God has a real essence only if he exists, so we can conclude nothing by merely analyzing this essence until and unless we can learn of God's existence by means other than the Ontological Argument.

HOBBES

The objections we have considered so far may be divided into two broad categories: factual and theoretical. Factual objections focus on the empirical premise of the Ontological Argument, according to which (in Descartes's version) we have an innate idea of a perfect being that is sufficiently clear and distinct to serve as a premise of a demonstration. The theoretical objections may be further subdivided into two kinds: one kind focuses on the internal logic of the demonstration, whereas the other kind focuses the metaphysical presuppositions that give credibility to the demonstration.

We find all three objections in Thomas Hobbes's brief criticism of the Ontological Argument.

First, Hobbes attacks the empirical premise of the Ontological Argument by maintaining that we have "no idea" of God. Thus, since "any idea of God is ruled out," we cannot begin with our (supposed) idea of a perfect or infinite being in an effort to prove the existence of an incomprehensible God (which is precisely what *both* Anselm and Descartes attempted to do).[15]

Second, Hobbes criticizes the internal logic of the Ontological Argument in a manner similar to Gassendi. That which exists has no essence; the nonexistent is literally nothing and so has no essential attributes whatever. As Hobbes puts it:

> If the triangle exists nowhere at all, I do not understand how it can have any nature; for that which exists nowhere does not exist. Hence it has no existence or nature. The triangle in the mind comes from the triangle we have seen, or from one imaginatively constructed out of triangles we have beheld.[16]

Hobbes continues with a fundamental insight that would later be elaborated upon by Immanuel Kant. Existence is not an attribute like shape, size, and color; it is not something that we predicate of things, because we must first suppose that something exists (either as an idea or external entity) before it makes sense to ascribe any predicates to it at all.

> Whence it is evident that essence in so far as it is distinguished from existence is nothing else than a union of names by means of the verb *is*.[17] And thus essence without existence is a fiction of our mind.[18]

Finally, Descartes repeatedly expressed contempt for Scholasticism, because its metaphysical theories, which analyzed nature in qualitative rather than quantitative terms, had retarded the advancement of science (especially physics, which depends on the mathematical formulation of natural laws). But Descartes, according to Hobbes, failed to rid himself of those very assumptions which he professed to despise. The Ontological Argument assumes that there are degrees of reality, that some beings are "more real" or "more perfect" than others. Hobbes will have none of this:

> I pray M. Descartes to investigate the meaning of *more reality*. Does reality admit of more and less? Or, if he thinks that one thing can be more a thing than another, let him see how he is to explain it to our intelligence with the clearness called for in demonstration, and such as he himself has at other times employed.[19]

KANT

"Existence is not a predicate"—with these words Kant summarized his celebrated and definitive refutation of the Ontological Argument. Although Kant was more thorough than preceding critics, his basic point was by no means original. We find germs of it, for instance, in Aristotle's *Posterior Analytics*, where it is maintained that we cannot establish the existence of something through its definition. The existence of something must be otherwise proved, "unless indeed to be were its essence." But this latter is impossible: "[B]eing is not a genus, it is not the essence of anything."

According to Aristotle, the essence of a being is stated in its definition: To define something requires that we identify specific characteristics (differentia) that distinguish it from a broader class (genus) of existing beings. From this it follows that the essence of something cannot be existence per se, because "being" is not a genus. This is so because "genus" refers to a common characteristic (essence) that exists in some things but not in others, so to say that the essence of a being is existence would be to claim that a being is literally *everything*.[20]

In other words, something must first exist before it can possess any attributes, essential or otherwise. The nonexistent has no characteristics whatever. To say that a being exists does not describe the nature of that being, but merely posits something with a nature that can be described. Or, as Kant would later put it, existence is not a predicate.

Immanuel Kant opens his critique of the Ontological Argument with a discussion of what it means to speak of an "absolutely necessary being." Before we set out to prove the existence of such a being, we should reflect on what we are talking about.

Of course, we can give a verbal definition of an absolutely necessary being (e.g., as something the nonexistence of which is impossible), but this does not tell us whether the idea itself is meaningful. Unfortunately, philosophers often substitute examples for explanations. Geometry is a favorite here. Since propositions like "A triangle has three angles" are necessarily true, they have been used to illustrate what is meant by an absolutely necessary being. But, as Kant points out, such examples pertain to *judgments*, not to *things*. This distinction is crucial, because an unconditionally necessary judgment does not require a similar necessity in that to which the judgment refers. For example, it is necessarily true that a triangle has three angles, because the predicate (three angles) is contained in the meaning of the subject (a triangle). We cannot conceive of a triangle without three angles, and if we conceive of a triangle, we must also conceive of three angles.

To say, however, that a triangle necessarily contains three angles is *not* to say that its three angles must necessarily *exist*. Rather, it is to say that three angles must necessarily exist *only if we posit the existence of a triangle*. This is the condition that must be fulfilled before we can affirm the necessary existence of three angles. In other words, *if* a triangle exists, *then* it logically follows that three angles must also exist—but we are not logically compelled to affirm the existence of either.

In "A triangle has three angles" (which Kant calls an identical judgment), we cannot conceive of the subject while annihilating the predicate, because the latter necessarily belongs to the former. But I can suppress the thought of both subject and predicate without contradiction. To suppose that a triangle exists without three angles is a contradiction, and is therefore inconceivable; but to suppose that neither triangle nor its three angles exist involves no contradiction whatever, and is quite conceivable.

The same reasoning applies to an absolutely necessary being. We can annihilate the existence of this being in thought without contradiction, for we annihilate the thing itself along with its predicates, and thereby leave nothing to contradict. As Kant puts it:

> If, in an identical proposition, I reject the predicate while retaining the subject, contradiction results; and I therefore say that the former belongs necessarily to the latter. But if we reject subject and predicate, there is no contradiction; for nothing is then left that can be contradicted. To posit a triangle, and yet to reject its three angles, is self-contradictory; but there is no contradiction in rejecting the triangle together with its three angles. The same holds true of the concept of an absolutely necessary being. If its existence is rejected, we reject the thing itself with all its predicates; and no question of contradiction can then arise. There is nothing outside it that would then be contradicted, since the necessity of the thing is not supposed to be derived from anything external; nor is there anything internal that would be contradicted, since in rejecting the thing itself we have at the same time rejected all its internal properties. "God is omnipotent" is a necessary judgment. The omnipotence cannot be rejected if we posit a Deity, that is, an infinite being; for the two concepts are identical. But if we say, "There is no God," neither the omnipotence nor any other of its predicates is given; they are one and all rejected together with the subject, and there is therefore not the least contradiction in such a judgment.[21]

If we define God as a being that necessarily exists, then it would indeed be contradictory to accept this concept of God while rejecting its existence. But there is no contradiction if we simply reject this concept of God altogether and suppose that God does not exist. By rejecting the subject (God), we also reject the predicate (necessary existence).

To say that a *judgment* is logically necessary is to say that, given the subject, we must accept its predicate on pain of self-contradiction. But if we deny the existence of the subject, we also remove its predicate from our thought, and this annihilation of both subject and predicate does *not* involve a contradiction. The only way to evade this objection is to assert that some subjects cannot be thought of as nonexistent, but this merely begs the question (i.e., it presupposes the existence of an absolutely necessary being, which is precisely what the Ontological Argument is supposed to establish).

The Ontological Argument maintains that the existence of an absolutely necessary being cannot be denied without self-contradiction. This concept of God, Kant says, is logically possible (i.e., it does not contain a contradiction), but we can never establish that something exits from a mere analysis of the corresponding concept. *Real* possibility can never be inferred from *logical* possibility. Indeed, a concept may be logically possible and yet cognitively empty, if it is impossible to conceive what it would be like to experience such a being.

This latter point is important because, according to the Ontological Argument, if we can possibly conceive of an absolutely necessary being (God), then God must necessarily exist. Why? Because it would supposedly be contradictory to deny the existence of a being whose existence is absolutely necessary. If it is possible for the most real being to exist, then it must necessarily exist, because existence is part of it means to be "most real."

This argument is fallacious, according to Kant, because it treats "existence" as a real predicate, incorporates this predicate into the definition of "God," and then "proves" the existence of God by unpacking this definition. But if the existence of God follows necessarily from our definition of "God," then to declare that "God exists" is to utter a tautology, since this merely restates what is already included within our definition of "God."

We should also understand that "existence" (or "being") is not a real predicate; "existence" is not an attribute or quality that adds something new to our concept of something else. Rather, "existence" functions as the copula ("is," "are," etc.) of a judgment, indicating the relationship of the predicate to the subject. For example, in the proposition "God is omnipotent," the copula "is" obviously does not add another predicate to our concept of God, but rather affirms a relationship between the two concepts of "God" and "omnipotence." Likewise, if we take the concept of God, complete with all its predicates, and assert that "God exists" (or "There is a God") the "is" contained in this judgment does not add another predicate to our concept of God, but rather posits the existence of God along with all his predicates. Therefore, to say that "God exists" is to posit a *relationship* between a concept and its referent; it is to affirm the existence of an external object that corresponds to my concept of God. Kant continues:

> By whatever and by however many predicates we may think a thing . . . we do not make the least addition to the thing when we further declare that this thing *is*. Otherwise, it would not be exactly the same thing that exists, but something more than we had thought in the concept; and we could not, therefore, say that the exact object of my concept exists. If we think in a thing every feature of reality except one, the missing reality is not added by my saying that this defective thing exists. On the contrary, it exists with the same defect with which I have thought it, since otherwise what exists would be something different from what I thought. When, therefore, I think a being as the supreme reality, without any defect, the question still remains whether it exists or not.[22]

To illustrate what Kant is saying here, consider these two scenarios: (1) I think of possessing $100 that I don't have; (2) someone actually gives me $100. How do these cases differ? Do the real dollars in (2) constitute something *more* than the imaginary dollars in (1)? No, says Kant: We have not added anything to our concept of $100 by positing their real existence. The concepts in both cases are identical; what is different about them is that the dollars in (2) actually exist, where in (1) they do not. In other words, in stipulating that I actually possess $100, I have not somehow added a new predicate (attribute, characteristic, etc.) to the concept of $100. Existence is not a predicate.

NOTES

1. "St, Anselm on the Existence of God," in *Medieval Philosophy: Selections from Augustine to Buridan* (New York: Modern Library, 1964), p. 109.

2. Ibid., p. 112.

3. Arthur Schopenhauer, *The World As Will and Representation*, trans. E. F. J. Payne (New York: Dover Publications, 1958), vol. 1, p. 511.

4. Wilhelm Windelbandt, *A History of Philosophy*, trans. James H. Tufts (New York: Harper Torchbooks, 1958), vol. 1, p. 292.

5. This objection is similar to that raised by the monk Gaunilon, a contemporary of Anselm: "I do not know that reality which God is, nor can I form a conjecture of that reality from some other like reality . . . [f]or that reality is such that there can be nothing else like it." See "Gaunilon in Behalf of the Fool," in *Medieval Philosophy*, p. 115.

6. Thomas Aquinas, *Summa Theologica*, trans. Fathers of the English Dominican Province, Great Books of the Western World, vol. 19 (Chicago: Encyclopedia Britannica, 1952), p. 11.

7. *Objections Urged by Certain Men of Learning Against the Preceding Meditations; With the Author's Replies*, Great Books of the Western World, vol. 31 (Chicago: Encyclopedia Britannica, 1952), p. 113.

8. Ibid., p. 107.

9. Gassendi, though little more than a name to many students of philosophy, was an extremely important figure, for it was he who was primarily responsible for reintroducing the "atomism" (i.e., materialism) of Democritus and Epicurus into modern philosophy, offering it as the most satisfactory model for scientific explanations. Gassendi was a priest who, despite his Epicureanism and materialism—two positions that had long been condemned as atheistic—managed to function quite well within the Catholic Church.

10. *Objections*, p. 183.

11. Ibid., p. 195.

12. Ibid., p. 196.

13. Ibid.

14. Ibid.

15. Ibid., p. 139.

16. Ibid., p. 142.

17. As we shall see, this is exactly what Kant was getting at when he said that "existence" is not a predicate but functions instead as the *copula* of a judgment. Note also that Hobbes refers to *names* rather than *concepts.* This reflects a difference between the *nominalism* of Hobbes and the *conceptualism* of Gassendi (and Locke). Universals, according to nominalism, are neither the metaphysical essences of realism nor the abstractions of conceptualism; rather they are general terms, or names, that signify more than one object. Despite some technical disagreements between conceptualists and nominalists, both groups have typically embraced empiricism in one form or another. Historically, therefore, both have tended to analyze their common opponents from the same critical perspective, as we see in their similar objections to Descartes.

18. *Objections*, p. 142.

19. Ibid., p. 139.

20. This is basically how Spinoza used the Ontological Argument to prove the existence of God, while maintaining that "God" is synonymous with "nature" (i.e., the totality of existence). It is not clear—to me at least—why Spinoza took this roundabout path rather than leave "God" out of the equation altogether, but it is clear why he was widely condemned as an atheist in theistic clothing.

21. Immanuel Kant, *Critique of Pure Reason*, trans. Norman Kemp Smith (New York: St. Martin's Press, 1929), p. 502.

22. Ibid., pp. 505–506.

The Roots of Modern Atheism (I)

THE HISTORY OF ATHEISM

It is sometimes assumed that "atheism," like other "ism" labels (materialism, positivism, etc.) refers to a nuclear family of ideas that can be shrink-wrapped into a single historical unit for the sake of convenience. But this is a troublesome assumption, one that can distort our view of intellectual history. Labels usually acquire their meaning over time, through the spontaneous dynamics of conventional usage, so the reason why some ideas have been tagged with the same label may have little or nothing to do with their essential similarities. (This is especially true with negatively charged words, such as "atheism" and "anarchism," that have functioned as terms of opprobrium in the smear campaigns of ideological warfare.)

Atheism, or the absence of theistic belief, is a general perspective that has arisen within many different (and often incompatible) belief systems. Virtually every species of Western philosophy (including Christianity) has spawned atheistic variations, so the history of atheism is extremely diffuse. Thus rather than refer to the history of atheism, as if we were dealing with a monolithic movement, it might be more accurate to refer to the *histories* of atheism.

We have previously seen how the words *atheism* and *atheist* have been abused for centuries, having been hurled as bugaboo epithets by believers against other believers with unorthodox views. But a serious point about the inner logic of ideas sometimes lurked behind this tiresome name-calling. Some philosophical, scientific, and historical ideas, when pushed to their logical extremes, were clearly incompatible with Christian doctrines (especially the appeal to infallible revelation), so orthodox Christians branded these ideas as "atheistic" in order to call attention to their subversive tendencies. The label of "atheism" was a red flag, in effect, alerting other Christians to the dangers that lay ahead.

Many of these warnings proved to be justified. Some ideas in philosophy and science, after being defended by progressive and well-intentioned Christians, would later explode like secular time bombs, wreaking havoc in Christendom from within. This occurred many times during the development of modern secularism, and we could scarcely ask for better examples of the inner logic of ideas. But these examples pose a curious problem for the historian of atheism(s). Modern atheism is indebted for much of its development not to atheists per se (who were few and far between during the sixteenth and seventeenth centuries), but to implicitly atheistic ideas that were developed by theistic and Christian thinkers, many of whom would have been dismayed by the results they helped to bring about.[1]

The kind of atheism we shall consider here belongs to a broader tradition known as *freethinking* or *freethought*. This tradition includes not only atheists, but agnostics, deists, pagans, and even some liberal Christians as well. In the early 1600s (especially in France), "freethinker" was used interchangeably with "libertine": Both labels referred to unconventional thinkers (many of whom had been influenced by Greek skepticism and hedonism) who spurned—at least in private—the conventional beliefs and mores of polite society.

Although "freethinking" did not achieve social respectability until the eighteenth century, it was never burdened with a stigma comparable to that of "atheism." Many eighteenth-century free-thinkers repudiated atheism in favor of deism, but all freethinkers were united in their opposition to Christian dogma. The essential meaning of "freethinking" was clearly expressed in 1713, when Anthony Collins (a close friend of John Locke) published his *Discourse of Free-Thinking*.

> By free-thinking I mean the use of the understanding in endeav-oring to find out the meaning of any proposition whatsoever, in con-sidering the nature of the evidence for or against it, and in judging of it according to the seeming force or weakness of the evidence.[2]

GREEK ATHEISM

Around 200 C.E. a Greek physician and skeptic named Sextus Empir-icus mentioned some atheists who had lived centuries earlier, during the classical age of Greek philosophy:

> That [God] does not exist is the contention of those who are nick-named "atheists," such as Euhemerus and Diagoras of Melos, and Prodicus of Ceos, and Theodorus, and multitudinous others. Of these Euhemerus said that those who were believed to be gods were actually certain men of power who for this reason had been deified by the others, and then were thought to be gods. Prodicus said that whatever benefits life was understood to be God—things such as sun, moon, rivers, lakes, meadows, crops and everything of that kind. . . . And Critias . . . seems to be from the ranks of the atheists when he says that the lawgivers of ancient times invented God as a kind of overseer of the right and wrong actions of men. Their pur-pose was to prevent anyone from wronging his neighbors secretly, as he would incur the risk of vengeance at the hands of the gods.

... Theodorus, "the Atheist," is also in agreement with these men, and according to some, Protagoras of Abdera. The former, in his treatise On Gods, demolished with various arguments the theological beliefs of the Greeks, while Protagoras in one passage wrote expressly: "In regard to the gods I can say neither whether they exist nor of what sort they are, for many are the things that prevent me." The Athenians condemned him to death for this, but he escaped, and then perished, lost at sea. . . . And Epicurus, according to some, leaves God undisputed when addressing himself to the public, but not where the real nature of things is the issue.[3]

Unfortunately, none of the writings of these atheists (except Epicurus[4]) has survived the ravages of time, so we must rely upon the accounts of later writers, such as Cicero and Sextus, for what little information we have. But the influence of these atheists on later freethinkers is unmistakable. We see it, for example, in the various speculations about the "natural history of religion" that became increasingly popular after the Renaissance. The Greek atheists offered a variety of sociological and psychological explanations for the origin of religious belief. The gods were great personages who were deified after death; the gods began as anthropomorphic explanations of natural phenomena; the gods were invented by rulers as a means of instilling civic virtue and obedience in the masses; the gods were a self-serving fiction of priests, who wished to maintain their positions of power and prestige; the gods arose from fear of natural disasters and other unpredictable evils; the gods began as apparitions that appeared in dreams.

Other Greek philosophers—Skeptics, Epicureans, Stoics, and the like—developed arguments that would later be drawn upon by modern freethinkers. Rather than delve into the sources and targets of these arguments (many were directed by one school of thought against another), I shall instead classify them by subject matter and present them in an integrated fashion. The result is a remarkable arsenal of arguments that became the basis for modern atheism. (Although many of these arguments were directed against "the gods," they could readily be applied to "God" as well, so I have taken the liberty of using the latter word.)

A philosopher should put public opinion and social pressure aside and consider the question of God's existence on its own merits:

> In this subject of the nature of the gods the first question is: do the gods exist or do they not? It is difficult, you will say, to deny that they exist. I would agree, if we were arguing the matter in a public assembly, but in a private discussion of this kind it is perfectly easy to do so.[5]

It is to arguments pro and con, not to the testimony of authorities, that we should appeal when discussing the existence of God.

> In a discussion of this kind our interest should be centered not on the weight of the authority but on the weight of the argument. Indeed the authority of those who set out to teach is often an impediment to those who wish to learn. They cease to use their own judgment and regard as gospel whatever is put forward by their chosen teacher.[6]

Some people feel that it is impious and sinful even to question the existence of God: "Far from it. More often it is this very superstition that is the mother of sinful and impious deeds."[7] Thus we return once again to the key question: "By what rational arguments do you persuade yourself that gods exist at all?"[8]

It is commonly said that God is a perfect and self-sufficient being who lacks nothing and experiences no desire. Are we therefore to imagine that God has spent an eternity doing nothing except contemplating his own happiness and thinking nothing except, "I'm all right," and, "How happy I am!"[9] Happiness results from purposeful activity, from a successful striving for a good that we don't presently possess. But such goal-directed actions are possible only for beings that do not already possess every possible good, which is not true of God. If God lacks nothing, if he already possesses every good imaginable, then he would have to reason to act at all. God would be completely passive, desiring nothing and doing nothing, because no additional satisfaction would be possible for him. And the term "happiness" makes no sense to us in this context; indeed, if anything, we are apt to regard an extremely passive person as deficient in the kind of happiness that comes from successful activity. Extreme indolence, such as we must attribute to God, is a recipe for boredom, not happiness.

Moreover, if God was supremely and eternally contented, then what motivated him to create the universe as we know it at a given point in time? "Why should God . . . wish to decorate the universe with lights and signs, like some Minister of Public Works?" Did he previously live in darkness and only later decide that stars would spruce things up a bit? "Or are we to suppose that he only later acquired a taste for variety, and so embellished heaven and earth just as they now appear?" If God did all this for his own pleasure, "then why did he so long forgo the pleasure?"[10]

This kind of argument is intended to demonstrate the incoherence of supposing, on the one hand, that God is perfectly happy and contented and, on the other hand, that he has taken particular actions. Action is purposeful behavior, a means to an end; so to act presupposes that one wishes to replace a less satisfactory state of affairs with one that is more satisfactory. But a perfectly happy being cannot experience dissatisfaction of any kind—there is no conceivable state of affairs that could improve his condition—so it makes no sense to suppose that such a being would ever "act" in any manner whatever. "A god has no business to transact: he is involved in no activity: he labors at no tasks. . . ."[11] Action means change, and for a being that is already perfectly happy, there can only be change for the worse, from a state of perfection to something less desirable. Thus, to suppose that God is perfectly happy and contented is to render incomprehensible the creation of the universe or any other action by God.

Other incomprehensibilities arise when we suppose that God is a living being. Any such being must be able to experience sensations, "for it is precisely the fact of possessing sensation that differentiates a living being from what is not a living being." But sensation is a kind of alteration: "[I]t is impossible for a thing which apprehends by means of a sense to escape alteration and remain, instead, in the condition it was in before the apprehension." This means that God undergoes change, including change for the worse, in which case he cannot be perfect and immutable. We can therefore say that the concept of a living God, since it contains internal contradictions, cannot possibly refer to something in the real world. God, in other words, does not exist, because contradictions cannot exist.[12]

The Greek skeptics offered a number of variations on this theme. Does God have a sense of taste? If so, he can taste the bitter as well as the sweet, in which case he will sometimes be displeased? Likewise, if he can hear, see, smell, and touch, he will find some things repellent and thereby experience vexation. And since this means that "God is subject to change for the worse," we may once again conclude that a perfect and immutable God does not exist.[13]

Furthermore, God is said to be omnibenevolent, or all good. If we are to make sense of this assertion, we must suppose that God possesses every virtue to the greatest extent possible. But virtues (such as self-control and temperance) are meaningless unless we suppose that God is subject to temptation and "unless there exist certain things which for God are hard to abstain from and hard to endure." Again, however, this would mean that God is not already perfect— that he confronts problems, is able to feel vexation, and may possibly fail in his endeavors. Likewise, if God possesses the virtue of courage, this means that "there must exist something which to God is fearful."[14]

And what of the claim that God is omniscient, that he knows literally everything? If this is true, then God must know the meaning of "pain" and other negative sensations. But we must actually experience this kind of sensation in order to understand its meaning—we could not, for example, explain the meaning of "pain" to a being who has never actually felt it—so "God cannot possess a notion of pain . . . without having experienced it."[15] If, however, God is capable of feeling pain, then he cannot be perfect, omnipotent, and so forth.

THE REFORMATION

Nineteenth-century histories of freethought were typically written from a Protestant outlook. These histories tended to view the rise of secularism, science, and freedom of conscience as logical extensions of the sixteenth-century Protestant Reformation. Freedom of conscience in particular was viewed as the great contribution of Protestantism. It was the spark that ignited intellectual progress and ultimately made it impossible to suppress new ideas.

Modern historians tend to be more circumspect in their evaluation of the Reformation. Although they acknowledge that the Reformation exerted a powerful influence on the rise of secularism, they also stipulate that this was in large measure an *unintended consequence*. The Reformation unleashed a number of intellectual and cultural forces that could not subsequently be contained, even by Protestants themselves; and it was owing to these unintended consequences that secularism emerged.

Many rationalistic historians have also stressed the progress of science as a decisive factor in the overthrow of the Christian worldview. In response, it has been repeatedly pointed out that many great scientists—from Copernicus to Kepler to Newton—were sincere Christians who did not view their teachings as in any way incompatible with their religious faith. Of course, these accounts are not necessarily incompatible, since their analyses operate at the different levels of ideas and individuals. This is yet another area where we must pay special attention to the inner logic of ideas. An individual scientist may propose a theory that, in his opinion, poses no threat to Christianity, but this theory may later be seen in a different light, as its logical implications are spun out by other thinkers with different religious convictions.

In the title of A. D. White's classic work, *A History of the Warfare of Science with Theology in Christendom* (1896), we see expressed what many freethinkers have regarded as the essential historical conflict. For centuries, the liberating forces of science were engaged in perpetual warfare with the regressive forces of theology, until light emerged victorious over darkness in this Manichean struggle.

Such accounts are examples of history through metaphor—for terms like *science* and *theology* are nothing other than metaphors when considered apart from particular scientists and theologians, or particular scientific and theological theories. History, however, is concerned with *individuals* (specific persons, ideas, etc.), not metaphors. Even in apparently clear-cut cases, such as the nineteenth-century controversy over evolution, we do not see science per se aligned against theology (or religion) per se. Some liberal theologians took Darwin's side in this dispute, while some freethinkers (such as the agnostic Herbert Spencer) criticized natural selection as an inadequate explanation of biological change.

The chief difference between science and theology is not one of doctrine, but of *attitude* and *method*. This method is illustrated in the aforementioned work by A. D. White. Kepler, as White points out, proposed two theories about comets. His first theory, that comets move according to a discernible law, is right; whereas his second theory, that comets move in nearly straight lines, is wrong. Thus when the latter was discovered to be incorrect, other scientists simply dropped it and focused their sole attention on the former—thereby enabling science to advance. White continues:

> Very different was this from the theological method. As a rule, when there arises a thinker as great in theology as Kepler in science, the whole mass of his conclusions ripens into a dogma. His disciples labor not to test it, but to establish it; and while, in the Catholic Church, it becomes a dogma to be believed or disbelieved under the penalty of damnation, it becomes in the Protestant Church the basis for one or more sect.[16]

Luther, Calvin, and other Reformers undermined the monopolistic authority of the Catholic Church by elevating the conscience of the individual to the ultimate arbiter of religious truth. Like all forms of individualism, however, this appeal to subjectivity led inevitably to diversity: Protestant sects sprang up by the hundreds, each with its own interpretation of divine truth. Thus was the genie of religious pluralism liberated from the bottle of institutional authority. And from this diversity came argument and counterargument, as various sects attempted to establish their own monopoly on truth by attacking the doctrines of their Protestant and Catholic competitors. And thus did religious skepticism emerge from this brew as an unintended by-product, as freethinkers adapted the critiques of this side or that to serve their own ends.

Luther rejected the view, which had been accepted for centuries, that the pronouncements of the church, whether contained in tradition or expressed by popes and councils, should be accepted as the criteria of religious truth. The proper rule of faith, according to Luther, is the Bible: "[T]hat which is asserted without the authority of Scripture or of proven revelation may be held as an opinion, but there is no obligation to believe it." Luther declared that his conscience had been "taken captive by God's word," thereby compelling him to believe his own interpretation of the Bible, while rejecting the contrary teachings of church authorities (who often contradicted each other). Church authorities are but fallible human beings with no privileged access to the truth, so all Christians have "the power of discerning what is right or wrong in the matters of faith."[17]

Luther's Catholic critics were quick to accuse him of advocating a type of religious anarchy, a situation in which conflicting claims to religious truth cannot be resolved by submitting them to objective standards. Some Catholics (such as Erasmus), pointed to the ambiguity of many biblical passages, which will inevitably be interpreted in different ways.

Luther's rule of faith—the subjective certainty of one's conscience—was widely condemned as the repudiation of objective certainty, thus giving rise to the common accusation that Protestants were nothing more than skeptics in disguise. If the conscience of one Christian compels him to accept a proposition as true, while the conscience of another compels her to reject the same proposition as false, then Luther's subjective criterion will be unable to resolve this disagreement. Only by accepting the church as the final authority in matters of faith can such epistemological conundrums be avoided.

Luther, meanwhile, vehemently attacked his critics, branding them as the true skeptics. The truths of Christianity are far too important to depend for their certainty on the testimony of human authorities. To suggest that we are unable to discern truth directly from Scripture, that reading the Bible must leave us in doubt as to its intended meaning, is nothing less than blasphemous skepticism. A Christian cannot be a skeptic; he "ought to be certain of what he affirms, or else he is not a Christian." Though some parts of Scripture are difficult to understand, and though it contains mysteries that surpass our comprehension, it nonetheless contains the essential truths of Christianity. These truths, expressed in clear and evident terms, cannot be misunderstood except by those who are willfully blind.

According to Luther, to distrust the Bible as a source of certain truth—to argue that it necessarily generates doubt about its intended meaning, which can be overcome only by relying upon the interpretation of human authorities—is to mock God and his divine revelation. The Bible communicates knowledge directly from God to man, knowledge of the utmost importance, which is unattainable by natural means. The Christian is compelled by his conscience to accept these revealed truths with complete assurance, free from all doubt. It is sheer blasphemy, therefore, to depict the Bible itself as a source of doubt and uncertainty. For this is to suggest that God has failed in his attempt to communicate with man, leaving us with a garbled text that only the Catholic Church can decipher. Luther insists that God rather than man is the source of our infallible knowledge of religious truth. The Bible, and the Bible alone, can give us certainty. God's word is not the source of doubt: "The Holy Ghost is not a Skeptic."

Luther's appeal to conscience as the ultimate judge of scriptural truth proved to be extremely effective against Catholicism, but it created serious problems among Protestants themselves. As dozens upon dozens of sects arose, many with bizarre and unorthodox beliefs, each claimed for its own doctrines the subjective certainty of conscience that had been defended by Luther. Luther found this pluralism and diversity abhorrent, as did the other great Reformer, John Calvin. But having unleashed the individual conscience as the final arbiter of religious truth, how could this anarchistic force be contained? The political aspect of this problem was easily solved: Both Luther and Calvin were determined foes of religious toleration, and both called for the extermination not only of Catholics, but also of heretical Protestants (such as Anabaptists and anti-Trinitarians) whose interpretation of Scripture did not comport with their own.

An idea, however, is far more difficult to kill than a person. The appeal to subjective certainty, if it justified the beliefs of Luther and Calvin, also appeared to justify with equal certainty the beliefs of their heretical cousins. Calvin, who had developed Augustine's notion of predestination into a systematic theology, also appealed to Augustine's theory of divine illumination. The elect—that fortunate minority with advance tickets to heaven, having been preselected by God as winners of the divine lottery—are blessed with the subjective certainty of divine illumination, "a conviction that requires no reasons." And it is this inner persuasion of the elect, which words cannot adequately describe, that gives them an infallible lock on religious truth.

FIDEISM

When, in 1562, the Renaissance printer Henri Estienne published the first Latin edition of *Outlines of Pyrrhonism*, he explained that this work by Sextus Empiricus (written c. 200 C.E.) had taught him that we cannot rely on reason, a fallible and unreliable instrument, in matters of religion, because this will only pave the way for atheism. Seven years later another publisher of Sextus, the French Catholic Gentian Hervet, also maintained that the skeptical arguments of Sextus could be used to defend Christianity.

In his summary of Greek skepticism, Sextus argues that reason cannot arrive at certain knowledge, because equally compelling arguments can be presented for or against the truth of any proposition. Thus Pyrrhonic skepticism refutes those philosophers who criticize Christianity in the name of reason. By demonstrating the impotence of reason, Pyrrhonism teaches us intellectual humility and prepares us to receive the doctrines of Christ through faith.

These interpretations of Sextus Empiricus set the stage for *fideism*, which was to become a popular method of argument among French Catholics for three-quarters of a century. Fideism is essentially an effort to vindicate faith at the expense of reason; by stripping reason of its cognitive efficacy, the fideists appealed to faith as the sole and ultimate source of certainty. If we look to reason instead, we will sink into a morass of uncertainty, where no belief can claim superiority over any other.

The modern freethinker may be surprised to learn that skepticism was welcomed into modern philosophy as an ally of Christian (and especially Catholic) beliefs. Skepticism and Christianity may strike the modern reader as strange bedfellows, to say the least, so it may help to explore some features of this alliance in more detail.

We must keep in mind that Pyrrhonic skepticism, unlike Academic skepticism, did not deny outright the possibility of certain knowledge.[18] The assertion that certainty is unattainable is, for the Pyrrhonist, a position which is itself uncertain. When examining a philosophic belief, the Pyrrhonists marshaled a battery of arguments for both sides, pro and con, in an effort to show that reason cannot justify one belief more than another. Given this dialectical standoff, the Pyrrhonists argued that we should disengage ourselves from useless philosophic controversies. Only in this way can we avoid mental anguish and achieve that state of mental tranquility known to the Greeks as *ataraxia.*

It is important to understand that Pyrrhonic skepticism was inherently conservative, because this explains much of its appeal to those Catholics who were attempting to defend the authority of their church against Protestant attacks. According to the Pyrrhonists, rather than engage in futile speculations about philosophic truth—which could be used to criticize the religious and political status quo—we should resolve instead to accept things as they appear to be, without attempting to judge them. This means that we should passively submit to the laws, customs, and traditional beliefs of our society, rather than challenging them with philosophic principles that cannot themselves be justified.

This conservative slant is what made Pyrrhonism so useful to Catholics during the Counter-Reformation. Pyrrhonic arguments, when directed against freethinkers and unbelievers, could be (and were) used by Catholics and Protestants alike, as a means of showing the superiority of faith over reason. But in the internecine battle between Catholics and Protestants, the conservative implications of Pyrrhonism proved to be of greater utility to the former. Protestants, after all, were the innovators, the radicals who had rejected the traditional authority of the church root and branch. And though Protestants did not seek to replace that authority with reason, they did appeal to personal judgment as the ultimate rule of faith.

The Catholic Pyrrhonists predicted that dire consequences would result from this religious individualism. The Protestants, in counseling people to rely upon their own judgment in religious matters rather than on the authority of the church, had embarked on a dangerous path. The feeble and unreliable judgments of individuals would result in diverse and conflicting religious beliefs, and terminate in atheism. As Montaigne, the major proponent of Catholic Pyrrhonism, put it:

> The mass of ordinary people lack the faculty of judging things as they are, letting themselves be carried away by chance appearances. Once you have put into their hands the foolhardiness of despising and criticizing opinions which they used to hold in the highest awe (such as those which concern their salvation), and once you have thrown into the balance of doubt and uncertainty any articles of their religion, they soon cast all the rest of their beliefs into similar uncertainty. They had no more authority for them, no more foundation, than for those you have just undermined; and so, as though it were the yoke of a tyrant, they shake off all those other concepts which had been impressed upon them by the authority of Law and

the awesomeness of ancient custom. . . . They then take it upon themselves to accept nothing on which they have not pronounced their own approval, subjecting it to their individual assent.[19]

Montaigne applied Pyrrhonic skepticism to the great theological question of his day: What is the proper rule of faith? By what criterion should we assess religious claims and accept one scriptural interpretation over others? In this area as in others, according to Montaigne, reason is unable to arrive at a definitive conclusion. Since reason cannot discern the rule of faith, to rely upon reason in this sphere will land us in a doubt that is fatal to Christian belief. The only alternative is to accept tradition, i.e., to submit to the authority of the Catholic Church.

Montaigne is one of the most ambiguous figures in modern thought. Was he a sincere defender of the Catholic faith, or was his fideism merely a smoke screen for disbelief? This question, debated for centuries, has become a cottage industry for philosophers and historians of the Counter-Reformation. For example, M. A. Screech presents Montaigne as a sincere Catholic who should be taken at his word; whereas Richard Popkin, while conceding that Montaigne (and other fideists) "seem capable of both a religious and non-religious interpretation," hazards the opinion that "at best, Montaigne was probably mildly religious. His attitude appears to be more that of indifference or unexcited acceptance, without any serious religious experience or involvement."[20]

Whatever Montaigne's own views may have been, his writings (especially *An Apology for Raymond Sebond*), provided a mine of information and arguments for later generations of freethinkers—who, as Screech puts it, "pillaged [the *Apology*] for anti-Christian arguments."[21] Fideism was clearly a double-edged sword. Montaigne's arguments could be used either to defend Christianity or to attack it, a point that was not lost on Catholic authorities who placed Montaigne's writings on the Index of Prohibited Books in 1697.

NOTES

1. Of course, to trace the history of ideas that are *implicitly* atheistic will leave the historian open to the charge of *selective* interpretation. This is a curious charge in a way, since all history is interpretation, and all interpretation is *necessarily* selective. If it means that the atheistic historian who investigates his own heritage will be prone to bias, causing him to see atheistic tendencies where others do not, I can only reply that this kind of disagreement is inevitable. It is inherent in the historical enterprise itself. Every historian has biases—or presuppositions, to use a more neutral term—that will influence his treatment of history, but such presuppositions do not make objectivity impossible. Indeed, it is precisely this inevitable bias that makes objectivity necessary.

2. Anthony Collins, *A Discourse of Free-Thinking*, in *Deism and Natural Religion: A Sourcebook*, ed. E. Graham Waring (New York: Frederick Ungar, 1967), p. 56.

3. *Sextus Empiricus: Selections from the Major Writings on Scepticism, Man, and God*, ed. Philip P Hallie, trans. Sanford G. Etherridge (Indianapolis: Hackett, 1985), pp. 188–90.

4. According to Epicurus, the gods, who exist in a separate world of their own, take no interest whatever in human affairs, so their existence is irrelevant to philosophy. This doctrine, however, was widely dismissed as an insincere concession to popular opinion, so we commonly find the name of Epicurus listed among the Greek atheists. This was the view of Cicero and Seneca, and this was the view of many later Christians; indeed, for many centuries, to be called an "Epicurean" or "hedonist" was tantamount to being called an "atheist." Although we don't have enough information to decide this controversy one way or another, my guess is that Epicurus was probably *not* an atheist in the strict sense. I say this because Epicurus and his followers repeatedly used the argument from universal assent to prove the existence of the gods, and closet atheists rarely go to this much trouble to conceal their true identity.

5. Cicero, *The Nature of the Gods*, trans. Horace McGregor (London: Penguin Books, 1972), p. 94.

6. Ibid., p. 73.

7. Lucretius, *On the Nature of the Gods,* trans. R. E. Latham (Harmondsworth: Penguin Books, 1951), p. 29.

8. Cicero, *Nature of the Gods,* p. 200.

9. Ibid., p. 116.

10. Ibid., pp. 78–79.

11. Ibid., p. 90.

12. *Sextus Empiricus*, pp. 206–207.

13. Ibid.

14. Ibid., pp. 208–209.

15. Ibid., p. 210

16. Andrew Dickson White, *A History of the Warfare of Science with Theology in Christendom* (New York: Dover Publications, 1960), vol. 1, p. 203.

17. Quoted in Richard Popkin, *The History of Scepticism from Erasmus to Descartes* (Berkeley: University of California Press, 1979), p. 2.

18. The two major schools of epistemological skepticism, as they originated in ancient Greek philosophy, are often called the Academic and the Pyrrhonic.

Academic skepticism, which derives its name from Plato's Academy, was inspired by the remark attributed to Socrates, "All I know is that I know nothing." As formulated by Arcesilaus (c. 315–241 B.C.E.) and Carneades (c. 213–129 B.C.E.), this version maintains that we can attain various degrees of probability, but never certainty, in our knowledge claims.

This claim was based on the standard Greek distinction between knowledge (*episteme*) and opinion (*doxa*). In this scheme, if a proposition cannot be demonstrated with complete certainty—i.e., if it might be false—then it does not qualify as certain knowledge and must be relegated to the status of mere opinion. According to Academic skepticism, both our senses and our reason are unreliable to some degree, so we can never lay claim to absolute truth, or real knowledge. And since nothing can be known with certainty, we must rely instead on opinions that vary in their degrees of probability.

Pyrrhonic skepticism is named after Pyrrho of Elis (c. 360–275 B.C.E.), an obscure figure who is portrayed in secondary accounts as a complete doubter, especially in ethical matters. Rather than endure the mental anguish and unhappiness that comes from seeking knowledge in the realm of values, Pyrrho is said to have suspended judgment, thereby attaining the state of mind known to Greek philosophers as *ataraxia* (quietude or unperturbedness).

Pyrrhonic skepticism was formulated as a distinct theory by Aenesidemus (c. 100–40 B.C.E.). It was Aenesidemus and his followers who first adopted the title of "skeptics" (from *skeptikos*, meaning "inquirer") and "doubters" (from *ephektikos*, meaning "one who suspends judgment").

Although both Academic and Pyrrhonic skeptics attacked "dogmatic" philosophers (such as the Stoics), who claimed to possess certain knowledge, their approaches differed significantly. ("Dogma," in its original meaning, referred to any proposition that can be known with certainty, not necessarily to a religious tenet that is accepted on faith.) The Academics, according to their Pyrrhonic critics, were not true skeptics, because they claimed to know with certainty that certainty is impossible—a position that is contradictory and therefore self-refuting. Thus Academic skepticism was sometimes called dogmatic skepticism.

The Pyrrhonists, in contrast, did not claim that knowledge is impossible; rather, they suspended judgment on all such theoretical questions, thereby avoiding the mental discomfort that comes from taxing one's brain with insoluble problems. For them skepticism was a mental attitude and a way of life, not an abstract philosophical position. The Pyrrhonists refused to judge or criticize the laws and customs of their society, resolving instead to accept things as they appear to be without committing themselves to any unorthodox position. In this way they attained the tranquility of ataraxia.

Of these two schools of skepticism, it was Pyrrhonism that was destined to exert the most influence on the course of Western philosophy, possibly because no major writings of the Academics survived the ravages of time. (Their arguments were transmitted through much later secondary accounts, such as those of Cicero and Augustine.) The Pyrrhonists were more fortunate. Around 200 C.E., the Greek physician Sextus Empiricus wrote an extensive summary of Pyrrhonic skepticism. Though virtually unknown to medieval scholars, manuscript copies of Sextus began to circulate during the Italian Renaissance and were eventually disseminated throughout Europe. His works were first published in Latin during the 1560s, and then in English three decades later.

Pyrrhonic skepticism, as summarized by Sextus, created a sensation—some called it a crisis—among European intellectuals. Some philosophers (such as Montaigne) embraced it enthusiastically, whereas others (such as Descartes) attempted with equal enthusiasm to refute it. But so tremendous was the influence of Sextus Empiricus that, by the end of the seventeenth century, "the divine Sextus" was widely hailed as the father of modern philosophy. For a brilliant account of the impact of Pyrrhonic skepticism on modern philosophy, see Popkin, *History of Scepticism*.

19. Michel de Montaigne, *An Apology for Raymond Sebond*, trans. M. A. Screech (London: Penguin Books, 1987), p. 2.

20. Quoted in Popkin, *History of Scepticism*, p. 55.

21. See M. A. Screech's introduction to Montaigne, *An Apology for Raymond Sebond*, pp. ix–xxxiii.

The Roots of Modern Atheism (II)

THOMAS HOBBES

Only humans exhibit religious beliefs and practices, according to Thomas Hobbes, so these must arise from characteristics that are peculiar to human nature. Foremost among these characteristics is the *"desire of knowing causes,"* especially those causes that seem to affect our welfare. Other animals are concerned only with their immediate needs and desires; we alone worry about the remote future, ponder our ultimate fate, and speculate about the causes of our calamities. But these things often remain beyond our grasp, so we tend to fabricate imaginary causes or believe what we are told by other people who we imagine to be wiser than ourselves.

Hobbes thus maintains that *anxiety about the future* is a primary motive, or "natural cause," of religious belief: "For being assured that there be causes of all things that have arrived hitherto, or shall arrive hereafter; it is impossible for a man, who continually endeavoureth to secure himself against the evil he fears, and procure the good he desireth, not to be in a perpetual solicitude of the time to come. . . ."[1] Unless this perpetual fear (the fruit of our inevitable ignorance) finds a concrete object on which to fasten itself, it will remain diffuse and unendurable: We will feel that we can neither control our future nor understand the causes of good and evil, and we will find refuge from anxiety only in sleep. And it was while in this semiconscious state that primitive man encountered dream apparitions that he could not explain, except to credit them with real existence as ghosts and spirits. Hence the origin of the gods.

Thus far Hobbes has done little more than summarize the theory of Epicurus, as expressed by "some of the old poets."[2] But having followed Epicurus to this point, Hobbes now veers off in a radical direction. He argues that people who ground their belief in God on "their own meditation" (in contrast to the testimony of others) will understand that the notion of an immaterial being is incomprehensible, repugnant to reason, and therefore should not be taken literally:

> [T]hough men may put together words of contradictory significa-
> tion, as *spirit* and *incorporeal*; yet they can never have the imagina-
> tion of any thing answering to them: and therefore, men that by
> their own meditation, arrive to the acknowledgment of one infinite,
> omnipotent, and eternal God, chose rather to confess he is incom-
> prehensible, and above their understanding, than to define his
> nature by *spirit incorporeal*, and then confess their definition to be
> unintelligible; or, if they give him such a title, it is not *dogmatically*,
> with intention to make the divine nature; but *piously*, to honour him
> with attributes, of significations, as remote as they can from the
> grossness of bodies visible.[3]

This latter contention—that the divine attributes should be understood as a way of paying homage to an incomprehensible God— was part of the Hobbesian solution to the problems of religious diversity and strife. Words like *omipotence* and *omniscience* should not be construed literally *or* metaphorically; rather, they are *emotive* terms that evoke feelings of reverence, awe, and submission in the believer. Consequently, it is senseless for theologians and metaphysicians to pontificate on the "true" meaning of God's attributes, or to engage in rancorous debates with dissenters over the same issue, because such terms have no cognitive meaning. The word "God" does not signify an intelligible concept at all, but refers instead to an incoherent "something" that defies our comprehension. Or, to put it more simply, *the term "God" is literally meaningless.*

Hobbes was probably the first modern thinker to make this outrageous claim, and it is hardly surprising that, after the publication of *Leviathan* in 1651, to be called a "Hobbist" was tantamount to being called an "atheist." Yet Hobbes professed to believe in God, as we see in the following passage:

> [T]he nature of God is incomprehensible, that is to say, we understand nothing of *what he is*, but only *that he is*; and therefore the attributes we give him, are not to tell one another, *what he is*, nor to signify our opinion of his nature, but our desire to honour him with such names as we conceive most honourable amongst ourselves.[4]

As with many of his freethinking contemporaries, it is difficult to tell how seriously we should take Hobbes's claim to believe in God. His frank repudiation of Christianity was highly unusual in his day, and it involved considerable risk; but to profess outright atheism was virtually unheard of (except in private conversations), and the risk would have been unacceptable to anyone with an unimpaired instinct of self-preservation. Thus, since we may reasonably assume that any seventeenth-century atheist would have been extremely reluctant to go public, preferring instead to remain in some kind of closet, however flimsy, it is necessary to read Hobbes "between the lines" in an effort to discern his true opinion.

In my opinion, this is a relatively simple task: Hobbes was an atheist, pure and simple. Unlike the similar problem with Spinoza's "atheism," where there is ample room for differing interpretations and scholarly disputes, Hobbes leaves little room for doubt. (Subtlety was not one of his strong points.) He was an avowed materialist, for example, so any supreme *being* in which he supposedly believed would have to have been a *corporeal* (i.e., material) entity. This point is implied (if not explicitly stated) in Hobbes's freewheeling discussion of angels. Are angels immaterial bodies, as many people believe? No, says Hobbes; this is a self-contradictory and nonsensical idea. The word "body" refers to that which fills or occupies space; a body "is a real part of that we call the *universe*":

> For the *universe*, being the aggregate of all bodies, there is no real part thereof that is not also *body*; nor any thing properly a *body*, that is not also part of that aggregate of all *bodies*, the *universe*. The same also, because bodies are subject to change, that is to say, to variety of appearance to the sense of living creatures, is called *substance*. . . . And according to this acceptation of the word, *substance* and *body* signify the same thing; and therefore *substance incorporeal* are words, which, when they are joined together, destroy one another, as if a man should say, an *incorporeal body*.[5]

According to Hobbes, angels, spirits, and other supposedly incorporeal bodies are "idols of the brain";[6] they are literally "nothing; nothing at all." If angels exist, they must be material substances of some kind. They must take up room, have dimensions, and move from place to place, "which is peculiar to bodies." Entities cannot be incorporeal, because this would mean "that they are in no place; that is to say, that are *nowhere*; that is to say, that seeming to be *somewhat*, are *nowhere*." The phrase "incorporeal substance" makes sense only if we suppose that "body" signifies "a thin substance invisible, but that hath the same dimensions that are in grosser bodies."[7]

There isn't much wiggle room here, to say the least, for the Hobbesian critique of angels and other spiritual entities applies equally to God, who is also said to be a "spirit." Hobbes deals with this problem in a characteristic way: In referring to God as a "spirit," we merely mean that "God" is utterly incomprehensible, that we have no coherent idea of what this word means, that we know not whereof we speak when we speak of "God." Thus, to say (as Hobbes sometimes does) that "God exists" is to say literally nothing at all. The only way to import meaning into this utterance would be to suppose that "God" refers to a *material* being of some kind—perhaps a "thin substance invisible," but a substance nonetheless—a body that occupies space, has dimensions, and can move (or be moved) from place to place. But this would also mean that God undergoes change, and, as we saw in our discussion of Greek skepticism, with this supposition the rest of the divine attributes (perfection, immutability, omnipotence, etc.) fall like cascading dominoes.

Methodological rigor was extremely important to Hobbes; indeed, he attempted to render his entire philosophy "scientific" by basing it on the model of geometric reasoning. The philosopher must begin with precise, well-defined terms and, proceeding from these to self-evident axioms, go on to draw scientific conclusions. None of this meshes with the incoherent belief in the existence of an incomprehensible "something" called "God"—so we must either conclude that Hobbes was really an atheist whose vague profession of theism was merely a sop to public opinion, or that he was able to rationalize a serious violation of his fundamental principles, a violation that he could not have failed to understand. (This latter is always possible, of course, for we know of many cases where philosophers have failed to embrace the inner logic of their own ideas, but in the case of Thomas Hobbes this seems extremely unlikely.[8])

SPINOZA

Spinoza, according to Pierre Bayle (1647–1706), was "a systematic atheist" who made use of equivocation and artifice "to avoid showing his atheism plainly." Spinoza's *Theologico-Political Treatise* is "a pernicious and detestable book in which he slips in all the seeds of atheism," so his followers "have hardly any religion at all." Friends reported that though Spinoza died "completely convinced of his atheism," he had avoided this label because "he wished not to give his name to a sect."[9] Bayle continues:

> Very few persons are suspected of adhering to his theory; and among those who are suspected of it, there are few who have studied it; and among the latter group, there are few who have understood it and have not been discouraged by the perplexities and the impenetrable abstractions that are found in it.[10]

Unlike other charges of "atheism" that were bandied about during the seventeenth century, Bayle's remarks should not be dismissed out of hand. For Bayle was no religious fanatic; on the contrary, he was one of the best-read and fair-minded scholars of his generation, who took pains to study the works of those writers with whom he disagreed. If it is true that many people misunderstood Spinoza because they read him carelessly, the same appears not to be true of Bayle, whose summary of Spinoza's ideas is generally accurate.

The reason why Bayle regarded Spinoza as an atheist is the same reason that occurs to most readers: While praising God to the hilt as a necessary and infinitely perfect being who is the cause of all things, Spinoza explicitly identifies "God" with "nature." Spinoza expressly denies the existence of a transcendent being, i.e., a being that exists apart from nature and acts upon it as an external agent. Every change that occurs, every instance of cause and effect, is immanent within nature and takes place according to the deterministic laws of nature.

Scholars continue to debate the question of whether Spinoza was really an atheist; and if this debate seems incapable of resolution, this is partially because the key term "atheist" is rarely used in a clear and consistent manner. The question "Was Spinoza really an atheist?" can be interpreted in (at least) three different ways. If we apply the label "atheist" only to writers who never employ theistic terminology, then Spinoza was not an atheist in this superficial sense. If, by "atheist," we mean a thinker who explicitly disbelieves in any personal, transcendent, or supernatural God, then Spinoza was indeed an atheist. If however, we mean "Did Spinoza view *himself* as an atheist?" then the issue becomes far more problematic.

Spinoza once remarked that "my opinion concerning God differs widely from that which is ordinarily defended by modern Christians. For I hold that God is of all things the cause immanent," and "I do not bring in the idea of God as a judge." Nature, according to Spinoza, "is the power of God under another name"; "in nature there is no substance save God, nor any modifications save those which are in God." As for the attributes of God: "By *eternity*, I mean existence itself"; "*reality* and *perfection* I use as synonymous terms"; by "infinite" is meant that "the nature of the universe is not limited," i.e., that it is "infinitely modified, and compelled to undergo infinite variations." Moreover, "God does not act according to freedom of the will," but is determined by the eternal laws of his nature. To suppose that God can intervene in the natural course of events through miracles is absurd: "I have taken miracles and ignorance as equivalent terms." "God can never decree, or never could have decreed anything but what is," nor does God act "with a view of promoting what is good."[11]

If these and similar positions do not represent an atheistic viewpoint (especially by seventeenth-century standards), then it is difficult to imagine what could possibly qualify. Spinoza's "God" is neither supernatural nor transcendent, he does not intervene in human affairs or "act" in any meaningful sense at all. In short, the God of Spinoza bears virtually no resemblance to what most people mean by "God." He is a prime example of what Pascal contemptuously referred to as the metaphysical God of the philosophers, in contrast to the personal God of religion.

Nevertheless, though Spinoza does not believe that God should be the object of religious worship or prayer, he does exhibit a profound reverence for this perfect being (while also noting that all of nature is inherently perfect). But we should keep in mind that Spinoza regards truth and reality as two sides of the same coin, so when he contends that lasting happiness can only come from the contemplation of God, this appears to express nothing more than the pursuit of wisdom—a quest for universal knowledge that is certain, immutable, and eternal—that has captivated philosophers for twenty-five hundred years. Indeed, in this respect Spinoza differs little from Aristotle, who also touted the contemplative life of the philosopher as the most desirable, and who labeled as "divine" our metaphysical knowledge of first principles.

Despite the fact that Spinoza's ideas are thoroughly atheistic, I am inclined to answer "no" to the question, "Did Spinoza view himself as an atheist?" Contrary to Bayle, I seriously doubt if he was a secret atheist who tried to camouflage his true opinions by dressing them in theistic garb. I say this because atheism was commonly associated in Spinoza's day with the materialism of Epicurus and his modern followers, such as Thomas Hobbes. And Spinoza, whatever he was, was no materialist.

Spinoza probably disliked the materialistic implications of "atheism" as much as he disliked Christianity, Judaism, and other conventional forms of theism. This is sheer speculation, of course, and whether I am right or wrong is of little consequence. The problem we are considering here is valuable, not for whatever answer it may yield, but because it provides an excellent focal point for understanding how a given philosopher viewed the religious controversies of his day, and how atheism was dismissed out of hand as an unacceptable alternative. Explicitly to advocate atheism was a virtual guarantee that one's ideas and arguments would be condemned without a fair hearing. Serious attempts to understand the nature of atheism were fairly scarce during the seventeenth century; indeed, the label itself was so odious that anyone who undertook an impartial investigation was sooner or later bound to be accused of harboring atheist sympathies.

It is safe to say that Spinoza's metaphysical theories exerted little influence on the subsequent development of freethought and atheism (if for no other reason than few people could understand them). But the same cannot be said of Spinoza's *critical* theories and investigations, especially in regard to natural causation, miracles, and the Bible. I have discussed some of these issues in a previous book, so I shall confine myself to a single but stunning example Spinoza's antitheological frame of mind.

Perhaps the most famous part of Spinoza's *Ethics* is the appendix to part 1. Although this discussion has often been cited for its repudiation of "final causes" (i.e., purposes in nature), its broader implications have rarely been recognized. What Spinoza presents, in effect, is a refutation of the Design Argument, an argument which many people have found to be more persuasive than any other "proof" for the existence of God. Indeed, it was this argument that prevented many eighteenth-century deists from taking the plunge into atheism. The Design Argument was embraced by some of the most celebrated names in the history of freethought, such as Voltaire and Thomas Paine, and it continued to be immensely popular well into the nineteenth century, until the Darwinian theory of evolution provided a naturalistic *method* of explanation for the complex, adaptive, and seemingly purposive nature of life.

According to Spinoza, we have a natural desire to understand the causes of natural phenomena (especially those that influence our welfare), and we also have a natural tendency to view nature in human terms. Thus, when we lack knowledge of natural causes, our imagination fills the void by attributing to nature the same kind of purposes and intentions that we observe in ourselves and other human beings. A kind of metaphysical transference is at work here. Many events and things affect us for good or ill. They are important to us, so we assume they were brought about with us in mind, by a being to whom *we* are important. We think that the world was specially created for our benefit, and that its complex structure and immense beauty must have been designed by a purposeful, powerful, and intelligent being.

The first problem with this theory, as Spinoza notes, is that "it does away with the perfection of God; for, if God acts for an object, he necessarily desires something which he lacks."[12] Some theologians tried to get around this problem (which had been proposed by the skeptics of ancient Greece), by stipulating that God created the world for his own sake, not for the sake of his creation. But this reply (or any similar to it) is unsatisfactory, for it still implies that God—a perfect being who lacks nothing and therefore can desire nothing—"lacked those things for whose attainment he created means, and further that he desired them."[13]

To ascribe purpose to nature is essentially an argument from ignorance. Nature is infinitely complex, so we can never claim to *know* that a given phenomenon could not have been produced by natural causes. So rather than attempt the impossible, rather than attempt to prove that a natural cause is impossible in a given case, theologians appeal to ignorance instead. Theologians attribute what we don't presently understand, or what science has failed to explain, to God—a "sanctuary of ignorance" that satisfies the imagination but not the understanding. Quoting Spinoza:

> [I]f a stone falls from a roof on to someone's head, and kills him, [theologians] will demonstrate by their new method, that the stone fell in order to kill the man; for, if it had not by God's will fallen with that object, how could so many circumstances (and there are often many concurrent circumstances) have all happened together by chance? Perhaps you will answer that the event is due to the facts that the wind was blowing, and the man was walking that way. "But why," they will insist, "was the wind blowing, and why was the man at that very time walking that way?" If you again answer, that the wind had then sprung up because the sea had begun to be agitated the day before, the weather being previously calm, and that the man had been invited by a friend, they will again insist: "But why was the sea agitated, and why was the man invited at that time?" So they were pursue their questions from cause to cause, till at last you take refuge in the will of God—in other words, the sanctuary of ignorance.[14]

Similarly, those who do not understand how nature could have produced the human body, will often "conclude that it has been fashioned, not mechanically, but by divine and supernatural skill. . . ." And "anyone who seeks for the true causes of miracles, and strives to understand natural phenomena as an intelligent being, and not to gaze at them like a fool, is set down and denounced as an impious heretic. . . ."15

Spinoza's use of the term "miracle" in this latter passage is highly significant. The argument from design is ultimately an appeal to miraculous causes, i.e., causes that do not, and cannot, occur in the natural course of events. This is why an "explanation" via design is not a legitimate alternative to scientific and other naturalistic modes of explanation. To refer to a miraculous "cause" is to refer to something that is inherently unknowable, and this "sanctuary of ignorance" explains nothing at all. However much it may soothe the imagination of the ignorant, it does nothing to satisfy the *understanding* of a rational person.

Another feat of the imagination is to "firmly believe that there is an *order* in things," and that things that further this order are metaphysically "good." Spinoza's objection to this view is the most radical part of his critique, for even atheists will often speak of an order inherent in nature. Spinoza disagrees. Nature is what it is, and things behave as they do in virtue of what they are. Thus nature exhibits neither order nor chaos, good nor evil, beauty nor deformity; these assessments are derived from human standards, not from nature per se. We evaluate a natural phenomenon as "well-ordered" when it can be easily understood or when it affects us favorably—whereas we speak of "confusion" (or "chance" or "chaos") when confronted with a phenomenon that eludes our understanding or brings unforeseen evils upon us.

In thus relegating "order" to the same status as "beauty" and other subjective16 evaluations, Spinoza undercuts the Design Argument at its roots. If the fundamental facts of nature—their ultimate explanation, so to speak—are that things exist, that things are what they are, and that things behave as they do in virtue of what they are, then to ascribe "order" to natural phenomena is simply to restate these fundamental facts in an abbreviated form. It is to say that these fundamental facts are comprehensible. If, however, we wish to say more than this—if, by "order," we mean that nature exhibits beauty, harmony, goodness, or the like—then we are merely importing additional evaluations into our set of fundamental facts. And this means that we need only explain these evaluations, not the facts they purport to describe.

Hence, according to Spinoza, if we wish to explain the "purpose" and "design" in nature, we need only to look within ourselves, to the reasons and causes that generate these evaluations. It is as unnecessary as it is absurd to posit the existence of an unknowable cause, God, who uses unknowable means (miracles) to bring about results that he could not possibly desire. Spinoza concludes:

> [A]ll the explanations commonly given of nature are mere modes of imagining, and do not indicate the true nature of anything, but only the constitution of the imagination; and, although they have names, as though they were entities, existing externally to the imagination, I call them entities imaginary rather than real; and, therefore, all arguments against us drawn from such abstractions are easily rebutted.[17]

DAVID HUME

Which cognitive discipline played the greatest historical role in undermining Christian orthodoxy? We might suppose that science or philosophy is the best answer to this question, but I would choose history over all other candidates. Christianity, after all, is a revealed religion, one that revolves around the Bible—and this means that it is principally a *historical* religion. A special revelation from God is a unique historical event, one that occurred at a specific place and time. And unless we receive a personal revelation immediately from God, we must rely on the historical accounts of other people, such as those found in the Bible.

This distinction between *personal* revelation and *historical* revelation was crucial to Hobbes, Hume, and other critics of Christian dogma. (By "dogma," in this context, I mean a revealed truth that, because it comes from an omniscient and nondeceitful God, is accepted as infallibly certain.) These critics generally agreed that if a person believes he has received a personal revelation from God, there may be little we can do to change his mind. But they also pointed out that the situation changes dramatically when this person *reports* his experience to *others* with the hope of winning their assent. A person may feel compelled to accept whatever (he believes) God has revealed to him, but others—those to whom he reports his experience—are in a radically different position. For they are receiving a report not directly from an infallible God, but *indirectly* from a *fallible* human being who, like themselves, is easily deceived and frequently errs.

When Protestants broke free from the authority of the Catholic Church, they were left in a somewhat embarrassing position in regard to the veracity of miracles. Neither side wished to cast doubt on biblical miracles (especially those attributed to Jesus), because the ability to perform miracles was widely regarded as the sign of a divine messenger; this was the fundamental criterion that distinguished the authentic prophet from his fake counterpart. And without this criterion, without the ability to identify true emissaries from God, the entire scheme of biblical revelation—and therefore Christianity itself—would quickly collapse, since there would be no basis for assuming that the biblical writers were anything other than deluded and foolish men.

Many different people with many different beliefs have claimed to be divine messengers, and, since not all of their contradictory messages can be true, the believer must find a way to separate his favorites from the pack. Every Christian theologian, Catholic and Protestant alike, understood this, so no theologian could dispense with miracles altogether. The veracity of miracles therefore involved far more than whether God can, or does, intervene in the natural course of events. What was at stake here was the very foundation of Christianity itself.

Protestants, however, faced a serious dilemma. For many centuries, from the beginning of the Christian era to the Protestant Reformation, Catholics had reported thousands of miracles performed by popes, saints, bishops, priests, and even Catholic laypersons. Indeed, if we believe the accounts of the church fathers and medieval theologians, miracles—including the resurrection of dead people—were commonplace occurrences, which had sometimes been witnessed by dozens (or even hundreds) of people.

It is understandable why Protestants found these reports disturbing. If the pope was the Antichrist, and if the Catholic Church was a tool of Satan, then why would God have favored Catholics with an abundance of miracles? Something was clearly amiss: Catholics were evil and deluded heretics who did not enjoy God's favor, so their alleged miracles could not be accepted at face value. And thus did Protestants repudiate Catholic miracles as mere superstition. They were nothing more than pious frauds that had been foisted upon the ignorant masses by mendacious and oppressive clerics.

It seems inevitable, owing to the inner logic of ideas, that the critical focus on Catholic miracles would eventually be applied to all historical miracles, including those which were dear to Protestants. And this is exactly what we find in the famous critique of David Hume.

According to Hume, although experience teaches us that some things are true, it also teaches us that our judgment is fallible, that we often commit errors when reasoning about matters of fact. This latter is evident when we rely, as we often must, on the testimony of other people as a source of information that we cannot verify for ourselves. Such testimony often turns out to be misleading, distorted, or downright false; and the testimonies of different people, or of the same person at different times, often conflict with one another.

Why, then, do we grant any credibility at all to secondhand testimony? This is clearly *not* owing to any *necessary* relationship between testimony and truth; if this were so, no testimony would ever be false, and testimonies would never conflict. Hume maintains that our confidence in testimony is based on experience:

> Were not the memory tenacious to a certain degree; had not men commonly an inclination to truth and a principle of probity; were they not sensible to shame, when detected in a falsehood: Were not these, I say, discovered by *experience* to be qualities, inherent in

human nature, we should never repose the least confidence in human testimony. A man delirious, or noted for falsehood and villainy, has no manner of authority with us.[18]

How much credibility we grant to a particular testimony—whether we dismiss it out of hand, view it as doubtful or probable to some degree, or accept it as a sufficient proof—depends on a number of factors. We are hesitant, for example, when witnesses contradict each other, or when they are of doubtful character, or when they appear to be promoting their own interests. In addition, our confidence diminishes as the reported event becomes more unusual and unlikely to have occurred. In this case, we have conflicting sets of experience that must be weighed against each other. We believe, on the one hand, that secondhand testimony is often reliable, while believing, on the other hand, that some events are highly unlikely (given our past experience) or impossible (given our knowledge of natural laws).

We must often judge historical accounts on a case-by-case basis. The historian, for example, must assess documents that give different accounts of the same event, or she must evaluate the credibility of a particular witness, or she must sift the probable from the improbable in one report. Many such problems confront us in our daily lives as well. We hear an unsavory rumor about a friend that conflicts with our own experience of his moral character, or someone in whom we have confidence claims to have witnessed an improbable event, or an authority (a doctor, scientist, etc.) tells us something that conflicts with the testimony of other authorities. In these and similar cases, we must weigh the probability of one experience against the probability of another experience and arrive at the best judgment we can.

As Hume points out, however, we are not obliged to consider the *particular* merits, the specific pros and cons, of every testimony that we come across. There are certain kinds of testimony that we should reject out of hand, without further consideration, because they report events that are *impossible*. And this brings us to Hume's celebrated critique of miracles.

"A miracle," says Hume, "is a violation of the laws of nature; and as a firm and unalterable experience has established these laws, the proof against a miracle, from the very nature of the fact, is as entire as any argument from experience can possibly be imagined."[19] Hume is here referring to *historical* miracles, i.e., to reports of miraculous events that we receive from other people. His argument is a deceptively simple one. If a person claims to have witnessed a miracle, i.e., if he testifies to the violation of a natural law, then how am I to evaluate his account? Here, as in other conflicts pertaining to matters of fact, I should weigh one probability against the other. So I ask myself, "Which is more probable—that what the witness says is false, or that nature did indeed take a vacation from its normal course?"

I have experienced many cases of being told something that is false, but I have *never* witnessed a violation of natural law. Thus, in evaluating the comparative probability of these events—a falsehood versus a miracle—I should decide in favor of the former. Upon being told of a miraculous event, I should *always* conclude that the "witness" has conveyed a falsehood. In Hume's words:

> There must . . . be a uniform experience against every miraculous event, otherwise the event would not merit that appellation. And as a uniform experience amounts to a proof, there is here a direct and full *proof*, from the nature of the fact, against the existence of any miracle. . . .[20]

Suppose someone tells me that he saw a dead man brought back to life. Here I should consider "whether it be more probable, that this person should either deceive or be deceived, or that the fact, which he relates, should really have happened."[21] There is no real contest in this case, because the possibility of resurrecting the dead conflicts with *all* of my previous experience, whereas I know of innumerable instances where people have related falsehoods. I therefore conclude that "no testimony is sufficient to establish a miracle, unless the testimony be of such a kind, that its falsehood would be more miraculous, than the fact, which it endeavors to establish. . . ."

This argument is more radical than it may appear at first glance, because it establishes not merely that I should reject this or that testimony as false, but that I should dismiss the entire *class* of miraculous reports as utterly devoid of *credibility*. Recall what I said about credibility in chapter 1:

> *To say that a proposition is credible is to say not that it is justified but that it is worthy of being justified.* A credible proposition is one that we regard as worthy of further consideration. Without credibility a proposition will simply pass through our consciousness without stopping long enough to be examined.

Rather than focus on this or that particular report, Hume's critique ("an everlasting check to all kinds of superstitious delusions") undermines the credibility of historical miracles in general. Whereas many freethinkers had attacked the miracles of Christianity by debunking the biblical accounts one at a time, Hume maintains that this kind of piecemeal criticism is unnecessary, because it mistakenly implies that particular reports should be taken seriously. A report merits close examination only if it is credible, i.e., only if it is attended with some degree of probability. But the probably is nil that *any* reported miracle is true, so, given this lack of credibility, we may dismiss *all* reports on principle, without bothering to investigate the details of specific claims.

This was an important strategic innovation in the battle against Christian dogma, because it removed biblical controversies from the realm of theologians, historians, and other "experts," who would often flaunt their credentials in an effort to silence their freethinking opponents (who were often self-educated). Moreover, given the innumerable "accounts of miracles and prodigies [to] be found in all history, sacred and profane," even the most meticulous critic will find himself overwhelmed. Theologians will demand that he refute one piece of "evidence" after another; and when this proves impossible—whether from lack of time, lack of interest, or for some other reason—the theologian will proclaim victory, because some of his arguments have remained unanswered.

Hume's critique, as I said, was designed to deal with this kind of strategic problem. It is "a decisive argument . . . which must at least *silence* the most arrogant bigotry and superstition, and free us from their impertinent solicitations."[22] The freethinker, in other words, needn't become a biblical scholar in order to justify his rejection of Christian beliefs. He need only apply the ordinary canons of philosophical criticism to the entire class of historical miracles, including those reported in the Bible. Then, after finding that such reports lack credibility, he can move on to more important matters.

EDWARD GIBBON

If we wish to gauge the progress of secularism during the eighteenth century, we need only glance at some of the works that made 1776 one of the most remarkable years in the history of publishing. That year witnessed the appearance of Thomas Paine's *Common Sense*, Thomas Jefferson's *Declaration of Independence*, Adam Smith's *An Inquiry into the Nature and Causes of the Wealth of Nations*, Jeremy Bentham's *A Fragment on Government*, and the first volume of Edward Gibbon's *Decline and Fall of the Roman Empire*.

Although it is quite remarkable that not one Christian is to be found among these influential writers, what is even more remarkable is that all of them dared to criticize religion openly, and none felt the need to camouflage his disbelief in a mantle of respectability (as might have been necessary just fifty years earlier).

In 1776, while England was facing revolution abroad, a freelance historian named Edward Gibbon was stirring up trouble of a different kind at home. For it was in this year that Gibbon published the first volume of his monumental work, *The Decline and Fall of the Roman Empire*. This volume contains two scandalous chapters on the early history of Christianity, which are introduced as follows:

> The theologian may indulge the pleasing task of describing Religion as she descended from Heaven, arrayed in her natural purity. A

more melancholy duty is imposed on the historian. He must discover the inevitable mixture of error and corruption which she contracted in a long residence upon earth, among a weak and degenerate race of beings.

Our curiosity is naturally prompted to inquire by what means the Christian faith obtained so remarkable a victory over the established religions of the earth. To this inquiry an obvious but unsatisfactory answer may be returned; that it was owing to the convincing evidence of the doctrine itself, and to the rule providence of its great Author. But as truth and reason seldom find so favourable a reception in the world, and as the wisdom of Providence frequently condescends to use the passions of the human heart, and the general circumstances of mankind, as instruments to execute its purpose, we may still be permitted, though with becoming submission, to ask, not indeed what were the first, but *what were the secondary causes of the rapid growth of the Christian church?*[23]

Gibbon notes that reports of early Christian miracles "have been lately attacked in a very free and ingenious inquiry, which, though it has met with the most favorable reception from the public, appears to have excited a general scandal among the divines of our own as well as of the other Protestant churches of Europe."[24] We might suppose that Gibbon is here referring to *An Enquiry Concerning Human Understanding* (1748), in which David Hume launches his famous attack on the belief in historical miracles. In fact, however, the "very free and ingenious inquiry" to which Gibbon refers was a work by Conyers Middleton, *Free Inquiry into the Miraculous Powers, which are Supposed to have Subsisted in the Christian Church* (1749).

Middleton's *Free Inquiry* played an important role in Gibbon's intellectual development, for it was upon reading this work that a young Gibbon lost his remaining faith in Protestantism. Indeed, it appears that Middleton excited more controversy than did his illustrious contemporary, David Hume.

Middleton exploited a latent weakness in the Protestant view of early Christianity. Focusing most of his attention on Christian theologians of the fourth century, Middleton argued that these revered apologists, however sanctified by tradition, had in fact resorted to deceit, forgery, and fraudulent history in an effort to defend their cause and win converts.

According to Gibbon, our beliefs about early Christianity will be determined not so much by the arguments advanced for this or that miracle, but primarily by "the degree of the evidence which we have accustomed ourselves to require for the proof of a miraculous event."[25] Though the historian should not allow his religious convictions to warp his historical judgment, he must nonetheless work from a theory of the relative probability of historical miracles, and then apply that theory to the specific case of early Christianity.

Gibbon notes that miracles have been reported by many Christians from the earliest days of Christianity through the eighteenth century (when Gibbon was writing). Yet the Protestants of Gibbon's day, while persuaded of the authenticity of early miracles, were far more skeptical of later reports, often rejecting them outright. But how can we draw a line between true and false reports, between authentic miracles and superstitious fables? It is while focusing on this question that Gibbon makes his most telling critique of historical miracles.

Reports of miraculous cures, which were commonplace in the early Christian community, are cited by the apologists as evidence for Christianity. But these mundane miracles should not surprise us, when we consider that "about the end of the second century, the resurrection of the dead was very far from being esteemed an uncommon event; that the miracle was frequently performed on necessary occasions . . . and that the persons thus restored to their prayers had lived afterwards among [Christians] many years." What is the historian to make of these reports? Given the frequency of resurrections during the second century, and given the easy availability of those former corpses who were now up and about and ready to testify for their faith—given the abundance of these and other contemporary miracles, Gibbon wonders why early Christians did not convince far more people than they actually did. How could anyone remain skeptical about a solitary resurrection in the past, when he could easily observe (or otherwise verify) many such resurrections in the present? And how are to interpret the curious response given by Theophilus (the bishop of Antioch) to a skeptical friend? The skeptic promised to embrace Christianity immediately upon meeting just one former corpse, but as Gibbon observes: "It is somewhat remarkable that the prelate of the first eastern church, however anxious for the conversion of his friend, thought proper to decline this fair and remarkable challenge."[26]

It is at this point that Gibbon, after noting how Middleton's *Free Inquiry* had caused a "general scandal" among Protestant theologians, makes one of his rare excursions into historical methodology. Gibbon does not think that the historian should play the role of religious partisan, defending one side over another in theological controversies, so he is reluctant to express his own opinion about Middleton's arguments against the veracity of early Christian miracles. But however the historian may strive to remain impartial, he must assess the evidence and testimony that have traditionally been offered to defend the claims of Christianity.

Consider, says Gibbon, that every age has its share of reported miracles, "and its testimony appears no less weighty and respectable than that of the preceding generation." How then are we to avoid inconsistency if we deny the miracles of the eighth or twelfth centuries, while accepting those in the second century? There is no appreciable difference in the number of witnesses or in their character from one age to the next, so all such miraculous accounts, in whatever era we find them, have an equal claim to our assent. Nor is there any difference in the usefulness of such miracles, for "every age had unbelievers to convince, heretics to confute, and idolatrous nations to convert; and sufficient motives might always be produced to justify the interposition of heaven."[27]

Despite these similarities, even the friends of revelation believe that there was *some* period in which miracles were "either suddenly or gradually withdrawn from the Christian church." Here Gibbon is thinking primarily of Protestants—those who affirmed the veracity of miracles during the apostolic age, using them as the foundation for their own religion, while repudiating later claims of the Catholic Church, which they despised.

Whatever era is chosen as the dividing line between authentic and bogus miracles, Gibbon calls it a "just matter of surprise" that the Christians who lived during that transition period were quite unaware of the dramatic change that was taking place. These Christians, who had previously been endowed with sufficient faith to discern authentic miracles, were now unable to distinguish between true and false accounts, as if their faith had insensibly degenerated into credulity.

After all, these Christians claimed to have witnessed miracles firsthand, just as they always had; and if we accept their earlier accounts (i.e., those before the transition period) as genuine, then we must suppose them to have been of sufficient discernment to recognize the marks of authentic miracles. "The recent experience of genuine miracles should have instructed the Christian world in the ways of Providence and habituated their eye . . . to the style of the divine artist."[28] But if this is so, then how did these discerning Christians lose this ability after the transition period and suddenly begin to defend bogus miracles with the same assurance (and using the same kind of evidence) with which they had previously confirmed authentic miracles?

Gibbon's point about those transitional Christians who, having previously been reliable witnesses of authentic miracles, were mysteriously transformed into credulous purveyors of bogus miracles, is a clever adaptation of the Humean critique. Gibbon, in effect, is asking the following question: Which is more likely—that experienced and credible witnesses should unaccountably become unreliable and superstitious? Or that their accounts were unreliable from the outset, and should not be accepted as grounds for believing in any historical miracles whatsoever?

In thus applying the critiques of Middleton and Hume to the early history of Christianity, Gibbon paved the way for the secularism of modern history, in which miraculous accounts are given no credibility.

NOTES

1. Thomas Hobbes, *Leviathan*, ed. Michael Oakeshott (New York: Collier Books, 1962), p. 87.

2. The principal source was undoubtedly Lucretius's *On the Nature of the Universe* (which we discussed in the previous chapter). Hobbes's discussion of fear and dreams is a restatement of material from this epic poem, which in turn is a restatement of Epicurus's theory of the origin of religious belief.

3. Hobbes, *Leviathan*, p. 89.

4. Ibid., p. 287.

5. Ibid., p. 286.

6. This reference to "idols" shows the influence of Francis Bacon, for whom Hobbes had previously worked as an amanuensis. Bacon's "idols" are erroneous tendencies inherent in the human understanding, natural defects that can be corrected only through rigorous and systematic thinking. For additional details, see my discussion of Francis Bacon in chap. 7, "The Career of Reason."

7. Hobbes, *Leviathan*, p. 291.

8. There is another good reason why Hobbes, though really an atheist, publicly claimed to believe in God. Like a number of Greek atheists, Hobbes regarded (some) religious beliefs as a necessary foundation for social order—a means of reigning in the unruly passions of the masses, who otherwise might not obey the laws of their country. Absolute sovereignty (i.e., unconditional submission to the ruling order) is a dominant theme of *Leviathan*, and it runs throughout the lengthy discussions of religion and God.

9. Pierre Bayle, *Historical and Critical Dictionary: Selections*, trans. and ed. by Richard H. Popkin (Indianapolis: Hackett, 1991), pp. 288, 299, 293, 301, 300.

10. Ibid., p. 300.

11. Benedict Spinoza, *The Ethics, Correspondence, and a Theologico-Political Treatise*, trans. R. H. M. Elwes, 2 vols. (New York: Dover Publications, 1951); Letter XXI, p. 298; Letter XXXIV, p. 338; *Theological-Political Treatise*, p. 25; *Ethics*, p. 69; *Ethics*, p. 46; *Ethics*, p. 83; Letter XXXII, p. 292; *Ethics*, p. 70; Letter XXIII, p. 302; *Ethics*, p. 72; *Ethics*, p. 74.

12. Ibid., p. 77.

13. Ibid., p. 78.

14. Ibid.

15. Ibid.

16. It must be understood that "subjective," in this context, means an evaluation that originates in the human *subject*, something that is not an *intrinsic* property of the *object* being evaluated. To call something "subjective" in this sense does not imply that it is (necessarily) arbitrary or unjustified. Many philosophers, for instance, have maintained that "beauty" is subjective inasmuch as it is not a metaphysical property inherent in the nature of things, while also maintaining that assessments of beauty are not arbitrary, but can be assessed by rational standards of one kind or another. The terms "subjective" and "objective" have been used in so many different ways by philosophers and scientists, that it is almost always necessary to specify their intended meaning in a given discussion.

17. Spinoza, *Ethics*, p. 81.

18. David Hume, *Enquiries Concerning Human Understanding and Concerning the Principles of Morals*, ed. L. A. Selby-Bigge and P. H. Nidditch (Oxford: Clarendon Press, 1975), p. 112.

19. Ibid., p. 114.

20. Ibid., p. 115.

21. Ibid., p. 116.

22. Ibid., p. 110.

23. Edward Gibbon, *The Decline and Fall of the Roman Empire*, Great Books of the Western World, vol. 40 (Chicago: Encyclopedia Britannica, 1952), p. 179.

24. Ibid., pp. 189–90.

25. Ibid., p. 190.

26. Ibid., p. 189.

27. Ibid., p. 190.

28. Ibid.

Some Irreverent Questions Concerning God

IS GOD AN ATHEIST?

Before the Christian dismisses atheism as irrational or condemns the atheist as immoral, he should consider the disturbing possibility that the God of Christianity is himself an atheist. And if this is true, it means that the Christian worships, obeys, and has devoted his life to an atheistic being who does not believe in any power superior to himself, never prays, is utterly without faith, and who does not acknowledge any authority, either cognitive or moral, external to himself.

If theism is loosely defined as belief in a higher power, a mysterious being whose essential nature cannot be understood (whether in whole or in part) by the believer, then God is an atheist. He does not believe in a power higher than himself, nor can there be anything that he fails to understand, for nothing can be unknown or unknowable to an omniscient being.

If theism is defined as the belief in a supernatural being, then God is an atheist. His own powers, though supernatural from a human point of view, are comprehensible to himself. Everything is "natural" from God's perspective.

If theism involves a relationship of subordination and dependence between a theist and her object of veneration, then God is an atheist. He is a self-sufficient being who disbelieves in any power greater than himself. He worships nothing, never prays, never seeks forgiveness, and never acknowledges his own errors.

If theism is the belief in a creator, or first cause, who is ultimately responsible for one's own existence, then God is an atheist. He believes himself to have existed eternally—though, as Kant suggested, even God must occasionally wonder where *he* came from.

If theism involves the belief an external moral authority, a being whose moral law is obligatory for his creatures, then God is an atheist. He does not believe in a higher law, nor does he think himself capable of doing wrong. He does not regard himself bound to respect the rights of any other being. God is morally autonomous, a law unto himself.

God is therefore an atheist. Moreover, he is a positive atheist of the most dogmatic variety, for he claims to know with absolute certainty that there exists no being superior to himself. He is never troubled by doubt, never reexamines any of his beliefs, and never feels obliged to justify them.

This raises some further questions: Why, if God is an atheist, should we suppose that that he disapproves of atheism among his creatures? Is not a benevolent father pleased when his children grow up to be like him? And how can the Christian condemn atheism per se without also condemning their atheistic God? Is not the atheist who strives to be like God more admirable than the Christian who merely believes in him?

IS SATAN A CHRISTIAN?

Satan is not an atheist—that much is clear—for he believes in the God of Christianity. We thus have the intriguing spectacle of a battle between two titans, with God the atheist on the side of good, and Satan the theist on the side of evil. And if the Bible is to be believed, the atheist will ultimately triumph over the theist.

Is Satan the theist also a Christian? Apparently so, because a Christian is defined in terms of his beliefs, not his actions. Satan clearly believes in the central tenets of Christianity. He believes, for example, that that Jesus, the Son of God, was sacrificed to redeem the sins of mankind—for if Satan does not believe this, why did he tempt Jesus in an effort to sabotage his divine mission? He also believes in the resurrection of Jesus, in the power of God to work miracles, and in the existence of a heaven and a hell he calls home.

Satan, a major player in many biblical events, does not have the least doubt about the veracity of God's word. Indeed, it is impossible to name one belief of the best Christian that Satan does not share. We may therefore conclude that Satan is a Christian, despite his rebellious spirit and competitive zeal. No one is perfect, after all.

CAN GOD TELL THE PERFECT JOKE?

Does God have a sense of humor? Has he ever laughed divinely? Has he ever cracked a spiritual grin? Has an omni-jolly chuckle ever punctuated the grim silence of eternity?

Can God, a perfect being, tell a perfect joke—a joke than which nothing funnier can be conceived? Can an infinite being tell a joke that is infinitely funny—and, if so, could it cause people to die laughing? Do those who populate the kingdom of heaven ever laugh, or does humor die with the body, along with sex and other innocent pleasures?

These questions are not as frivolous as they may first appear. Humor plays an important role in human life. Laughter is an intrinsic value, something we enjoy as an end in itself rather than a means to something else. Laughter is a moveable feast, something we can take with us anywhere and enjoy at our leisure. To laugh with another person is among the purest forms of social interaction, a spontaneous intermingling of thoughts and emotions.

It is nice to think that God deliberately bestowed upon us the gift of laughter; if so, it was one of his better ideas. A traditional method of exploring this kind of issue is to speculate on the nature of prelapsarian man, i.e., human nature before Adam's *lapse*, or fall, into sin.

According to St. Augustine, for example, prelapsarian man would have engaged in sexual intercourse for the purpose of procreation, but the pleasure of sex would not have been nearly as intense as it now is. Sexual lust (including the orgasm) is a consequence of original sin and was therefore unknown to Adam and Eve prior to the Fall.

May we apply the same logic to laughter? Were Adam and Eve capable of laughter before the Fall? If they had never sinned, would humor have been a part of prelapsarian life? If our present nature had never been vitiated by original sin, would we still tell jokes? Would there have been a place for stand-up comedians in the Garden of Eden—or is George Carlin solely the product of original sin?

There are problems in supposing God to have a sense of humor. Comedy is the art of the inappropriate. We laugh at the unexpected, not the routine. But nothing can be unexpected for a God who knows everything—past, present, and future. There can be no punch lines or novel twists for a God who is incapable of being surprised. Everything happens on schedule according to a divine plan; and God, the author of that plan, is never taken aback. Thus, if God is to laugh at all, he must provide his own humor and laugh at his own jokes, because there is nothing to surprise or amuse him in the course of human events.

Of course, to say that we cannot make God laugh is not to say that he cannot make us laugh. But this laughter, if it is to be authentic, must be the product of natural humor rather than supernatural decree. An omnipotent God who can turn a woman into a pillar of salt could easily generate as much laughter as he likes by merely willing it to happen. But this would be cheating, reducing God to the level of a bad comedian who provokes laughter in his audience by drugging their drinks. The question is not whether God can cause people to laugh, but whether he can do so through humor.

It seems that a perfect God should be able to tell a perfect joke, one that can generate more laughter than any joke that is merely human. But this is where things get complicated. Suppose God were to reveal the perfect joke, the joke than which nothing funnier can be conceived. This joke is absolutely funny, not relatively so, because it emanates from God's absolute sense of humor. To understand this joke is necessarily to understand that it is the funniest of all possible jokes, and to laugh accordingly.

But what if I don't laugh at this divine joke? Do I sin if I fail to laugh hard enough or long enough? This question seems to require an affirmative answer. For consider: If whatever God says is necessarily true, and if he says that his joke is the funniest of all possible jokes—one that merits the greatest amount of laughter—then for me not to respond appropriately would be to defy the will of God.

Suppose I laugh less at the divine joke, which God has declared to the be the funniest of all possible jokes, than I do at a joke by George Carlin. Since I assess the quality of a comic by his ability to make me laugh, my response to Carlin would mean that I regard him as funnier than God. This is a blasphemous notion, however, because it suggests that the supreme being, whose nature is synonymous with perfection itself, is less than supreme in his capacity as a comic.

If both Carlin and God framed their jokes with the intention of provoking laughter, and if I laughed more heartily at the former than the latter, this means that Carlin was more successful than God in accomplishing what he set out to do. And if Carlin is better able to evoke laughter, if his power in this sphere is greater than God's, then God is neither supreme nor perfect in all things, because his ability to tell a good joke is inferior to that of a mere mortal. And this implies that God was either mistaken or lying when he proclaimed his joke to be the funniest of all possible jokes, because there is at least one joke that I find funnier than his.

A perfect being, as we noted before, can tell a perfect joke, a joke than which nothing funnier can be conceived. Now let us suppose that God, having decided to bless us with his infinite humor, reveals his perfect joke, to wit: "The cat is on the mat."

So now we have it, the perfect joke, straight from the mouth of the supreme comic, an infallible being who has declared it to be the funniest of all possible jokes. The problem is that few people will laugh spontaneously upon hearing "The cat is on the mat"—and they will fail to understand why this should even be dubbed a joke at all, much less a perfect one.

We are thus confronted with a dilemma. We have been told by an infallible being that this joke is supremely funny, so we feel that we ought to laugh. But we don't laugh, because we don't find it funny at all. So who is to blame—God or man—for this discrepancy between *ought* and *is*, between the response that we should have *in theory* and the response that we do have *in fact*?

The main issue here is whether we have a *moral* obligation to laugh at the perfect joke. This will doubtless strike many as a senseless question, because genuine laughter is a spontaneous reaction that is impervious to moral imperatives. If I don't see any humor in the perfect joke, "The cat is on the mat," but am commanded by God to laugh at it nonetheless, how can I possibly do what is required of me? I could fake it, of course, like an actor in a comedic role, but my insincerity would be transparently obvious to a God who knows my every thought and feeling. God demands that I respond with genuine laughter, not hypocrisy, but how is this possible if I don't see any humor in his perfect joke?

The problem of the perfect joke generates two schools of interpretation: the believers and the free-laughers.

According to the believers, the perfect joke is indeed supremely funny, so our failure to laugh is our problem, not God's. God, after all, knows better than we what is truly funny, so we should have absolute faith in what he tells us and strive to understand his transcendent humor. We should not presume to judge God's joke by human standards, but should accept it as supremely funny and work from there. Belief must precede humor, and faith is the foundation of belief.

The believer, having accepted God's humor as an act of faith, will learn to laugh at his perfect joke. "The cat is on the mat" will eventually strike the man of faith as supremely funny, causing him to tingle with a spiritual laughter that will seem foolish to the unbeliever.

The free-laugher, on the other hand, is unwilling to subordinate his sense of humor to the demands of an external authority. The perfect joke is simply not funny, regardless of who originated it, and it does not become any funnier merely because God demands that we laugh at it. And why would God endow us with a spontaneous sense of humor and then punish us for a reaction over which we have no control?

It seems that the perfect joke, like the Trinity and other Christian doctrines, will forever elude our understanding. But the perfect joke, though it transcends our sense of humor, does not contradict it. Taking our cue from Thomas Aquinas, we may say that the perfect joke supplements, or perfects, our natural sense of humor. Thus, however much the Christian may fail to understand the humor of the perfect joke, he must place his trust in God and laugh on faith.

CAN GOD HAVE AN ORGASM?

Can God have an orgasm? The mere posing of the question is bound to offend the religious sensibility of many people, and many would refuse even to consider the question from fear that God—who is privy to their every thought—would seriously disapprove of any such blasphemous curiosity. But this question raises a serious problem about the nature of God that dates back to the skeptics of ancient Greece.

If we suppose that God can feel physical sensations of any kind, then we must also suppose that God is a corporal entity, a physical organism with the capacity to experience sensations. And this supposition, aside from conflicting with the notion that God is a purely spiritual being, carries with it the disturbing implication that God is subject to change and so cannot be immutable. To experience a sensation, after all, is to experience a change from one state to another, so if God is able to feel anything we cannot regard him as immutable, because this means the absence of any change whatsoever.

Moreover, the notion that God can feel sensations and is therefore subject to change is clearly incompatible with the absolute perfection of God. For consider: If we suppose God to be perfect, then any change must necessarily be for the worse, after which he will no longer be perfect. If, on the other hand, we suppose that any change in God is necessarily for the better, then this means that God was less than perfect prior to the change.

These and similar arguments were first proposed by the skeptics of ancient Greece, who showed that the traditional conception of God (or the gods) is self-contradictory and therefore incoherent. The only way out of this conceptual morass is to say that God, who never changes, does not experience sensations or feelings of any kind, as we understand those terms. But this assumption brings with it a new set of problems. For example, if God is unable to experience pain, then there is at least one thing that we humans (who are quite familiar with this sensation) know that God does not, in which case God cannot be omniscient. For we can never know the meaning of "pain" unless we have experienced this sensation for ourselves. "Pain" must be defined ostensively, i.e., through direct experience, so a being who has never felt pain can never *know* the meaning of "pain."

Thus if God has never felt physical sensations of any kind, then there are many things of which he is necessarily ignorant, things that are known to his creatures but not to their creator. Most people have experienced an orgasm, but can the same be said of God? If the answer is yes, then we confront the previously discussed conflict between change and immutability, as well as that between change and perfection. If the answer is no, then we might ask why God has never had an orgasm. Is this because he *will not* or because he *cannot* have this experience? In the former case, although many things are presently unknown to God, he could acquire this knowledge if he so chose. In the latter case, God is forever barred from knowing many things that we humans know quite well. In either case, however, God cannot be all-knowing, because he must totally ignorant of sensory knowledge.

Matters of Life and Death

ETHICS WITHOUT GOD

Let us consider two hypothetical scenarios. Both involve Thomas, a Christian who has always tried to live a moral life and obey God's commandments.

In the first scenario Thomas is awakened in the early morning by a clear and distinct voice. "Arise Thomas," says this voice, "for your Lord God wishes to speak to you."

As Thomas gets up, he senses a divine presence as a holographic image of Jesus descends into his room. "I am well pleased with you," says this image, "for you have always been a man of great faith. But I enjoin you to be more charitable in your actions. You must help the poor, comfort the oppressed, and assist the downtrodden. Go forth, Thomas, and do as I have bidden you." Then the image floats upward and disappears.

Thomas, needless to say, is stunned. It occurs to him that he might be dreaming, so he goes to his kitchen for a glass of water. He stays up for the rest of the morning, running over in his mind the details of this remarkable event. He was wide awake, the voice was distinct, and the image clear, so Thomas concludes that his experience was indeed an authentic revelation from God.

Now consider a second scenario, which is identical to the first in every respect except one. Thomas hears the same audible voice, sees the same image of Jesus, and feels the same divine presence, except this time the image says: "Thomas, I am well pleased with you, for you have always been a man of faith. Now I will test your faith. I command you to take your firstborn child to a mountain top, lay him upon an altar, and plunge a dagger through his breast. I command this in the name of the Father, Son, and Holy Ghost."

Again, Thomas reflects on his experience, but this time he is more skeptical. He thinks he may have been dreaming, or hallucinating, or perhaps the visitor was really Satan, who was attempting to deceive him. In any case, Thomas finds it hard to accept this second experience as a true revelation from God.

But why? Why would Thomas be inclined to doubt the second experience more than the first? They are, after all, identical in every respect except for the content of the command itself. If the circumstances of the first experience—a clear voice, a distinct image, and an inner feeling—are sufficient to qualify it as a genuine revelation, then why wouldn't the same conditions also qualify the second experience as a genuine revelation? Clearly, the thing that troubles Thomas about the second experience is the command to kill his firstborn child. This, he thinks, is not the kind of thing that God would require of him.

Perplexed, Thomas searches the Scripture for guidance, where he runs across the Old Testament story of Abraham and Isaac. There he reads that Jehovah (or "Yaweh," depending on your taste in vowels) commanded Abraham to kill his firstborn son, and that Abraham did not question this revelation, but did precisely as he was told. Only at the last minute, as Abraham was ready to plunge a dagger into Isaac, did God intervene to save the boy's life. But Abraham, of course, didn't know this would happen. He truly believed he would have to kill his beloved child. Indeed, if he had harbored mental reservations and merely gone through the motions, while expecting that God would intervene to stop the killing, then this would not have been a real test of his faith.

Abraham is praised by Christians and Jews alike for his willingness to kill his beloved son. He was willing to act against his moral convictions, suppress all of his doubts and reservations, and obey what he believed to be the will of God. And for this he praised as one of the greatest religious figures in history.

What, then, is Thomas to think of his second experience? He cannot automatically dismiss its authenticity on the ground that God would never command him to kill his eldest son, for he knows that God commanded precisely the same thing of Abraham, who did not hesitate to do as he was told. And who is Thomas to question the will of God? How can he presume to know what God would and would not demand of him? And by what right does he ignore a divine revelation merely because he disapproves of, or does not understand, its content?

Suppose that Thomas were to solicit some of his Christian friends for advice. What would they tell him? I suspect they would be far more skeptical of the second "revelation," which demanded that Thomas sacrifice his son, than the first, which called upon him to be more charitable.

But why? There seems to be only one plausible answer. Most Christians simply will not accept the possibility that God would require Thomas (or any one else) to kill an innocent child. And this belief persists, despite the biblical account of Abraham and despite their conviction that God acts in mysterious ways, that he need not justify himself to man, and that he should be obeyed unconditionally, without mental reservations.

Thus, in calling upon his moral principles to assess the authenticity of a revelation, the Christian presumes to judge God. He presumes to know what God would and would not demand of him. He presumes that his own moral judgment is sufficiently reliable to serve as a test of what should qualify as an authentic revelation. He presumes that his own moral principles are so well grounded that even God himself would not violate them. And this means that *the fundamental values of the Christian are based on something other than the will of God.*

We needn't rely on hypothetical scenarios in order to prove this point; we can find may examples of it in real life. Consider, for example, the typical reaction when a Muslim terrorist straps a bomb to his chest, walks into an Israeli marketplace, and kills himself along with many innocent victims. The faith of this terrorist is doubtless sincere, since he is willing to sacrifice his own life. He believes that Allah has appointed him to wage a holy war against the infidels, and that his act of self-destruction will ensure him a fast track to paradise. Thus whatever the political motives for his act of terrorism may be, it is ultimately grounded in his religious faith.

From Muslims, Christians, and Jews alike we would hear the same objection, namely, that the true God would never call for the murder of innocent people. Yet this assertion is impossible to justify on biblical grounds. Throughout the Bible (especially in the Old Testament) we find many cases where innocent people are killed, either directly by God or at the hand of his appointed agents. Time and again we read that the Israelites, acting on God's behalf, massacred entire populations of conquered cities, men, women, and children. In the sixth chapter of Joshua, for example, we find that the victorious Israelites "utterly destroyed all in the city, both men and women, young and old, oxen, sheep, and asses." There were exceptions, however. In Numbers (31:17–18) we find the following commandment attributed to Jehovah: "Now therefore kill every male among the little ones, and kill every woman who has known man by lying with him. But all the young girls who have not known man by lying with him, keep alive for yourselves."

Suppose the general of a modern army, having overtaken an enemy city, were to give the same order to his troops: to kill everyone, young and old alike, except the young virgins, who should be kept alive for the benefit of his soldiers. This general would be condemned as a moral monster by every conscientious theist. Would it make any difference to these religious critics if the general sincerely believed that he was acting on a personal revelation from God? No, because these critics would not accept his purported revelation as genuine. God, they would insist, would never command such horrible deeds, so we can know with certainty that the general was either mistaken or lying when he claimed to be obeying a commandment from God.

It will perhaps be said that I am taking the Old Testament stories too literally, and that we should take into account the primitive conditions and customs that prevailed when these unsavory accounts were written. But this merely reinforces my point. Our moral standards (or at least some of them) have improved over the last several thousand years, so the Christian is unwilling to believe that God would sanction the same kinds of actions now that he sanctioned then.

God, we are told, never changes: He is the same now as he ever was and ever will be. It is we, not God, who have changed. Thus if God appears to change, this is because the modern Christian does not work from the same moral assumptions as his ancestors; he perceives God through different moral spectacles and evaluates him by different criteria. It was not difficult for an ancient Jew to believe that God would command the massacre of a defeated people, for this behavior was fairly routine for a tribal god of war like Jehovah. But standards have changed and, consequently, so has the Christian view of God.

Whatever religious people may say about the divine source of their moral beliefs, in practice they often give priority to their moral principles, using them to assess the validity of various religious claims. They accept some claims as authentic (or at least credible) while rejecting others as spurious, depending on their moral implications.

In this sense, therefore, we may say that many Christians implicitly accept the possibility of an ethics without God, inasmuch as they use their ethical principles to evaluate religious claims. Having accepted certain actions as morally reprehensible, they will question or reject altogether any religious belief that runs counter to these moral convictions. Returning to our original example of Thomas and his two experiences: If an apparent revelation commands something that religious people regard as moral, then they may accept it as legitimate. If, however, the revelation commands something they regard as manifestly immoral, then they will almost certainly reject it.

Let me put this issue in different terms. If you are a religious person who believes that God can, and does, communicate with human beings, and if you believe that God's will should always be obeyed without reservation, then under what circumstances would you accept a personal revelation as authentic, if that revelation required you to do something that contradicts your moral principles? Suppose God snatched you up to heaven for a brief visit, showed you around the place, introduced you to some angels, allowed you to visit with some of your deceased loved ones, and then gave you explicit instructions that, upon returning to earth you must sacrifice five children, randomly selected, as a demonstration of your faith.

Furthermore, suppose that you were given permission to discuss this project with God before implementing it. What would you ask him? Perhaps you would ask why he wants you to kill five innocent children. At this point, however, God's countenance becomes dark, and he replies in a stern voice, "Who are *you* to question *my* will?"

Now, sensing trouble ahead, you back off and try an approach that is less confrontational. You decide to engage God in a philosophical conversation about the nature of good and evil. You say: "Have you not written, Lord, that we shall not commit murder, and is it not murder to kill innocent children?"

God seems more receptive to this approach: "True," he replies, "I did say that. But murder is wrong only because I have said it is wrong. I am now telling you that, in your case and in your case only, the killing of five children is a good deed, because I have so decreed. What I have previously declared to be evil, I now declare to be good. And just as murder is evil because I say it is, so it is now a good thing, because I say it is. I am the creator of good and evil, and just as I make these things what they are, so I can remake them into something different. Any *more* questions, earthling?"

Here you may wish to pose an old philosophical question to God. "Lord," you ask, "is something good because you will it, or do you will it because it is good?" A great many Christian theologians, both living and dead, would love to hear how God responds to this question, because it has given rise to one of the great debates in Christian theology.

Some Christians, such as the thirteenth-century philosopher Thomas Aquinas, have said, in essence, that God necessarily wills what is good and that, given the nature of his creation, even God's omnipotence cannot transform what is good into something evil, or vice versa. According to this approach, which is often called "natural-law theology," an omnipotent God could have created an alternative universe with characteristics radically different from the one in which we now live. And, if this had happened, then the moral laws governing our actions might also be radically different. But given the present world as God created it, good and evil flow necessarily from the nature of things, and even God cannot invert this relationship between the true and the good.

Why is this so? Because God, according to the natural-law theologians, cannot will a contradiction. He cannot, for example, violate a law of logic by willing A to be non-A at the same time and in the same respect. Similarly, God cannot will a moral contradiction, nor can he contradict himself. By creating a world in which murder is wrong, he has created an inexorable relationship between the nature of human beings and this moral prohibition. Therefore, to imagine that God can arbitrarily declare murder to be right, contrary to the nature of his own creation, would be to imagine, in effect, that God can contradict himself, which he cannot.

This natural-law explanation did not satisfy many theologians, such as the fourteenth-century philosopher William of Occam and, later, the leaders of the Protestant Reformation (most notably Luther and Calvin). The natural-law approach of Thomas Aquinas, according to these Christians, is mistaken, because it tries to impose human limits on the omnipotent power of God. "Omnipotence" means precisely just what it says: God is all-powerful; he can do literally anything he wishes. Murder is wrong because God has so willed. Thus, if God were suddenly to declare that murder is right and obligatory, then we would be required to obey him in this case, as in every other, by committing murder. Because this view attributes moral good and evil solely to God's will, to his volition rather than to his reason, it is commonly known as *voluntarism*.

These two approaches, natural law and voluntarism, comprise the two basic answers to our previous question, "Is something right because God wills it, or does God will it because it is right?" The voluntarists contend that something is right because God wills it, whereas natural-law theologians say that God wills something because it is right—that good and evil flow necessarily from the nature of things, as God created them.

Let us now consider the implications of these approaches for an atheistic ethics, an ethics without God. Is a rational ethics possible without God? Can we justify a code of ethics by appealing to reason alone, without recourse to faith and revelation?

If the voluntarist is right, if good and evil depend solely upon God's will, then an atheistic ethics is clearly impossible. In the voluntarist scheme of things, everything would be permissible in a godless universe. There would be no objective right and wrong, no justice and injustice, no virtue in compassion and charity, no evil in cruelty and murder.

But this does not follow from the natural-law approach, which grounds its moral principles in the nature of human beings and social interaction. Consider how this approach is compatible with an atheistic ethics. "Granted," the atheist will say to the natural-law Christian, "we disagree about whether our world was created, but we do agree that our world is here, that it exists, whatever its origin may have been. We agree that human beings have a specific nature, that they require certain things to survive, to prosper, and to be happy. We agree that humans have the power of choice, that we have no automatic means of survival and no instincts that will lead us infallibly to happiness, that we must learn which actions are good for us and which are bad. We agree that humans, as purposeful and volitional beings, require a code of values, a system of normative principles, to guide our choices and actions. Therefore, we can also agree that moral principles are absolutely necessary for a good life." This is the foundation for a rational theory of ethics, one that is acceptable to both the atheist and to the natural-law Christian.

I mention this compatibility of natural-law theology and an atheist ethics because it illustrates an important point. The atheist is far from being alone when he claims that ethics can be justified rationally, without referring to the will of God. This position has been defended for many centuries by some of the greatest figures in the history of Christianity, Judaism, and Islam. If we add to this the long list of Greek philosophers who defended a secular ethics, such as Plato, Aristotle, Epicurus, and the Stoics, then we have a formidable list of great thinkers who held that a rational ethics, an ethics without God, is possible.

Please note that I am *not* using an argument from authority. I am not suggesting that we should accept a theory of ethics merely because it has been upheld by many outstanding philosophers. True, we sometimes appeal to authorities and experts in the realm of science, when we lack technical knowledge or the means to verify a scientific experiment. But this appeal to authority has no place whatever in philosophical discussions. Philosophical knowledge does not depend upon experiments, specialized observation, or technical skills. Rather, philosophy is, in effect, refined common sense; it derives its knowledge from the common experience of humankind, from observations and experiences that are accessible to every normal adult.

This is particularly true in the field of ethics. One need not engage in orgies in order to have a moral opinion about them, or become a drug addict in order to assess its desirability as a way of life, or own slaves in order to condemn slavery. The competence of a moral philosopher is not based upon an abundance of diverse experiences; indeed, many philosophers have lived rather sheltered lives. Rather, a philosopher's competence flows from his ability to discriminate, evaluate, and present logical arguments for a given opinion. The conclusions reached by moral philosophers are often commonplace. After years of reflection and deliberation, a philosopher may proclaim that, yes, murder is unjust, and ought to be legally prohibited. To this, the average person is likely to respond with a yawn. "What's the big deal?" he will ask. "I, along with millions of other people, already believe this to be true."

Well, the big deal lies in the fact that the philosopher, though she may arrive at mundane conclusions, is better able to justify those conclusions than is the average person. She can give reasons and arguments for her beliefs, and she can counter the arguments of moral skeptics. The ancient Greeks had a word for this kind of reasoned knowledge; they called it *episteme.* And they distinguished this reasoned knowledge from the beliefs of ordinary people, who rarely attempt to justify their beliefs with rigorous arguments. They called this *doxa*, or opinion.

Thus, according to the Greeks, if we hold a belief uncritically, accepting it because this is how we have been taught, or because we are too lazy or too timid to analyze it, or because an authority tells us we should, then our beliefs are mere opinion, not true knowledge. Opinions can qualify as true knowledge only after they have been critically assessed and can be justified with reasoned arguments.

We may say, therefore, that the philosopher, not content with moral opinions, seeks to acquire moral knowledge. People may generally hold the opinion that murder is wrong, but the philosopher wants to know *why* it is wrong. She examines every plausible counterargument she can think of, she explores various reasons that have been given for the immorality of murder, and then, having sifted and evaluated this information, she arrives at a reasoned judgment. She may be wrong, of course; no one is infallible. But the well-reasoned error of a philosopher is often more instructive than the unreasoned truth of a credulous mind.

In knowledge, as in many other areas of life, we usually get what we pay for. A philosopher who has invested a great deal of thought in her opinions will usually produce something of value, something that will be of use to other people, even if she turns out to be wrong. Conversely, a credulous person who has invested little, if any, mental labor in his opinions, will produce nothing of real value, nothing that others can learn from, even if he turns out to be right. We can learn more from the reasonable errors of great mind than we can from the true opinions of a fool.

I have stated that a rational ethics, an ethics without God, is possible, and that this belief is accepted, if only implicitly, by many religious people as well. Now I would like to underscore this claim with a final hypothetical example.

Suppose that you have been a deeply religious person throughout most of your life, but that, for some reason or other, you suddenly abandon all of your religious beliefs in favor of atheism. If this were to happen, if you were now a confirmed atheist, how would this change your moral behavior? Would you now say to yourself: "Aha! There is no God, and therefore no binding principles of morality. I am now free to murder, rob, and rape as I please. I have always been tempted to do these things, but have restrained myself in order to please God. But now, since I no longer believe in God or his commandments, I am morally free to become a murderer, a thief, or a rapist. Oh, glorious day! I am free at last—free to live the kind of life that I have always desired, the kind of life that will bring me happiness and inner peace. I am free at last to abandon the phony virtues of justice and kindness and take up instead those appealing characteristics related to viciousness and violence. No longer am I forced to accept the likes of a Jesus or a Gandhi as moral exemplars; now, without God to order me around, I can freely profess my admiration for Stalin and Hitler and follow their glorious example of how to live a happy and fulfilling life."

It is highly questionable whether most people would drastically change their moral principles upon deconverting to atheism. Yet many people still cling to the belief that religion is an essential foundation for ethics. They fear that if religion goes out the window, morality will follow close behind. And this assumption tends to generate a resistance to critical thinking in matters of religion, for fear that too much rational analysis will weaken or destroy the moral fabric of society.

DEATH

"Look back at the eternity that passed before we were born," wrote the Roman poet Lucretius, "and mark how utterly it counts to us as nothing. This is a mirror that nature holds up to us, in which we may see the time that shall be after we are dead. Is there anything terrifying in the sight—anything depressing—anything that is not more restful than the soundest sleep?"[1]

As with all of the material in *On the Nature of the Universe*, Lucretius was relating the views of his philosophical hero Epicurus, who attributed the fear of death to the superstitious belief in an afterlife. The fear of death, according to Epicurus, originated with the religious doctrine that we will be rewarded or punished in a future life, depending on how we act (or what we our believe) in our present life. The doctrine of personal immortality, by generating an irrational fear of the unknown, is therefore responsible for a good deal of needless suffering—so it is up to the philosopher to eradicate this superstitious fear by exposing the fraudulent claims of religion, thereby removing a major obstacle to tranquility and peace of mind. (I shall henceforth dub this the "Epircurean Remedy.")

What if Epicurus was right? What if the soul (i.e., consciousness) does indeed die with the body and take with it every trace of personal identity? Is not the prospect of our extinction, our descent into the oblivion of nonexistence, a dreadful thing? No, said Epicurus, because with death comes the cessation of all desires and emotions; death will liberate us from pain and suffering, so there is no reason to fear death as something terrible. But what about the brute fact of nonexistence? How can any person be expected to confront this fate without some degree of trepidation, if not fear?

It is here that the previously quoted passage from Lucretius comes into play. If you want to know what nonexistence is like, simply think of the time before you were born. You were eternally nonexistent before birth, just as you will be eternally nonexistent after death. These situations are essentially identical, so why should you fear one more than the other? If you do not anguish over your nonexistence before birth, then why should you anguish over your return to that same condition after death?

It would be difficult to overemphasize the influence of the Epicurean Remedy: It appears again and again in the writings of atheists, deists, and others who rejected the doctrine of personal immortality. Consider, for instance, this passage from Arthur Schopenhauer:

> If what makes death seem so terrible to us were the thought of *nonexistence*, we should necessarily think with equal horror of the time when as yet we did not exist. For it is irrefutably certain that non-existence after death cannot be different from non-existence before birth, and is therefore no more deplorable than that is. An entire infinity ran its course when we did *not yet* exist, but this in no way disturbs us. . . . I can then console myself for the infinite time after my death, when I shall not exist, with the infinite time when I did not as yet exist, as a quite comfortable state.[2]

Despite the impressive pedigree of this argument, I do not find it especially convincing. Although it may have a soothing effect, although it may provide some consolation to compare my future state of nonexistence to that of the past, I cannot agree with Epicurus that this mental exercise should eliminate the fear of death altogether, even when it is coupled with the additional insight that with death comes an end to pain and suffering.

It is of course a good thing to face facts squarely, especially when the fact in question has momentous implications, Indeed, as the atheist Joseph McCabe once remarked, death is simply "the final fact." Beyond this there seems to be little more the atheistic philosopher can say, because philosophy deals in general principles that apply universally to every human being, whereas how we face death is an intensely individual matter that will vary from person to person.

In other words, if the Epircurean Remedy fails to accomplish its intended purpose, this is not because it is not true or useful to some degree, but because philosophy cannot deal adequately with the many psychological variables that determine how a particular individual views death. Epicureanism (along with Stoicism, Skepticism, and some other rival schools of thought in Hellenistic Greece) spurned the theoretical conception of philosophy that had been advanced by Plato and Aristotle, maintaining instead that the ultimate goal of philosophy should be practical. The philosopher seeks knowledge not for its own sake but as a means of attaining contentment and happiness.

This preference for practical over theoretical wisdom led Epicurus to pit philosophy against religion as a superior means of attaining happiness. We should be guided by the facts of nature, not by the fears of superstition, because only the former enables us to understand man as he truly is—a natural entity who will eventually die. And it is because many people cannot accept this final fact that they turn to the fables of popular religions. They believe that man— who was created according to a divine plan and endowed with an eternal soul—enjoys a privileged exemption from natural causation. Why, after all, would God have favored us with a special creation (and provided us with a world for our use and benefit) if he intended that we should perish into everlasting nothingness after death?

In defense of the religious viewpoint, it might at least be said that the doctrine of personal immortality, however unjustified it may be, is at least a comforting belief, one that provides consolation for the fear of death. And if this is true, then religion is by no means inferior to philosophy when it comes to eradicating this fear.

Epicurus, as we have seen, would have none of this. He insisted that the consolation of religion is fraudulent, because the very fear that religion claims to assuage is itself the product of religion. For consider: If we believe in a creator, God, who takes a personal interest in human affairs, and who is either pleased or displeased by human behavior, then we will feel the need to placate this god as a means of avoiding divine retribution. Moreover, since it would be presumptuous to tell God what he ought to do, we can never be absolutely certain that our ultimate destination will be heaven rather than hell. Thus has religion exacted a high price for its consolation, for in addition to manufacturing extravagant hope, it has also manufactured extravagant fear, anxiety, and terror.

The philosopher, according to Epicurus, plays an important practical role. He debunks the popular religion of his day, and in so doing he eradicates the fountainhead of superstitious fears. This view of philosophy—that it should function as a solvent of superstition, and that this is a praiseworthy task in and of itself—became a recurring theme of seventeenth- and eighteenth-century philosophy. When Spinoza, for example, said that superstition "is engendered, preserved, and fostered by fear,"[3] he was merely echoing Epicurus; as was David Hume when he wrote: "Weakness, fear, melancholy, together with ignorance, are . . . the true sources of SUPERSTITION."[4]

NOTES

1. Lucretius, *On the Nature of the Universe*, trans. R. E. Latham (Harmondsworth: Penguin Books, 1951), p. 125.

2. Arthur Schopenhauer, *The World as Will and Representation*, trans. E. F. J. Payne (New York: Dover, 1966), vol. 2, pp. 466–67.

3. Benedict Spinoza, *A Theological-Political Treatise*, trans. and ed. R. H. M. Elwes (New York: Dover Publications, 1951), p. 4.

4. David Hume, "Of Superstition and Enthusiasm," in *Essays: Moral, Political, and Literary*, ed. Eugene F. Miller (Indianapolis: Liberty Classics, 1987), p. 74.

Index